T0371184

OUTCAST

OUTCAST

A History of Leprosy,
Humanity and the
Modern World

OLIVER BASCIANO

faber

First published in 2025
by Faber & Faber Limited
The Bindery, 51 Hatton Garden
London EC1N 8HN

Typeset by Typo•glyphix, Burton-on-Trent, DE14 3HE
Printed and bound by CPI Group (UK) Ltd, Croydon, CR0 4YY

A CIP record for this book
is available from the British Library

ISBN 978–0–571–38430–3

Our authorised representative in the EU for product safety is
Easy Access System Europe, Mustamäe tee 50, 10621 Tallinn, Estonia
gpsr.requests@easproject.com

2 4 6 8 10 9 7 5 3 1

In memory of my sister, Anna

CONTENTS

PROLOGUE

The USA was busy building its border wall and the country's right-wing media were in a state of absolute frenzy. It is strange how grimly odd North American television is: the anchors with their blocks of static hair and immoveable opinions, the manic shouting for no apparent reason, the agitated ticker scrolling endless anxiety across the bottom of the screen. It is a self-contained world; brightly lit, loud and paranoid. The screen filled with footage of cranes hauling huge black girders into a line that would end up snaking a great swathe of the US frontier to Mexico.

The news anchor lamented that progress was too slow; the number of immigrants escaping drought and crime in Central America had barely abated. The country was being 'swamped'. He welcomed a guest: David Ward, a former US Immigration and Customs Enforcement agent, popped up on a split screen as footage of people walking from Guatemala into Mexico played. With unblinking blue eyes and goatee on the verge of grey, Ward griped that an army was heading to US soil, 'not only from Central America but they're coming in from Africa, from the Middle East'. This is nonsense, I thought to myself.

As I went to change channels Ward thundered that, worse still, the caravans of immigrants harboured diseases such as 'leprosy and TB that are gonna infect our people in the United States'. It made me stop. I knew first-term President Donald Trump had claimed 'tremendous infectious diseases' were running rife because of immigration – it had become one of his minor refrains. Tuberculosis, maybe, at a push – but leprosy? Surely 'fake news', the newly minted phrase of the moment. Surely there is no leprosy now? In another

1

time the question might have evaporated into the hyperbole it obviously was. Yet it lingered. The bait and switch Ward performed on-screen, between the othering of disease and the othering of the immigrant, seemed, and seems still, to be everywhere. The idea of leprosy began to consume my thoughts.

The next day, the day after. The immigrant as walking pathogen, the immigrant as criminal. Crime as a disease, disease as the other: build the wall, stop the boats, keep them out. It's a health emergency, it's a political calamity, it's a moral imperative. Our society is sick; the demigod populist has the cure. This book was born of this time, a moment in which, despite this shrinking world and our interconnected lives, the other is seen as more contagious than ever.

———

Leprosy, or Hansen's disease, is caused by an intracellular, rod-shaped, environmentally sensitive pathogenic bacterium known as *Mycobacterium leprae*, first identified in 1873 by Gerhard Armauer Hansen, a Norwegian physician. It is spread in water droplets transported by sneezes and coughs. The bacterium, which thirty-six million years ago shared a common ancestor with *Mycobacterium tuberculosis*, evades the immune system by seeking out the cooler extremities of the body, hiding as an outlaw in the nervous system. There were 202,485 new cases reported across more than a hundred countries in 2019. (Central American cases were in the single digits.) The global frequency in 2023 dropped dramatically to 182,815, but as with many health problems, the Covid-19 pandemic catastrophically skewed detection. Compared to other bacteria, *Mycobacterium leprae* is incredibly slow to replicate itself, and this has long hampered attempts to trace the spread of the infection: by the time it is visibly apparent, a person who has leprosy is likely to have been asymptomatically carrying and perhaps proliferating the disease for an average of five years, sometimes as many as twenty.

The first sign for the majority of patients will be numbness, most likely affecting the ability to gauge temperature, followed by sensitivity to light touch. A patient with tuberculoid leprosy – who will have better natural immunity to the attacking bacteria – might only exhibit a few discrete lesions, one- to two-centimetre red or white patches with slightly raised borders, possibly appearing decades after the initial signs. A person with untreated lepromatous leprosy (in which far more of the bacterium is present) is likely to suffer damage to the skin, the upper respiratory tract, toes and fingers, the eyes and the inside lining of the nose; they will experience blocked nostrils and swelling of the legs. If they seek medical attention, with luck, a doctor can order a slit skin smear, in which a small cut is made to the earlobe, forehead, chin, buttocks or, if they've already appeared, the lesions themselves. The doctor will scrape out a sample, which will be analysed under a microscope. The current multidrug cure – a combination of dapsone, rifampicin and clofazimine – has been available internationally since 1981. It was a major medical breakthrough and succeeded in reducing new cases from more than five million a year to the current hundreds of thousands.

Neither strain is as infectious as mythology dictates, and 95 per cent of the world's population is naturally immune to the bacillus. Most people with a good diet and the privilege of hygiene could spend a lifetime living with someone who is actively affected by the disease and not contract it. In areas where leprosy is still endemic – with India, Brazil and Indonesia topping that chart – a staggering 7.8 per cent of people have been found to carry the bacteria in their nasal passage.

Yet the disease's dark reputation perseveres globally. In an 1886 essay, the French dermatologist Henri Leloir wrote that the leprosy patient suffers their condition twice, first as mycobacterial infection, second as stigma. A century later, in *Illness as Metaphor*, Susan Sontag notes: 'Nothing is more punitive than to give a disease a meaning – that meaning being invariably a moralistic one . . . In the name of the disease (that is, using it as a metaphor), that horror is imposed on other things. The disease becomes adjectival.' While this book does serve as a history of leprosy, *Outcast* is not a medical biography, but the story of this stigma – how the secondary infection identified by Leloir spread: how it came about, and how this particular stigma, the ur-stigma, was used as the blueprint for other forms of discrimination. Leprosy has become a geography, the world divided into ever-shifting territories of the unclean and clean; those who are subjects of Sontag's 'kingdom of the sick', and those looking across the border wall in abject fear.

———

A condition called 'leprosy' has much footprint in later translations of religious scripture, its sufferer hailed as ritually impure from Sanskrit hymns to the Old Testament, but these often prove unreliable evidence with which to trace the modern condition. A great deal of today's medical knowledge first emerged from the cultural and intellectual hub of third-century BC Alexandria. Among the ancient city's doctors was Straton, who, on encountering great sickness among Alexander the Great's soldiers returning from India (leprosy and war continue to dog each other today), described in detail a condition that resembles the effects of *Mycobacterium leprae* to a tee. 'Its symptoms are not hidden: they consist in livid and black embossments that resemble ecchymoses; some on the face, others on the arms, still others on the legs.' This bruising he named 'elephantiasis', long before the lymphatic infection that swells the legs took the name.

Attracted by Alexandria's reputation for tolerance, though keeping to their own quarter in which they might make their religious observances without hindrance, the Jewish scribes of the city were busy at their desks too, translating the Tanakh into Greek. Where today's reader finds reference to 'leprosy' there, and in the Old Testament, in the original text the Hebrew word *tsa'arat* (צָרַעַת) was used. The first use of *tsa'arat* these scholars needed to translate occurs in Leviticus 13, as God appears to Moses and issues a complex series of commands regarding ritual cleansing in the case of a person with a skin condition. Such a person is deemed unclean and is forbidden from entering the temple or touching sacred objects. They must live outside the camp. While symptoms persist, a priest must undertake regular examinations to see if the infection is spreading. 'If the priest look on it, and, behold, there be no white hair in the bright spot, and it be no lower than the other skin, but be somewhat dark; then the priest shall shut him up seven days.' For the examining religious man this was regarded as a risky job, and the passage not only forges the connection between this skin complaint and sin, but also charity and martyrdom. Crucially, however, we don't know what condition was being described, and nor would the rabbinic scholars have done – unlike Straton's scientific description, the verse is light on visual clues – but in their upper-case script, laid down on parchment, they inked their translation as *lepra* (λέπρα), which at the time was a more generalised term. Taken from the Greek word for scales, as in of a snake (the scholars perhaps relishing the link to the Garden of Eden), it covered a vast range of dermatological conditions, from boils to vitiligo and psoriasis, all annoying, but comparatively harmless.

If a single – identifiable – health complaint were to become synonymous with such passages, it would create the conditions for the societal stigma that was to come. That is of course what happened. In using *lepra* the scribes of Alexandria had translated *tsa'arat* carefully, reflecting the vagueness of the scripture, but as the years passed, the more general nature of the label of *lepra* slipped away and it came to replace elephantiasis as the name of the more serious, specific, disease that we now know as leprosy. Medical men tried to arrest the trend, but language was never consecrated in books but in the lanes, squares and markets of the ancient world. By the fourth century, Gregory, bishop of Nazianzus, was using *lepra* to describe a horrifying spectacle: sufferers who were 'disfigured, unrecognisable, identified only by their names; avoided, shrunk from, detested, despised by relatives, fathers, mothers, spouses, children; wandering night and day, naked, destitute, exposing their loathsomeness to the gaze of passers-by to move them and obtain alms'. The die was cast: leprosy was etymologically linked with sin; it was the disease iconic of Christian charity. By the sixth century, this was the stigma summoned rote by congregations whenever the rabbi or priest mentioned *lepra* from their bimah and pulpit, an image not of mild eczema or persistent psoriasis, but the terrible deformations of leprosy at its most severe. If the image of the biblical 'leper' is more at home in Sunday school classes than academia, more parable than fact, it nonetheless laid the foundations for the persecution that was to come.

––––––

To be called a 'leper' is now a mark of the other and a slur. Leprosy is a cultural artefact, a costume and a mask; a turn of phrase, a metaphor. It is a receptacle for nightmares and prejudice, a synonym for the lost and the cast-out. Leprosy is a lazy descriptor, a word so full of meaning and meanings that it has become meaningless. It is a linguistic construction. Erving Goffman, the American sociologist, argued that to understand stigma 'a language of relationships, not attributes, is really needed'. Stigma – the 'spoiled identity' of the leper – occurs not because of a person's particular characteristics, but because of those characteristics in relation to the people who surround the subject. I will only use, in quote marks, the word 'leper' – today highly offensive to anyone affected by the disease – in such moments when it would be ahistorical not to, or if I am precisely referring to the social construct rather than the patient themselves. The word 'leprosy' has been superseded in many languages with deviations of 'Hansen's disease' but retains common usage in English, so I too will continue to use it, with acknowledgement that it is contested.

When Goffman sets up those whom he calls the 'normals' versus the stigmatised, I can't help thinking of the 'ordinary' Americans for whom the likes of Fox News claim to speak, the 'hard-working Britons' that the right wing of my own country valorise. All stigmas, leprosy the ur-stigma included, are ultimately a combination of language and politics, or language weaponised in pursuit of a particular politic. In labelling and categorising we are attempting to produce an 'other' beyond our self, to build a wall between 'us' and 'them'. If we consider who is stigmatised in today's society, merely as absolute numbers, whether by race or gender, disability or belief, those affected by leprosy are a statistical footnote (an issue that frustrates NGOs raising funds and patients battling for political attention). And yet the history of leprosy is also the history of colonisation and oppression in Africa, Asia, South America and the Pacific, a history that has entangled the Jewish people for millennia. There's a reason so many individuals that identify – or might latterly be thought of – as LGBT or queer are found woven into this story. The 'leper' takes many forms.

When David Ward lied about leprosy among the Hondurans, Guatemalans and Salvadoreans heading for the USA, he knew what he was doing. Leprosy has been used as a means to persecute and subjugate throughout history, a trigger word for fear and panic, an age-old excuse for racism and repression.

————

My journey to the root of this stigma started in the northern hemisphere – Britain, Norway, Russia – partly out of pragmatism, partly because the presence of colonies and sanatoria in the temperate world so obviously refutes the racist idea of leprosy as a 'tropical disease'. Following in the wake of imperialism, I traced leprosy south into South Africa and Mozambique, to Hawaii, until in 2019 I moved to Brazil. Working as a journalist amid the turbulence of that country's lurch to the right, the political mismanagement of which created a 'regional leper colony', *Bloomberg* thought, I saw how leprosy remained endemic in the world's fourth-largest democracy. I also found that while the country harboured the disease, and a very dark biopolitical history, it was also at the vanguard of a remarkable social movement seeking to right the wrongs of the past. A community once isolated has given rise to an international network of patients, activists and advocates, a people who refuse to be outcast.

They are the heroes of this story, and they sent me from one to the other, recommendations and introductions that I am eternally grateful for. A certain amount of travel is necessary to tell the story of a people pushed to the periphery, though the cruel irony never left me that the freedom of movement I enjoyed was a privilege that had long been denied many of them. Scribbled-down phone numbers turned into flight bookings; tentative emails precipitated planes across Siberia and boats to Japanese islands, Land Cruisers off-road during an insurrection, buses through the backlands of Brazil and hundreds of interviews across five continents. Albert Camus wrote in *The Plague* that 'perhaps the easiest way of making a town's acquaintance is to ascertain how the people in it work, how they love, and how they die'. I adopted his methodology but with trepidation: all those are delicate points of connection, made infinitely more so considering I was a stranger arriving with power and a pen among some of the most marginalised people in the world. I was received with remarkable generosity and grace, though, and made to feel welcome wherever I went.

What follows – the story of leprosy's stigma since that fateful misunderstanding in ancient Alexandria – is pieced together from three sources: the words of those I met, my own observations, and historical records. The last of these is more often used to corroborate the first, but on occasions, as is the way of telling the story of a people who were purposely disappeared, this has not been possible. I've included such testimony nonetheless, signposted with the thought that personal mythology, even with its veracity uncertain, tells you more about how a person has experienced the world than facts and figures ever could. *Outcast* is partly about acknowledging a wrong of the past, but it also asks a difficult question, one with which patients past and present have long grappled. Does a society's sense of itself always rely on ostracisation?

PART ONE

'What strange ideas people have about leprosy, doctor.'
'They learn about it from the Bible, like sex.'

Graham Greene, *A Burnt-Out Case*

ST ALBANS, UK

I n 1178 a small procession set out from the English village of Redbourn, a box of bones carried aloft. Their destination was St Albans, an old Roman town a few kilometres south, then, as now, dominated by its abbey. More than eight centuries later, on the first good day of a bad spring, I'm walking the same route they took. I pull my cap down to shield my eyes and push towards the sun. It is a country road, cracked, potholed and patched up, that I have taken before: I was born close by and went to school in St Albans, now a commuter hub of chain restaurants and spiralling house prices, but filled still with the urban remnants of two millennia. In the distance, across the farmers' fields, I can hear the muffled rumble of the A road that I used to travel by bus each weekday, dressed in the uniform of my Catholic comprehensive. Today, though, I'm looking for a leprosarium.

The medieval troop carried with them the relics of St Amphibalus, the priest who inspired St Alban, the protomartyr of the British, to embrace Christianity. Alban was decapitated as he protected his mentor from the Romans around the year AD 304. The skeleton of Amphibalus, it is said, lost on his own death the following year, had been unearthed after a local man dreamt of its whereabouts, a miraculous vision that proved correct. Tramping along, my younger self feeling as ancient a history, newborn lambs amble the fields to the right and cows plod to the left. The grass they browse stretches out unstintingly flat, each side reaching asymmetrical copses of trees that stitch the luminescent green to the cloudless blue sky above. After half an hour the blocky spire of the abbey peeks above the distant horizon, the crown to a millennium of architectural additions and extensions. When the faithful from Redbourn neared the town's wall

850 years ago, the Norman building their destination, ahead they saw a small group coming in the opposite direction. It was a band of monks carrying their own relics, the bones of St Alban, out to meet them, reuniting the saintly pair on this path and in death. As each parade approached the other, their loads are said to have become miraculously light; the normally heavy caskets – which had until then required the strength of the whole group to lift them – could suddenly be borne by a single monk 'without difficulty'. This supernatural sign may have ended just as a tale being told there and then, but yet another vision occurred a short while later.

Chroniclers tell of an otherworldly light flashing before a local man as the spirit of Amphibalus appeared. The man was told that the meeting place should be honoured with fitting reverence. To the right of the lane, on this magical spot, St Mary de Pré Priory was built, expressly founded in 1194 for thirteen women with leprosy. It joined a similar establishment in the town, a monastery called St Julian's, built five decades previously for men with the disease, though that site has long been lost to time, tarmac and suburbia, preserved only as the name of the neighbourhood. I know there is little to see today of St Mary de Pré too, just an oddly steep verge, one that leads to slightly uneven terrain, before heading down to the boggy ground of the ancient River Ver. I notice it only because I'm looking, a local historian having furnished me with rough co-ordinates, the incline carpeted with the white skeleton heads of cow parsley, the dips and troughs of the pasture beyond trampled by cow's feet. I climb over a wooden fence, carefully avoiding a length of barbed wire strung between the planks, and trace the boundaries of the field, all the while eyeing the grazing cattle nervously. Somewhere under the tangled ground, a few hundred years of earth between, lie the remains of the priory. This weed-ridden stretch of nothingness conjures up a disease disappeared, a history buried far underground, the Middle

Ages and its ailments dissipated to a place of fairy tales. The analogy of leprosy seems acceptable, because for many in the West the living, breathing disease is dead.

———

Even without the sacred nature of the spot, St Mary de Pré's location at the entrance to the town, along what was then a busy thoroughfare on which alms could be begged, might be considered a prime position – it was beyond the town's walls but in sight of the abbey and the first building any traveller would encounter. The sisters, who took their vows on diagnosis, would have been happy with the ad hoc charity, but neither were they forgotten by the powers that be. St Mary de Pré boasted glazed windows, tiled roofs and a fire in each dormitory, and the newly crowned King John bestowed them with over thirty acres of land on which they could farm, while also decreeing 'that they may have one festival every year at St Mary's. In the meadow near the village of St Alban . . . with all the liberties and free customs pertaining to such a holiday'. The abbot granted various tithes and the income provided a lifetime allowance in food and clothing for the religious order. Living alongside the sisters who had the disease were healthy nuns, both ranks of the religious order overseen by a prioress, and they would dine together, neither permitted to be late or leave before grace had been said. They were given access to local mills to grind oats and malts, and every week a cartload of wood would arrive. The sisters whose health allowed would pray, cook and clean, and haul sacks of grain or the bails of logs into the religious house.

This all seems at odds with the cliché of the 'medieval leper', outcast, feared in their rags, shunned as they rang their bell or sounded their clapper, seemingly to signal their unwanted presence; this was the dirty figure I'd seen depicted by Hollywood, the one I'd been taught about in some offhand fashion at school. Unless St Mary de Pré was an aberration, to judge from my home town, the mythology of the 'medieval leper' seems no more real than that of the vampire or ghoul. That figure, I come to realise, is more than a story we have scared children with on a dark night or an image invented to provide a pleasingly coherent picture of the past. It is a bogeyman constructed carefully, with a political and social purpose, a nightmare assiduously made with perennial human fears in mind.

When the first sisters entered St Mary de Pré, Christianity had found firm roots in England for little more than 500 years. Their disease was a mark of sin in the Old Testament, but now, inspired by the New Testament, it had also become a condition of divine blessing. In Numbers 12, Miriam is smitten by 'leprosy' after she and Aaron speak derogatorily of their Ethiopian sister-in-law. Whether it really was leprosy or not is irrelevant – the medieval faithful reading in translation now believed it was. 'And the cloud departed from off the tabernacle; and, behold, Miriam became leprous, white as snow: and Aaron looked upon Miriam, and, behold, she was leprous.' This God was a wrathful one. Were you to move from the synagogue to hear the priest in his pulpit, however, you would be told of Jesus meeting ten men with the disease on the border of Samaria and Galilee, their belief in his ability to perform miracles rewarded by instantaneous emancipation from ill-health's grip. Matthew 8 tells the story of a man with leprosy approaching Jesus and saying he believed a miracle could happen and he could be cured by a touch of the hand. And so it came about. These were shining examples of good Christians. The gospel writer goes on to quote a passage from Isaiah, in which the prophet predicted the divine coming would take 'our infirmities / And . . . our sicknesses'.

No vampire or ghoul, then, but a man or woman with leprosy *was* a supernatural being in medieval times, an age in which the empirical and spiritual were intertwined to a cosmological extent that today's secular society might never fully comprehend. No lumpen 'Dark Ages' of post-Enlightenment myth, but certainly this was a world in which God and the Devil were everywhere, in which every action was a transaction with the afterlife, and in which such a visible condition can only ever have been interpreted as a message, divine or diabolical, from up above or down below. The 'leper' was a phantasmagorical being, a small bit of God made spoiled flesh: a visage to be feared, but honoured too. As the centuries passed, however, it was the medieval devil who took hold of the disease – or rather, he was handed the condition by the politics not of the medieval world, but of the nineteenth century.

———

To understand the disease in medieval times is not an exercise in history so much as in historiography. In our own great-grandparents' lifetime, when imperial powers used the spectre of leprosy as a means of controlling their colonised populations, they reached for a mythologised picture of another time, conjuring the 'leper' as pure horror show, a manifestation of disorder and racialised primitivity. To create an outcast, it is helpful to have the weight of the past on one's side – if it isn't, reinvent the history.

The more nuanced story is that a person with leprosy in the Middle Ages was an exemplar of sin and divinity simultaneously. To be a sinner was not the exception though, but the baseline of medieval humanity. And that original sin – as Augustine of Hippo had it – would only be added to in a lifetime. A person with leprosy manifested this devilishness physically but if he or she were to bear such sickness with patience and humility, they would be justly rewarded in unprecedented fashion. Until the Reformation turned the world upside down, medieval Christianity operated on a system of 'spiritual credit' in which every good deed, every prayer or mass, every suffering, could be used as payment against the time one was condemned to spend in purgatory. (Pilgrims to the castle church at Wittenberg, for example, where Martin Luther would start his revolt against Rome, could commute 1,902,202 years and 270 days from their torment by viewing the 19,013 holy bones contained there; visitors to the relics of Saints Albans and Amphibalus would be making similar calculations, the bones a potentially lucrative income for the abbot.)

To have leprosy was deemed so uniquely awful, however, that it was considered a living purgatory, and come the moment of death, a person with the disease had already paid their debt to God. With their sentence spent, they would go straight to heaven. When Gregory of Nazianzus, who in his infamous funeral address memorialising the charity of Basil of Caesarea described the *lepra* as 'men already dead except to sin; often dumb, with festering bodies whose insensible limbs rotted off them; heartbreaking and horrifying spectacles of human ruin; objects of repugnance and terror', he was not really describing the leprous of this world, but the awful, lengthy spectacle that awaits everyone in his audience (though heretics in particular), come their final breath and journey to the purgatorial flames. Faced with this, for some, leprosy seemed the better deal, 'misfortune considered blessed', Gregory said. The English-born chronicler Orderic Vitalis wrote of a monk named Ralf who successfully prayed for the disease; Yvette of Huy, the Belgian saint, went to live in a community of leprosy sufferers, yearning to join their number.

If one couldn't cancel purgatory with leprosy, one could at least bank some spiritual goodwill by practising charitable deeds or financial generosity towards these Christ-like figures (as Basil of Caesarea had done, establishing what has been characterised as the first hospital). The leprous sisters of St Mary de Pré would have prayed for their patrons' souls in the next world, in return for the food and succour they had received in this one.

———

After I've climbed back over the wooden fence, scraping a cowpat off my boot sole, it takes me fifteen minutes to walk through Verulamium Park, past the crumbling, fenced-off Roman walls I used to sit out on as a teenager and on to the foot of the hill that leads to the cathedral. So close to the city, it is clear that the placement of the hospital was an act of display, too, advertising the Christian charity of the priory's benefactors and its abbot. Social solvency and spiritual credit through an easy bit of patronage: the equivalent of sponsoring a night at the opera or bankrolling an art exhibition.

The set-up in St Albans was not odd. One of the earliest leprosaria in London was established in 1117 by Henry I's wife, Queen Matilda, a feverishly Christian woman who would wash and kiss the feet of the sick out of penitence (ensuring such acts were well-publicised among her subjects). It was situated in the gardens between the City of London and Westminster, where St Giles in the Fields church and the brutalist Centrepoint building now stand. The site was chosen to allow the up-to forty inmates to seek charity and barter for goods from those making their way between the two settlements. Matilda set a fashion, and the rich and ennobled of medieval England established such houses in East Anglia, the Midlands, the North and the far west of England. By 1350, at least 320 were established throughout the country, with Matthew Paris, the St Albans-based Benedictine monk, estimating that there were 19,000 leprosaria across western Europe.

Land registries, archaeological evidence and other primary sources show that these ranged from cloistered religious communities such as St Mary de Pré to near-democratic spaces in which residents had a large degree of autonomy due to the patronage they received. In the substantial collection of Byzantine artefacts of the Dumbarton Oaks Museum in Washington, DC, there is a sixth-century seal with the appearance of a coin, just over two centimetres in diameter and made of lead. The seals were used to verify that a document came from the sender and to demonstrate it had not been opened or tampered with. With a rough, chipped edge, this particular one shows St Zotikos on one face with an inscription in abbreviated Greek on the other: 'Seal of the brothers of St Zotikos' (St Zotikos was canonised for saving hundreds of people with leprosy who had been condemned to die by Emperor Constantine). These monks belonged to a large leprosarium that was established in the mid-sixth century in Constantinople. In a remarkable bit of detective work, for which the seal proved the smoking gun, historians were able to establish that any sale of assets or property from leprosaria needed the consent of the leprous residents themselves, which in the case of large institutions such as St Zotikos, where they outnumbered staff, effectively gave them a stake in the governance of their own institution, including, possibly, the budget itself. With that would have come power: no decision could be made without the residents' seal of approval.

Signs of similar agency could be found in western European institutions across the full run of the Middle Ages. In thirteenth-century Brive, south-west France, the residents regularly inspected the accounts and if they found the master of the leprosarium, elected from their number, to be corrupt, they were able to hold him to account. There is copious material showing that women had managerial roles. One document notes that a leadership meeting featuring four female and three male patients at a leprosarium in Genoa was, on one occasion in 1408, moved from its usual room in the institution to one of the women's bedrooms because she was confined sick to her bed. They would have crowded in, huddled round her, to discuss the immediate issues of the day. I imagine it was as long and winding as all residents' meetings, with the kind of grandstanders and rule sticklers who are uniform to any age. The patients themselves could accept philanthropic gifts as legal representatives of the institution in which they lived: in early-fifteenth-century Crete, a woman named Irene Ambelakianes had enough responsibility to sign a receipt for one such cash bequest. For many patients, life inside the walls of the leprosarium therefore was better than anything they had experienced outside – materially and politically – a privilege they guarded anxiously. At St Julian's, one of the richest of these establishments, patients were given a pig at Martinmas, with the resident who had lived in the leprosarium the longest enjoying first dibs. Where else would you get such treatment?

According to the statute books for various institutions across Europe, were any resident to prove continually disruptive, the ultimate sanction was expulsion from the community: a sign that these were places the residents wanted to be part of, not prisons they dreamt of escaping. Robert and Agnes Waldshaf, a married couple both with leprosy, lodged a petition with the English Crown in approximately 1328. Their institution beyond the East Gate of Chester, they moaned, had been founded 'for lepers alone' but 'is now charged with other people who are not sick', and would the king please ensure 'that they might be served with what he granted them there'. Indeed, St Bartholomew's in Dover has been likened to a 'medieval equivalent of a workers' co-operative under the direction of their leprous master', in which the sixteen male and female residents divided their garden produce and shared grain, milk and eggs between them, with enough surplus to pay the rent for the hospital land.

Completing this bucolic image, they made their own clothes from wool shorn from the leprosarium's own flock of sheep.

————

While the abbot of St Albans was planning St Mary de Pré, Henry II sat on the English throne. If some Victorian accounts are taken at face value, the kind that have since passed into popular imagination, the monarch oversaw a regime in which the leprous were burned alive – barbarous stuff that seems at odds with the archaeology beneath the grass. In debunking such fabulation, Carole Rawcliffe, now emeritus professor of medieval history at the University of East Anglia, emerges as something of a hero, forensically tracing the origins of this and other similarly horror-inducing readings of the past not just to the source material, but also the points in history where the misunderstanding – or deliberate misreading – of the archives occurred.

Henry II was draconian in his suppression of foreign religious heretics, introducing laws that promised death to anyone found importing banned religious texts or harbouring nonconformists in their homes. Leprosy was often used as an analogy for heresy in the Middle Ages: both spread by breath, one deforming the body, the other corrupting society. William of Newburgh, a chronicler, called those agitating against Church orthodoxy a 'pestilential disease'. As this analogy passed through texts and books of later centuries it became distorted, materialising in lurid descriptions of the English king ordering the sick to the stake. The narrative of Henry II conducting a cruel war against those affected by the disease is countered by the monarch's personal patronage of patients – not least in St Albans, where he not only confirmed the endowments already bequeathed to the residents of St Julian's, but added his own donation, in perpetuity, of 1d. a day (equivalent to what a skilled tradesman might earn in a week). The figure of the 'leper' was, after all, a bulwark against the Reformation, as much a part of Catholic theology as indulgences and transubstantiation.

Rawcliffe suggests another source for the claims of immolation was probably Thomas Becket – the monarch's sworn enemy, and eventual murder victim, so not exactly unbiased. It was, however, a nineteenth-century woman, Agnes Lambert, who painted the image of 'lepers' in flames most vividly for the modern reader. Lambert's historical misdirection was featured in the second of two articles she wrote in *The Nineteenth Century*, a pre-eminent monthly journal that took a strong interest in the subject of leprosy as Britain's imperial conquests flourished. The first article in August 1884 spilled out over two dozen pages of hyperbolic prose, suggesting the disease was an imminent threat:

> Leprosy has not ceased to be of living interest and concern to Englishmen; . . . with the expansion of England, it has been brought back to our very doors. For wherever the eye may rest throughout our vast Indian Empire, or the further-stretching limits of our colonial possessions, the dark cloud of leprosy is at this moment, whilst I write and others read what I have written, overshadowing the fairest spots of earth and the most fruitful territories of our commonwealth.

Committed to the doctrine that those with leprosy should be kept away from the rest of society, even at the cost of their own rights, she used her second commission in September 1884 to complain that the colonial authorities didn't take the danger as seriously as they, she claimed, had done in the Middle Ages. 'Whether they were the outcome of charity or selfishness, the one great general object in view was, not the cure of leprosy, for then as now leprosy was deemed incurable, but to arrest the spread of it: to prevent the contamination of the sound by contact with the infected'; to this end they were 'rigidly excluded'. She seems to excuse Henry II's supposed cruelty because, she writes, the king was acting 'through fear, not through greed'. Whatever repressive methods the new segregationists of the imperial powers might employ, they could at least claim they weren't indulging in mass executions. The medieval 'leper' and all the apparent degradations they suffered were concocted and exaggerated not only to strike fear into nineteenth-century hearts, but also to bolster colonial missionary programmes. 'Again and again we come across the stern decree of banishment and confiscation pronounced by the secular authority against the leper,' Lambert writes of the Middle Ages. 'And again and again we find the Church mercifully extending its protection to them.' The picture she paints of the past, bar the death sentence, seems above all a blueprint for imperial authorities tackling the disease by bayonet and Bible in her own time.

The myth of the 'leper mass' is just as fanciful. In 1931 Édouard Jeanselme, a French leprologist, wrote a detailed summary of a funereal ceremony which he alleged was performed in the Middle Ages on the discovery that some unfortunate harboured the disease. Jeanselme describes how the 'leper' was allowed to enter a church one last time. There they knelt before the altar under a makeshift awning of black material with a black veil over their face. In Amiens, France, the service would take place in the cemetery, the condemned required to stand in a freshly dug grave. Inside or out, three spadefuls of soil would be thrown in the face of the victim and, breaking from the Latin, the rules governing their new life would be read in the local language. They were told they could never again enter a church, nor 'fair, mill, marketplace, or company of persons. I forbid you to ever leave your house without your leper's costume.' They were told they couldn't use a stream or the water fountain. They couldn't enter a tavern, or touch anything that they might buy until it was theirs.

They were given a bell, rattle or clapper, which they must sound by way of warning. With that in hand, the diseased was led to their new accommodation.

The sisters of St Mary de Pré would have certainly had to go through a ceremony, just as the healthy nuns they lived alongside would have done when they took their habit. There was no 'funeral'. The leprous monks of St Julian's certainly had a uniform – a tunic and cowl of russet colour in which the sleeves were to extend to the hand and down to the ankles, black cloaks to be worn over the top when they attended church – and were dead to the earthly world, because like all religious they had taken their sacred vows. There were rules too: the leprous monks were to walk downwind of others, they weren't to linger gossiping in the street, they couldn't play with children – but the notion of a strict universal ostracisation is grossly overstated. For Chaucer to write of his lackadaisical friar, 'He knew the taverns well in every town / And every innkeeper and barmaid / Better than a leper or a beggar-woman' suggests a person with leprosy must have been a reasonably common sight for those swigging ales in the fourteenth century. Other apparent injustices are similarly questionable. On diagnosis, a person often lost legal rights, particularly rights to property, but the relinquishing of one's worldly possessions, to put it another way, was standard procedure for entering religious cloisters. And what about the bell and clapper, so iconic of the 'leper', used so much in religious art of the period? A tool not to scare away the public, but to summon their charity, the disease affecting the throat and speech. The equivalent of a British ice-cream van's tune calling for custom.

The macabre vision of the 'leper', misrepresented and distorted, proved too alluring a thought, though, taken up by poets such as Alfred, Lord Tennyson and Algernon Charles Swinburne – both close to the literary milieu of *The Nineteenth Century* – chiming with the dark Romantic imagination, and for far darker political ends. Before Jeanselme, Lambert too had relished the 'leper mass' as a common event. Reporting the priest's commandments, she pauses at number four – the rule which apparently forbade someone with leprosy from touching anything at the market until they had paid for it – and makes implicit her reason for retelling this history. Referring back to her first article for *The Nineteenth Century*, she writes: 'The fourth of these commandments would certainly have been appreciated by the people of Jamaica, where, as we saw, the lepers exhorted contribution by putting their fingerless stumps upon the articles they wanted that were exposed in the stores.' She notes approvingly of the seventh law, which commanded 'lepers' to avoid narrow streets, that even if those in the Middle Ages had been cogent with modern germ theory and had seen bacillus under the microscope, 'would it have been possible to devise a more minute and searching law?' Jeanselme was an equally unreliable historian, in fact no historian at all but rather the president of the eugenicist French National League Against the Venereal Peril, who among other things, personally advocated rigorous screening for leprosy, mental health issues and sexually transmitted diseases prior to the issuance of marriage licences in early-twentieth-century Paris. At every turn, there seems to be a figure of the later imperial age manipulating the image of medieval leprosy to suit the prejudices of their present.

———

Across a vast geography and numerous centuries, the experience of the medieval European with leprosy was not universal. Their fortunes waxed and waned. Civic and religious law differed, monarchs and popes left their mark, attitudes in the markets and taverns didn't always accord with the letter of the statute book. Not everyone was gifted a holiday pig. Leprosy was a constant presence until the fifteenth century, but the 'leper', the outcast, came and went. There *were* pockets of horrendous repression in the Middle Ages, and the so-called 1321 'lepers' plot' is surely the most infamous.

In the middle of Lent that year, during an unseasonable bout of snow, a rumour circulated the towns and villages of southern France that people with leprosy were behind a plan to poison the wells and drinking fountains. Their weapon was a witchy concoction of urine, human blood, three unspecified herbs and a consecrated host. These were apparently ground down to paste and placed in small bags containing weights which would sink to the bottom of the water sources. It was a wild fabrication, the kind that had long plagued other groups, such as Jews, who would soon be embroiled in this catastrophe. Like all conspiracy theories, it is hard, however, to say where the rumours sprang from or why it caught the imagination in quite the way it did. (Strangely, it did foreshadow another apocryphal incident some hundred years later, in which Catalan–Aragonese forces retreating from a Neapolitan village were said to have left their adversaries caskets of wine contaminated with the blood of leprosy patients.) Soon anyone with leprosy was being rounded up for inquisition and torture – at least two of those apprehended were women who had been elected 'masters' of their leprosaria. On the Maundy Thursday before Easter, the mayor of Périgueux ordered all the inhabitants of the leprosy houses to assemble in the town square. Men and women were separated and each subjected to interrogation with the order for general execution coming ten days later. Messengers were dispatched to King Philip V to tell him what had occurred.

With Easter gone, one of the most ferocious enforcers of Church orthodoxy, Bernard Gui, was put in charge of the investigation. He never seemed to doubt the plot 'against the safety of the people', said to be two years in the making. Bernard declared that 'these persons, unhealthy in body and insane in mind, had arranged to infect the waters of the rivers and fountains and wells everywhere . . . so that healthy men drinking from them or using the water thus infected, would become lepers, or die, or almost die, and thus the number of the lepers would be increased and the healthy decreased'. With the type of violence and lines of questioning employed by medieval inquisitors, often using torture, Bernard soon gathered the evidence he needed. Initially he claimed their motive was to take 'the lordship of towns and castles, and had already divided among themselves the lordship of places, and given themselves the name of potentate, count or baron in various lands, if what they planned should come about'. Come June, in a royal edict, those who had admitted their apparent guilt had their possessions seized by the Crown. Yet a person who had to beg for alms in their lifetime often had little to offer in death and so the pickings were relatively slender.

The detainees were coerced into extending the apparent plot, and admit they were in league with the Jews. In this lurid fantasy, Jewish people had paid the leprous to carry out the poisoning of the water, knowing that if they had done it themselves, they would be immediately suspected. It provided the flimsiest of excuses to arrest and kill any number of Jewish people and confiscate their property – possibly always the real aim. Given this alliance was already surely stretching credibility, it seemed logical to bring in yet more groups who were hated under Philip V's reign. Muslims, of whom there were few in France at the time, were undoubtedly the ones ultimately pulling the strings, the conspiracists reasoned, with the king of Granada and the sultan of Egypt taking on Mr Big roles. This seems the first anti-leprosy hysteria, a pogrom against the sick. It is a devilish story, but one that happened in just a few months, and the horrors proved short-lived. Something approaching sanity began to prevail in Périgueux by autumn when free movement resumed gradually, and soon after across the rest of France. The innocence of those with leprosy was acknowledged – they were even compared to the blameless children killed by Herod at one point – and the Pope agreed a decade or so later to a request for the return of one community's assets. No apology was forthcoming to the Jewish people, however, and when the Black Death arrived two decades later, history repeated itself, with fear once again stoking anti-Semitism.

———

In 1327, just a few years after the 'lepers' plot' across the Channel, Richard of Wallingford was made abbot of St Albans at the age of thirty-five. He showed no sign of leprosy during his ratification in Avignon, a city that had borne much of the persecution, but soon after a pain in one eye was the harbinger for worsening health. His monks refused calls for his removal, however, and demanded that a coadjutor be appointed to carry out his more strenuous duties while Richard was allowed to devote himself to his passions of horology, astronomy and trigonometry.

Stepping into the shade of the abbey is a relief after the walk; the stone walls and auburn floor tiles, with their crest motif, are cold to touch. The abbey, or cathedral as it is now, is the kind that is popular and big enough to need an extensive gift shop and a small platoon of jolly retirees to give guided tours. The interior is a mall of chapels, bays and vestries that line what is boasted as the longest nave in England. Stretching eighty-five metres, filled with rows of wooden pews, its gothic decoration was relatively new to Richard's time; the abbot inherited a building in disarray and bad shape following neglect and two earthquakes. From above, the whole place has the floorplan of a cross. You could spend hours touring what was once the mother-house to St Mary de Pré. The body of the cathedral has a pictorial ceiling and medieval wall paintings scratched out in red pigment from pillar to pillar. At the top, the altar is flanked by ornately carved choir stalls. The small crowd of tourists I pass at the entrance are diluted by the sheer size of the place, but their footsteps echo and mix with the sound of the organ practice drifting from the other side of the building. The stone shrines of Alban and Amphibalus, with their statuary and red and blue cloth roofs, are grandiose affairs left alone on this weekday.

At the information desk, I ask an older lady in a twinset where the modern re-creation of the clock Richard invented can be found. Her reply – that it is in 'the north ambulatory by the back of the watching loft' – is opaque, though signposts and the map she provides soon take me there. The original timepiece was destroyed by Henry VIII's Reformation and the dissolution of the churches, and this is one of a few versions built using Richard's notes. Located in a dark corridor around the corner from Amphibalus' memorial, it is a complex amalgam of freestanding black cogs, levers and dials, almost shoulder-height, more resembling agricultural equipment or an engine than a clock. Richard's father, who died when the boy was ten, had been a blacksmith, and metalworking obviously ran in the family. The largest element, a circular tabletop of brass, reflects the slight light of a stained glass window above. With the numbers one to twenty-four lattice-cut into the metal dial, and a large bell hanging to one side, this element was designed by Richard to give the hour; a second disc visible beneath, painted blue, details the movements of the sun, moon and stars. It would help the monks tell when an eclipse was due or when the religious festivals were to be celebrated.

It was a great leap forward in engineering and astronomy, a leaflet tells me, but this mechanism seems to say something too about the inventor's disease, which is barely mentioned in the otherwise informative text. Richard's own body was a clock, the advancement of leprosy marking the passing of days into months and years. Over in his chambers, across the abbey, his voice became hoarse, the sight in one eye fading to a blur. As the bacterial timepiece ticked, patches spread across his body and face. There are near-contemporary miniature drawings of him in a manuscript titled 'The St Albans Benefactors' Book': Richard is depicted in his black gown with his mitre and crosier, as he would have still worn at the main altar, but here he points proudly to his horological invention. The artist doesn't shy away from showing Richard's face besmirched with speckles and spots either, nor his ears engorged and nose snubbed, but there is no sign of the fabled leper's cloak and bell, no people screaming in fear. For the abbot and medieval society, these disfigurements were a sign of devotion; a finite, measurable hell, one through which his ascension into the celestial heavens could be counted down. They were a blessing at odds with the infinite-seeming, unmeasurable fires of purgatory that awaited healthy mortals. No wonder Richard's monks refused to shun him. Their abbot was a greater conduit to safety than that of any other bishopric. Whatever was to be written later, for the medieval world, leprous time could be divine.

BERGEN, NORWAY

Magnus Vollset is as neatly turned out and smiley as you might imagine a Norwegian academic to be. He is in the kind of jumper – cream and thickly knitted – that is regulation wear against the cold and wet of Bergen, his home city, along with blue slacks, trendy dad sneakers and a groomed goatee. I would have forgiven him for being tired when he picks me up outside my hotel. Not only does he have his three-month-old baby in a pram, but it is a mere week since he helmed an international conference on leprosy, in which he and the University of Bergen, his employer, played host to medical experts, politicians, activists and NGOs from around the world. These kinds of gatherings happen frequently and have done since the first leprosy conference in 1897 in Berlin, inaugurated as the disease became the bogeyman of imperialism. This 2023 iteration was particularly auspicious as it marked the 150 years since Gerhard Armauer Hansen, Bergen's most famous name, identified the bacteria that causes the disease.

Vollset and I walk away from the port and its fishing boats and up the hill to the university, weaving the pram between the town's bike-riding denizens and cruise-ship tourists, the latter clutching little souvenir Norwegian flags and gift-shop bags of toy trolls and Viking paraphernalia. These prosperous crowds give no hint of the impoverished place this was in Hansen's time. The university campus occupies a two-storey, H-shaped building, which when it was built in 1857 was among the largest wooden buildings in Norway. Now painted white with a pitched roof of terracotta tile, the weathervane of its central tower points to the coniferous mountains that watch over the city; above, the sky battles between sunshine and drizzle. This place was originally a leprosarium, the third institution dedicated to the disease in the city. It could house 280 people across forty dormitories while also functioning as a new research centre tasked with investigating Norway's epidemic leprosy numbers.

'Getting rid of leprosy was a step out of medieval times for Norway, a country in which conditions had barely changed,' Vollset says as we enter the college reception. Patients would first be assessed. If their condition was very advanced with no treatment likely to be effective, they were sent to the dark cells of the fifteenth-century St Jørgen's charitable hospital nearer the port, now a city museum dedicated to the disease. If the condition of a patient might present fertile ground for study, however, it is here or the more modern state-run care hospital, established in 1849, that they would come. Inside the university, on first inspection, there is not much sign of its previous function – it houses the usual maze of offices and study rooms of any college, empty and echoey as it is the holidays, enlivened only by the odd potted plant or bust of an esteemed former don. There's a cafeteria in the round room of the sanatorium's old chapel with an altar of paper coffee cups and a silent congregation of stacked chairs under the domed roof where patients used to pray. Climbing to the floor above, we pass an upright piano on the stairwell, the steps landing in a long corridor. At the end, a locked door, through which is the reason I came to Norway. With a modicum of flourish, Vollset pulls out a set of keys.

———

Hansen's laboratory – two small rooms retaining most of their original fittings, the wood panels painted a medical mint green – is not routinely open to the public. In the first room, a wooden lab desk overlooks the courtyard garden. From here Hansen would have been able to see across to the men's wing of the institution or observe the patients taking the air on the lawns below. On the workbench to the right of where he likely sat is an oven-like contraption, its outside lined with fur, that worked as an incubation chamber for bacteria. A stack of four shelves climbing up the wall between the windows heaves with empty medicine bottles and long glass jars with cork stoppers: white transparent on the top shelf, brown and blue below. Some of these, Vollset admits, may not be the exact ones Hansen touched, but were bought from Svaneapoteket in Bergen, Norway's oldest pharmacy, which has been operating across town since 1595 – a strange slice of decorative artifice for a place rarely seen. Some objects are periodically sent over to the leprosy museum at St Jörgen's, but there are books, files and boxes here, as well as Hansen's purse and lighter. There are bygone scientific machines, the purposes of which I can't work out, a Bunsen burner, pestles and mortars, test tubes, weighing scales and several other portable stoves on which sit enamel pots. In a glass display box nearby is a taxidermy armadillo – one of the few non-human animals that can harbour the disease – a gift from the Brazilian contingent to the Tenth International Leprosy Congress. Undermining the aura of the place is the fact that no one is sure if this is the exact room in which he first observed the rod-shaped *Mycobacterium leprae* or not. Nonetheless, here is Hansen's microscope, here are his notes, here are the monuments to a great man of history.

Hansen was born in Bergen in 1841, one of fifteen children, and soon after weaning was sent to live with an aunt and uncle on a farm twelve kilometres out of town. He was, when he returned to the city at school age, 'not an outstanding student' he admitted, preferring to spend more time scrapping with pals, riding his toboggan and tormenting the local parson (for laughs Hansen and his friends would wait until the religious man snoozed or was writing his sermon and kick footballs hard against the wall of the clergy house). Despite this waywardness he did well enough to enrol at university in Kristiania, as Oslo was then known, and as his family were not rich he took various jobs along the way to support himself. Vollset relays the story with a historian's objectivity as we potter through the vestiges of Hansen's life. In the memoirs Hansen wrote when famous and old, he comes across as a laddish, humorous presence, someone with whom it would be fun to get drunk but who you'd probably want to leave before things got too boorish and out of hand: on news of German victory in the Franco-Prussian War Hansen says he was 'up all night drinking' with friends; he moans that on a trip to Bremen he was forced to share a stagecoach with 'two pastors and an unattractive woman'; in Venice he complains of the Norwegian tinsmith he gets stuck with, moaning that the simple man doesn't understand his intellectual chat. Such comments hide a youthful sensitivity, though, that stumbles out in both personal and professional settings. 'I was invited to many parties, where I enthusiastically ate and drank and talked. I was unable to dance, though, and this bothered me,' he writes at one point.

More seriously, though he would receive a gold medal for his studies of the lymph gland, his first post-mortem was a disaster, performed on a man who had drowned. 'I felt myself growing ill but managed to hold out until they started sawing the skull. That noise was more than I could take and I fled the place.' On graduating, and after a few years working in Kristiania, he took a position on the Lofoten Islands working as a medic to the cod fishermen. In 1868 a job back home became available and, tired of treating drinking accidents and diagnosing scurvy, though knowing little about leprosy, he jumped at the chance to work at the new research hospital. It was the making of him. 'During the first month I suffered terribly. I had never seen so much misery concentrated in one place,' he recalls. 'Gradually, though, as I commenced handling the patients, my aversion disappeared and was replaced by a great desire to learn the illness in detail', a thought that hints his interest was more academic than pastoral.

———

Norway was far from the oil-rich nation beloved of dubiously weighted 'quality of life' surveys it is today. In the early nineteenth century, still ruled by its then more prosperous neighbours, rural poverty was endemic. On being led into the Napoleonic Wars while under the control of Denmark, the Norwegians had been placed under naval blockade by the British, starving the population and depressing the timber industry. On defeat, Denmark was forced to cede its possession to rival Sweden, but the conflict ignited long-suppressed Norwegian nationalism. An attempt to declare independence failed, but much of a proposed new constitution, drafted in case of victory, was accepted by Stockholm, and a greater sense of autonomy prevailed. A massive cultural project to cultivate a Norwegian sense of identity, invariably romantic and idealised, began to unfold. Traditions and cultures were either rediscovered or more frequently invented, from the coining of the Viking Age as a period (instead of just early medieval times) to the stitching together of a national costume. The writers Peter Christen Asbjørnsen and Jørgen Moe set off for the far corners of the country to collect fairy tales and cultivate patriotic myths; Olea Crøger travelled from hamlet to hamlet recording the folk tunes; Ludvig Mathias Lindeman developed a new hymnal tradition that was uniquely Norwegian.

While culture blossomed, the country remained mired in poverty and the great many Norwegians with leprosy suffered the most in the aftermath of the war. There are no records of how many people had the disease at that time (which was part of the problem), but in 1852 there were approximately eleven cases for every 10,000 people, around 2 per cent of the country, with some areas in the western counties seeing symptoms among half the population. Those in St Jørgen's were in a pitiful state, crammed into tiny rooms with little medical attention. Johan Ernst Welhaven, the priest there, decried this destitution: if romantic Norway was so great, how could it let this happen? The connection between disease and the country's sense of self was an emotive one. The Black Death, which had decimated Norway's population across the classes, was cited as a reason the fourteenth-century kingdom lost its power and status and entered into what Ibsen satirised in *Peer Gynt* as 400 'years of darkness'. A carefully worded 1816 report by Welhaven is powerful. The opening paragraph described the 'tearful eye, and greatest anxiety of his heart' that he felt every time he was confronted with the patients in a place that was no hospital but 'a graveyard for the living'. Even more affecting are the twenty-eight watercolour portraits of the residents he included, together with four plates showing details of some of the worst physical manifestations of the disease. These stood in stark contrast to the kind of paintings that were being celebrated at the time. Johan Christian Dahl's *Mountain Landscape with Waterfall, Castle and Traveller on Horseback in Front of a Hut* (1816), an early example of the artist's glowing pastoral landscapes, is typical of the prevailing tone. It's a bucolic vision shared by many artists of this apparent 'golden age', which reached its zenith in the smiling folk of Hans Gude and Adolph Tidemand's *Bridal Procession on the Hardangerfjord* (1848), singing and chatting as they row across a beautiful sun-drenched fjord. Away from those fresh faces, Welhaven's portraits of his patients tell a different story. There is Olaf, in his blue waistcoat, his skin covered like a cheetah in black blotchy marks; Anna, staring sadly from behind drooping eyelids that hang pendulous down her face; a second man named Olaf, his face slowly morphing, his features overtaken by the condition. They aren't particularly accurate, medically speaking, and slightly voyeuristic in the way they hover over the person's disability, but if Welhaven painted them himself he did so with artistic flair and a political purpose that spurred the authorities into action.

———

It is bewildering as to where we might start in Hansen's lab, given how many curious objects it contains. I want to pore over the books, take out the papers, climb up and look at the top shelves. Vollset is game for me to do so but it is also clear he has a tour he has developed over years of showing around other intrigued visitors. He first directs my attention to three roller maps that hang at the entrance. 'Leprosy was thought this ancient disease; getting rid of it therefore became a priority for the nationalist programme,' he says. It was embarrassing that Norwegians arriving in the USA, for example, had to undergo a medical examination before being allowed entry. 'It was a disease associated with the colonies, and we didn't want to be a colony,' Vollset adds, not without a sense of dark irony. At over a hundred years old, the maps are yellow with age and frayed at the edges, a cliché of the treasure maps I dreamt of finding as a kid and faked using paper stained with coffee. One shows the world with a varying palette of deep red to orange to yellow, the tones indicating the density of leprosy cases as they invade the geography of the poorest nations. Hanging on the wood-panelled wall to the right is a map of India, and a third map, the largest, features Norway. Each one is as blotchy as the others, a visualisation reflecting the type of epidemiological registry Norway commissioned off the back of Welhaven's protest, the first of its kind and with a methodology still used today. There are stacks of censuses to be found too, with their cursive ink scrawl detailing the names and addresses of the diagnosed from all over the country. The data didn't lead Norway to the right scientific conclusion straight away, that leprosy was contagious, Vollset notes, but it did bolster the case for more research.

Seeing the clusters accumulate around certain villages in which multiple generations of the same families had lived for centuries, authorities initially convinced themselves that the disease was hereditary. The solution therefore seemed obvious: castrate or sterilise the patient and their family. The mathematical – not to mention the ethical – implications were extraordinary, however, entailing medical intrusion into not just the lives of the almost 3,000 people identified with the disease in 1856 but multiples of ten, if the doctors were to operate on parents, siblings and children of the diagnosed too; and more so if extended family were to be brought into the equation. Your cousin has leprosy? No children for you.

It was the physicians who protested against the idea. Their position among the public was still tenuous and it was a struggle to encourage people to trust modern medicine over local herbal doctors. (On a similar matter, Hansen once observed 'the wisdom of old folk . . . is usually just bunk'.) Instead, a milder solution was put forward, one by no means unique to Norway, and that was to ban marriage among those diagnosed and their families. It was now the clergy's turn to reject this apparent 'cure'. Vollset lays out the two arguments from the Church for me: 'The first argument was that marriage is a pact with God, that you can't interfere with. The second is more modern, in that banning someone from marriage doesn't stop them being human. The only thing we achieve by a policy like that is children being born out of wedlock. So for the clergy that would be creating a new social problem.' For now, while the data accumulated, the quandary of how to be a modern nation lay unanswered in the Nordic country.

The more progressive response to Welhaven's protest was the research hospital in which Hansen landed his job. His new boss was Daniel Danielssen, who, together with dermatologist Carl Wilhelm Boeck, had written the study *On Leprosy*, and produced *The Atlas of Leprosy*. The former, a first edition of which is kept in a vitrine that Vollset opens, each leaf carefully separated by tissue paper, provided the best contemporary written description of the disease; but the latter proves an even more extraordinary document when we lift it out of a display cabinet. What Welhaven's watercolours lacked in medical use, Danielssen and Boeck rectified in commissioning twenty-four detailed paintings that helped identify the appearance of leprosy over any other skin condition. The subjects do not provide the emotion of Welhaven's sitters; the pictures were scientific documents, lithographs sent around the world and used in diagnostic settings: we see the macular lesions in the cheeks of a young girl, the swelling of the joints in a man's hand, images of interior wastage and external decline.

Doctors from overseas were invited to observe Norway's epidemiological mapping – this was the first time anyone had gone out and conducted a door-to-door survey hunting out the disease – and the hospitals built in its wake, the inmates entering voluntarily at this point. Soon science rivalled the arts as a form of soft power. In 1874, Henry Vandyke Carter, an English surgeon working for the Indian Medical Service (and nowadays best known for his illustrations in *Gray's Anatomy*), came to study Norway's newfound focus, reporting back to the Under Secretary of State for India with enthusiasm. Robson Roose, a fashionable physician who counted many of the British political establishment as patients (and who more often considered questions of gout and wrote guides such as *The Wear and Tear of London Life*), also penned a whole book in admiration of Norway's leprosy model. As recently as 1989, the US historian Zachary Gussow subtitled a chapter on Norway's way of dealing with the problem

'The Enlightened Kingdom'. When less complimentary reports of the 'cheerless and desolate' Norwegian hospitals were made in Britain's *Nursing Record*, with institutions cited as lacking 'warmth' ('there is . . . no welcome, no touch of a sympathetic hand to invest these bare, dreary wards with some semblance of a home for these unfortunates'), it produced a furious response from Danielssen, professional and national pride piqued, who in the following issue combed through the article for whatever errors he could find.

Hansen got on personally with his boss, to the extent he even married Danielssen's daughter, Stephanie Marie, though she was to die of tuberculosis within a year of their vows. Professionally, though, they began to drift apart. Seeing how cases clustered only affirmed to Danielssen that leprosy was inherited. 'Once leprosy has entered a family it spreads to all sides and in a horrifying way,' he wrote. 'It sometimes looks as if it has become extinct . . . it is only a lull in the wind, only a slumber in which the terrible enemy has lain.' For Hansen, this made no sense – the younger doctor began to ask awkward questions. How is it that disease seems to spread sideways? Why doesn't everyone in the same family get the disease? How is it that it seems to skip generations? Why are non-blood relatives affected? Could it be a disease of poverty? Almost half the residents of some districts were suffering from this single debilitating illness: the poor-relief system was overwhelmed, the budget consumed, and the poor grew poorer. That cases then snowballed was evidence, to Hansen, that something else was at play.

Younger and more versed in microbiology, Hansen began pursuing the contagion theory. By the 1840s, with microscopes that could magnify over a thousand times, it was established that the body was an amalgam of trillions of cells. Scientists knew that bacteria could enter the body, but what they could not yet ascertain was if bacteria caused disease. 'At that time I had a remarkable work endurance. I could work tirelessly for hours on end, focussing through the micro-scope with great enlargement,' Hansen wrote. There are photographs of him doing just that: bald, his beard not yet turned white, hunched forward on an upholstered armchair, staring down the eyepiece tube, the lab even more cluttered than it is now. There's no doubt he was committed to his research for the sake of it, but it's not cynical either to suggest that leprosy provided a space in which the ambitious scientist could make his name. Every scourge needs a saviour, and for Hansen the disease would mean fame as the man who modern-ised Norway.

On the evening of 28 February 1873, the hospital was quiet before the weekend. Hansen was yet again at his desk. 'I found sufficient cells that appeared suspiciously like bacteria,' he notes – it was a breakthrough, but not the end of the matter. 'Then began a time of interminable testing.' In a footnote to his report, Henry Vandyke Carter mentions meeting Hansen – the Norwegian showed him 'minute organisms' in his telescope, which if proven to be a bacterial cause, Vandyke Carter acknowledged, would change everything. 'One day I was positive I had discovered the bacteria,' Hansen recalled. 'The next day the magnificent certainty had collapsed and I would be back where I started. It was always again and again and again. Finally when I wrote my first record of my research I could say no more than that I had found bacteria in the knots of leprosy and that I thought they were poison causing the disease.'

For Hansen himself, this was when leprosy became as much a political issue as a medical one. Two years after his discovery, he was appointed Chief Medical Officer for Leprosy, and he immediately set about lobbying to make segregation compulsory. The confinement of patients was gradual and uncontroversial at first: those impoverished by the disease were exempted from workhouses and sent to hospitals, which few, least of all the patients, complained about. They could still come and go, often making saleable objects in their cells to hawk around the streets; Henri Leloir, the French doctor, recalled being offered cobbling services from a man with leprosy during a visit to Bergen and seeing others sell 'eatables' in the market. The Seclusion of Lepers Act of 1885, more draconian, caused a great deal more debate before passing. 'There was an emotional outburst and strong opposition to this, the cry going up that such treatment of human beings was cruel, that it was a case of punching them because they had an illness which fate of the Almighty had wished on them,' Hansen wrote with increasing militancy:

> I maintained that healthy people must have the same humane treatment as the sick. If the fit found that the diseased could be a danger to them and consequently the community as a whole, they had the right and duty to isolate them as long as it was done com-passionately. Fortunately the healthy were in majority and ultimately responsibly prepared to exercise their power.

It is worth pausing over that last sentence as it contains the calculation that would set the terms of the debate across the globe. In defining 'biopolitics', Michel Foucault, the French philosopher, outlined how historically a monarch reserved the right to take life, either indirectly (by ordering subjects into battle, for example) or directly in such circumstances that the divine life of the royal was at stake (the gallows for a traitor or usurper). In modern times the role of the absolute monarch is replaced by 'the social body to ensure, maintain or develop its life . . . Wars are no longer waged in the name of a sovereign who must be defended; they are waged on behalf of everyone; entire populations are mobilised for the purpose of wholesale slaughter in the name of life.' Society's power lies not in its ability to command death but its reign over life, a life the purpose of which is the expansion of extractivist 'modernisation'. It is no coincidence, then, that the proposed mass segregation of leprosy patients, even if not as strictly maintained as in the countries that Hansen inspired, came at a point of Norwegian desperation after ten years of economic stagnation.

———

At the Twenty-first International Leprosy Congress in Hyderabad, in India's Telangana state, in 2021, in front of many advocating for changing the name of the condition from leprosy to Hansen's disease, Vollset presented a paper asking 'Armauer Hansen: Hero or Villain?' When relating the history to me, the historian uses 'we' to refer to Norway and it is clear he wrestles with the notion of national pride. 'We have this research institution, we're turning this shameful disease into a sign of progress, unity and everything positive, but as the optimism behind finding a cure begins to wane, things get stricter and stricter, things get darker,' he says.

While the Seclusion of Lepers Act of 1885 did not make institutionalisation universal, it gave authorities the power to detain patients who did not meet various hygiene standards in their own homes, including using separate rooms, beds, clothing, plates, utensils and kitchenware to the rest of the household. This was fine if you lived the life of a middle-class Ibsen character, in effect allowing the minority wealthier patients to stay home. Those living with a large family in, say, a one-room wooden cabin, were soon forced into hospitals, with inpatient numbers increasing dramatically in the years following. It was the sick's responsibility 'not to contaminate the healthy' under the prevailing culture and if they were not able, willing or too 'stupid' – Hansen's word – to take on that responsibility the doctor believed there was 'no other alternative than to use force'. Hansen lectured across the country about the importance of sanitation and hygiene in disease prevention, but admitted the primary purpose of the talks was to whip up fear against the sick. It is 'important that [the healthy] do not want contact with the lepers. If I achieve that then my goal is reached,' Hansen wrote to an American colleague. The aim? Even if the middle classes had the means to follow the hygiene rules that on paper ensured their freedom, they would find life unbearable. 'In Norway we have achieved that a leper who wants a servant does not find one,' Hansen proclaimed with a sense of satisfaction. The intention was to mould a specific health policy, contested as much as supported by science, into reflexive 'common sense'. Of course you wouldn't want your house cleaned by a leprosy patient, even though a year or two ago you'd had your shoes mended by such a person. This dims the aura around Norway's national hero. 'Stigma was used as a public health tool – spreading fear, spreading the message that these people were dangerous; that was used as a way of combating the spread of the disease,' Vollset says.

Soon Hansen's war on leprosy was taken up far beyond Norway's borders, a cooked-up horror among Europeans inverse to the prevalence of the disease in their midst. The number of new leprosy cases across the continent by the late 1800s was vanishingly small, and concentrated in a few tight geographical spots. On the yellowing map of the world in Hansen's lab, Norway is the only bit of the continent inked red; those burning blotches of colour, however, sprawl across the colonised populations of East, West and South Africa, India and South Asia, and vast swathes of South America. Ironically, the transformation of leprosy into a 'tropical disease', a term steeped in racist undertones, began in wet and windy Bergen. Danielssen and Boeck's mapping project gave colonial administrators the tools to conduct their own surveys, providing not only the most accurate data to date on the spread of the disease, but justification for the importation of Hansen's segregationist model. For many colonial powers, an excuse to introduce future control measures on their overseas subjects was too good to be true. 'This is rhetoric, an argument,' Vollset says of the maps. 'This is telling you that what we're doing works and if you too want to solve your leprosy problem, we have a solution for you.'

———

The British press at home and across the empire, both medical and popular, carried sensational descriptions of the disease's symptoms, lurid in detail, heavy with racism. A correspondent for the *Madras Mail* described a man whose 'cheeks had swollen, the hair on his eyebrows had dropped, his fingers and toes has swollen and gradually began to cut away, weal-like ulcers broken on various parts of his body and limbs – in fact he was a most horrible object to look at'. The *Madras Mail* reporter's words are reflected in 'The Mark of the Beast', a grotesque short story by Rudyard Kipling, first published in *Pioneer*, the Allahabad journal at which the writer worked. It centres on a drunk Englishman who, after blasphemously stubbing his cigarette out on a temple shrine, is bitten by 'a leper of some years' standing'. The Englishman becomes demonically possessed until the narrator of the story, a countryman, apprehends his attacker, who has 'no face' for 'his disease was heavy upon him'. The narrator physically tortures the faceless man until he lifts the spell off his friend. The demonisation of India in particular reached the highest level with Edward VII, then Prince of Wales, bemoaning the possession as the 'chief seat of the disease'.

In 1889 Father Damien, a Belgian missionary to a Hawaiian leprosy colony, died of complications from leprosy. In response, Reverend Henry Press Wright, a former British army chaplain, who had become rector to the English village of Greatham, pleaded: 'Are Europeans liable to leprosy? Is England in danger? I answer yes. Europeans and their descendants freely exposed to the disease take the malady just as readily as others.' The advances in science were partly behind this sudden reckoning. Hansen's discovery and those of other researchers dispelled any vestige of the belief that the disease might only, in the words of *The Times*, be a problem in countries 'to a greater or lesser extent, generally speaking, in proportion to the physical and moral degradation of their people'. It meant the non-white colonised world.

With the knowledge that the 'civilised' Westerner was as much in danger as those on the poorer streets of Calcutta or toiling in the sugar plantations of Hawaii, the banging of this war drum became deafening. In Wright's 1885 pamphlet *Leprosy and Segregation* he rallied, 'Ere we are aware of it the fearful scourge may again be actively in our midst; and England, who thought herself so safe, be with her closely packed population again in the field of its cruel ravages.' Written a year after Agnes Lambert's *The Nineteenth Century* articles, this *again* would have been a nod to the medieval mythology of the disease. With the British relationship with India in flux, Henry Vandyke Carter suggested direct rule would see an increase in the number of English people in India beyond those already present. 'Should the colonisation of India by Englishmen be ever attempted on a large scale, there would be a decided risk of the new population becoming tainted with leprosy . . . therefore strict regulations would have to be enforced.' The London School of Tropical Medicine was part of the response, established with colonial funds in 1899 – not for the benefit of colonised populations, but to counter the high death rate among white administrators, and the consequential financial burden borne by the British government.

The Palestine-born literary critic Edward Said has described Thomas Mann's novella *Death in Venice* as a fable in which an 'Asiatic' plague, a 'combination of dread and promise, of degeneration and desire',

threatens the very heart of a Western civilisation 'no longer invulner-
able, no longer able to ignore its ties to its overseas domains'. It is an
international fever dream that descends too on another, more populist,
short story, Arthur Conan Doyle's 'The Adventure of the Blanched
Soldier', set just after the end of the Second Boer War (though published in 1926). Sherlock Holmes is tasked with solving the mystery of
a missing soldier. Spoiler alert: the opium-partial detective deduces the
man has leprosy, or at least the man thinks he has it, contracted after
accidentally taking shelter in a South African field clinic. On the
stricken soldier's return to his bucolic English manor, fearful he will be
taken away and put into a life of segregation, his family keep his condition shrouded in secrecy and hide him away in an outhouse.
Emerging from his hermitude, the man describes to Holmes the
moment he encountered the leprosy patients.

> The African sun flooded through the big, curtainless windows, and
> every detail of the great, bare, whitewashed dormitory stood out
> hard and clear. In front of me was standing a small, dwarf-like man
> with a huge, bulbous head, who was jabbering excitedly in Dutch,
> waving two horrible hands which looked to me like brown
> sponges . . . A chill came over me as I looked at them. Not one of
> them was a normal human being. Everyone was twisted or swollen
> or disfigured in some strange way. The laughter of these strange
> monstrosities was a dreadful thing to hear.

The tale is both a satire on the fear that consumed the Western
world – so many of Conan Doyle's characters are colonialists whose
return to England catalyses some sort of crisis – while the description
taps into the contemporaneous reader's prejudice against both the
sick and the African continent. The story only ends happily because
the soldier is revealed to not actually have leprosy, merely a skin condition, the 'purity' of his complexion soon restored.

The 1897 Berlin international leprosy conference was the set piece to the global mania Conan Doyle leverages in his tale. Hansen was the star turn, but with sponsorship from the German state, this was not to be a purely academic occasion. Doctors across the world had been assembling into two camps: the contagionists, who supported quarantines and segregationist measures, and the anticontagionists, who argued that such measures were ineffective or unethical. Neither India nor Britain sent representatives, constituting a third group, who largely accepted the contagion theory but queried the large-scale construction of leprosaria. This position was not a benign one, but simply economic: the number of leprosy patients in India was never fully established with any certainty, but in 1881 an estimated 120,000 people had the disease, a number that the authorities thought likely to be wildly conservative. The British administrators of India were left with a stark choice. It would be financially impossible to incarcerate so many people. They could either accept the contagion theory and show the world that they didn't have control of the empire – a very dangerous move given that the agitation for Indian independence was gaining momentum – or reject the theory on spurious grounds. It was a weaselly position, barely softened by the various charitable organisations that provided perfunctory aid. When, after independence, an Indian doctor was challenged by a Japanese counterpart on the lack of any proper policy from the Nehru government, the medic's exasperation was clear. 'I had to explain to him the economic and other conditions of India and the difficulties which the Government of India had to face after independence. With hundreds of unsolved health and other problems, India had 1,500,000 leprosy patients . . . When segregation even in mainland colonies was a difficult problem, India could not even think of island colonies.'

The 180 delegates that did travel to Germany found themselves treated well. A specially commissioned train took them to the New Palace in Potsdam for a reception with the German emperor, Wilhelm II; the most prominent visitors, Hansen included, were given a private audience amid the rococo decor of the Grotto Hall, the thousands of inlaid shells eavesdropping on their conversation. The conference was watched carefully by governments of 'all civilised states', the news wires claimed, with many imperial powers nominating a scientist to specifically represent their interests (Édouard Jeanselme, the eugenicist leprologist, was there for France). Jules Goldschmidt, the Portuguese superintendent of a leprosarium on Madeira, called for 'a stern denial of entry to all diseased subjects [to Europe], and surveillance of all suspected individuals'; Hansen also spoke out for walls and closed borders. Summing up the mood, one correspondent noted: 'Every leper is a danger to his surroundings, the danger varying with the nature and extent of his relations therewith, and also with the sanitary conditions under which he lives.' While it was admitted the wealthy were as susceptible to the disease, in lines that reflect Norwegian law, it was deemed that 'among the lower classes every leper is especially dangerous to his family and fellow-workers'.

There was much reference to Europe's distant past and its lessons for the colonised world. The treatment of the medieval leprosy sufferers – the myth that they were universally feared and ostracised – was cited as an effective strategy in tackling the disease. Few present in Berlin denied the 'influence of Middle Ages' segregation in reducing leprosy in Western Europe', a British doctor recalled of his fellow delegates. Among those that did was Rudolf Virchow, a German physician who maintained people possessed a hereditary predisposition to the disease, and the British surgeon Jonathan Hutchinson, who argued leprosy was a condition of diet, particularly fish if badly cooked. Citing the apparent prevalence of the disease in Catholic countries, where fish would traditionally be eaten on a Friday, his view contradicts the report that a British government committee on which he sat had stated a few years earlier. Then there were those who accepted Hansen's hypothesis of contagion, but argued segregation by force only led to families hiding patients in the fashion of Conan Doyle's Blanched Soldier. 'Love and affection prove superior to the loathing and disgust which the disease naturally inspires,' one unsigned British newspaper editorial countered.

The conference, however, passed three motions, all authored by Hansen with the barest of amendments, that would have untold consequences for millions:

1. In countries in which leprosy forms foci or has a great extension, isolation is the best means of preventing the spread of the disease.
2. The system of obligatory notification and of observation and isolation, as carried out in Norway, is recommended to all nations with local self-government and a sufficient number of physicians.
3. It should be left to the legal authorities, after consultation with the medical authorities, to take such measures as are applicable to the special social conditions of the districts.

With these resolutions signed, the attendees, all men, were entertained by a 'smoking concert' at which, given the mood was turning in favour of such draconian control, it is perhaps notable that the top brass of the German Empire's military and police were on hand to chat with the medics and scientists. The British for their part, observing from afar, relented in their India strategy; as proposed years before by Henry Vandyke Carter after his visit to Norway, the authorities passed the All-India Lepers Act of 1898, mandating for forcible exclusion but backed by woefully few facilities. For the second leprosy conference, twelve years later, held in Bergen itself, London sent a representative and there was little debate over whether the disease was contagious or whether the segregation that had been pursued the decade previous had been the right course (though Hutchinson was still talking about fish).

———

In Bergen, Vollset leads me into a second, slightly larger room, just as crowded. It is dominated by a grand oak writing desk and a small island of vitrines, presumably later additions, in which Hansen's papers and research effects are shown. One wall is obscured by floor-to-ceiling glass-doored bookshelves, in which leather-bound titles report the state of leprosy from around the world. Another wall is filled with black-and-white studio portraits of Hansen and his peers, but you would be forgiven for not noticing those – more arresting are the wax faces which stare out of an open display unit. Like death masks, they are cast from real people, the material replicating the nodules and caverns of a face with advanced leprosy; masks of this time often still exhibit skin samples on their underside. But for tiny slits, their eyes are all but shut, the mouths swollen and blistered, the genders indeterminate as the bacteria does its grim work. Mounted underneath are moulds of infected ankles and wrists and elbows. The cast of a foot rests on the bottom of the cabinet. More unnerving still is a display which Vollset asks me not to photograph, even for reference. Across two shelves stand eight or so large glass jars, filled with discolouring formaldehyde and preserving alcohol. 'There's a certain controversy, a sensitivity that must be respected. We don't, after all, know where these came from or under what circumstances,' he says. Inside, swollen and ghastly, are the feet and hands of at least two leprosy patients. Terribly deformed, they might have been severed during the life of a patient, or they could have been removed after death. Either way, the question of medical consent hangs in the air as Vollset and I stare at them in the dimly lit room.

Utopian ideas underpin their gruesome preservation. They were saved by doctors – not necessarily Hansen; Vollset thinks they originated from a leprosarium in Trondheim – as time capsules. The assumption was that the future would always have better investigative tools than the present, that scientific progress was inevitable, and so it proved. Such samples have been extensively used in modern archaeobiological research, comparing their make-up to ancient and medieval skeletons as well as current DNA samples, tracing the routes different strains of the disease have made around the world. Preserved amputations helped establish how leprosy affects the joints, how the bacteria damage the hands and the feet. That knowledge, and the subsequent research, helped ease the pain of many. This history does not change the ethical murkiness of their procurement, nor is this a case of judging the past by the values of the present. The patients in Norway's hospitals were very vocal in proclaiming their rights. It was known among those at St Jørgen's that Danielssen was performing dissections on the bodies of residents after their death. It caused a great deal of grief but was perfectly legal and came at a point when little attention was being paid to Norway internationally. Things came to a head, however, as Hansen's fame spread. He wasn't particularly well-liked by his patients – it was known he was the godfather of segregation – but his brilliance in the laboratory shielded him from criticisms of his high-handed bedside manner.

He met his match, however, in the figure of Kari Nielsdatter Spidsøen. She was born in Bømlo, the last municipality on Norway's western coast as the country splinters into the sea. Her family of eleven was equally fragmented: her mother's family and step-family had a long history of leprosy and two of Kari's older sisters were diagnosed when she was four. As the first census of patients was being made, her brother died after contracting leprosy, and a year later her sister Synneva Christine and brother Øystein Johan, aged twenty-two and twelve respectively, were diagnosed and sent to the new hospital in Bergen. Brita, the oldest of the siblings, followed a year later. It seemed inevitable then that Kari would enter the public health data herself and in 1863, when she was sixteen, the local doctor ordered her to the city institution. Transported by rowing boat to the city, she carried with her a bag sparsely packed with two sets of clothes which 'will become the property of the institution after death'. With such finality weighing heavy on her mind, on entering the hospital the teenager would have found 300 more residents aside from her own family, all in cramped dorms.

By the time Hansen arrived four years later, Kari might have become acclimated to the crushingly uniform routine of waking at the same time, drinking the same carefully measured 360 ml of tea each morning; she'd certainly have known it was broth four days a week for dinner, with fish served three times, always potatoes and bread on the side, and that lights were extinguished at 10 p.m. without fail. Her body was the only thing that changed as her years ticked by into adulthood, and her symptoms are recorded as including necrosis of the leg – a problem that required amputation – and minor paralysis of the face, hands and the remaining foot. On the whole, however, her condition was on the milder end of the spectrum compared to others sharing the dorms.

Hansen was getting frustrated too, juggling his job as resident physician with his research as the Chief Medical Officer for Leprosy. After the initial burst of publicity over the potential identification of the bacteria, his progress in the laboratory had slowed. His correspondence with Robert Koch, the German scientist who would go on to publish the criteria needed to prove the causal effect between microbes and disease, was the source of his discouragement. Koch would later rule that, in order to prove a specific organism caused a disease, it must be shown that the bacteria was present in everyone with the condition and not found in the healthy; that it could be isolated and cultivated in the lab; and that it must cause a disease when administered to a healthy individual. While he was fairly certain of the first, Hansen had not been able to grow the bacteria artificially, despite the incubator in his lab (nor has anyone since), and his experimentation with animals had proved unfruitful. Worse still, his attempts to stain the microscopic rod-shaped forms and prove that they were bacterial had not only failed, but a German doctor, Albert Neisser – to whom Hansen himself had provided a sample and collaborated with when the rival visited Norway – had succeeded, publishing his results first. This threw Hansen into paroxysms of indignation, a fury shared by his colleagues in Norway, distraught that credit for the discovery might be taken away from the country. An indignant Hansen immediately published his research in Norwegian, German, English and French, concluding 'this paper effectively established the fact that it was I who found the cause of leprosy'.

The pressure to maintain his burgeoning fame was keenly felt when, during his hospital rounds on 3 November 1879, he asked Kari to come into his surgery. She was thirty-two years old by this point, feeling vulnerable after the death of Brita a month earlier, her last surviving relative in the institution. Walking down the corridor, one of those that the students during term-time crowd through today, she did not know why she had been summoned but was anxious enough that she burst into tears on reaching the door of Hansen's office. We know from the later court transcripts that once she was inside physical force was used, the hospital superintendent, also present, holding Kari as Hansen took out a cataract knife and raised it towards her face. She pushed him away and started protesting until the doctor's assistants calmed her down. Eventually she sat and submitted to his authority; Hansen pricked her eye twice, placing behind the conjunctiva a pus sample from a nodule of another patient with the more severe tubercular leprosy. Hansen was desperate to see if this more malignant form would spread, thus fulfilling the final criteria for contagious bacteria. Hansen said he believed he would be able to remove the nodules from Kari's eye at a later date, were they to grow, as he had done with patients who suffered from the issue naturally. Moreover, he maintained – a belief he retained despite the subsequent repercussions – that the advancement of science outweighed the personal considerations of the patient. Hansen said he kept the purpose of the operation secret from Kari as he could not 'presuppose that the patient would regard the experiment from the same point of view'. He presupposed correctly. The woman, distressed and angry, complained to the hospital chaplain, badgering the minister repeatedly over the course of a month to take up her cause.

Hansen would be in breach of Norwegian law if he had caused Kari pain, which seems an open-and-shut case, but given his fame and government position the matter was referred to the Chief Magistrate. He proposed charging Hansen with actual bodily harm, but then thought it prudent to seek the opinion of the Director of Public Health. The latter, spooked that Norway's greatest scientist faced such scandal, suggested that the question of the longer-term consequences of Hansen's actions be discounted, and the prosecution concentrate on punishing him for the use of the needle alone.

The legal sleights of hand didn't end there. The court noted that after the initial distress, and having been reassured by Hansen's colleagues, Kari's calmer demeanour could be read as acquiescence. Hansen's defence also countered that as the patient had leprosy, her sensitivity would be lessened anyway, and the needle in the eye, rather than constituting an assault might be merely uncomfortable. Kari herself said that aside from the mental distress and the future dangers of the experiment, she experienced so much pain that she had sleepless nights and still couldn't read with that eye, complaints which were dismissed as exaggerated. It would be difficult to allow Hansen to go completely unpunished, though. Among the patient body, the treatment of Kari had become a symbol of their wide-ranging grievances. They threatened to leave the hospitals and march through the streets. This would have been a major embarrassment to a country that had sold itself on the modernity of its leprosy policy, that wanted to be at the forefront in the 'science' of segregation. Instead, to quell the unrest it was suggested Hansen be charged with the misuse of a public office that had resulted in injury. The punishment under the legal code was loss of that professional position but no more; prior to Hansen's conviction however, the Ministry of Health quietly separated his two jobs: doctor at the hospital and Chief Medical Officer for Leprosy. As Kari was a patient under the auspices of the first role, the result was that he would lose that position, plus court costs of 90 kroner, likely a few days' wages. The second, far more politically important and prominent role, Hansen maintained.

———

The doctor's name has been adopted by those wishing to lose the stigma that 'leprosy' conjures: today 'Hansen's disease' and local translations thereof is the preferred term in dozens of countries including the USA, Japan, Portugal and Brazil. At the Eighth Leprosy Congress in Rio de Janeiro in 1963, the meetings now a quinquennial event, it was agreed 'leper' should never be used to describe patients, and in 1995 the Brazilian government went further and legislated against the official use of both 'leper' and 'leprosy', replacing the latter with *hanseníase*. The move has admirable intentions and follows the understanding that a person can't be defined by their medical condition – that a person made noun will always be stigmatised. 'Spastic', 'midget', 'retard': let 'leper' join these terrible slurs in rhetorical redundancy. For many patients around the world, whom Vollset rightly says should have the last say on the matter, 'Hansen's disease' symbolises the doctor's scientific breakthrough and the path it opened towards leprosy becoming a curable disease like any other. Either way, most have long divorced the term from the biography of the man.

As we are closing the vitrines in Hansen's lab, I ask Vollset what he thinks of his subject. 'Ambivalence. In a word.' Norway might have the most generous parental leave in the world – an enlightened kingdom indeed – but I'm feeling guilty about taking up so much of his time, so I start to give my thanks. He hasn't quite finished, though. 'In some aspects Hansen was definitely a progressive. He was a person who believed in Darwinism. He was very secular in a very Protestant country. He believed in women's rights and stayed in and looked after his stepchildren while his second wife went out with friends. He was also horribly elitist. He did not like his patients. He thought people with leprosy smelled bad. He thought they were uncivilised and he thought he was the representative of civilisation.' And what is the reaction Vollset gets when he delivers home truths about his home town's greatest hero? He waves the last question away. 'I'm in the business of problematising rather than celebrating.'

In 2015 the World Health Organization (WHO) issued advice on the naming of newly discovered diseases, and while the suggestion that place names and geographical regions should not be invoked garnered the biggest headlines (Spanish flu, West Nile fever and Ebola, for example), it also advised scientists not to add their own names to any discovery (or that of any other person: amyotrophic lateral sclerosis is often called Lou Gehrig's disease after the baseball player who was diagnosed with it). The WHO did not go into its reasoning for this latter advice, other than stating that the name of a disease should ideally give some indication as to its nature. They might have noted, however, that while the guidance makes the medical dictionary a far less colourful affair, it avoids such controversies as Hansen's legacy.

The court ruling against the scientist caused consternation among Hansen's colleagues, who felt that it might curtail research, but otherwise, unpublicised outside of Norway until decades later, it did little to hamper his career. It's only since, in the pages of *The Lancet* and other journals, in a conversation that grapples with now-familiar questions of how we deal with sins of the past, that his reputation has been reassessed. Within that discussion the biggest legacy of the court case is one often overlooked. Quietly, the judgment established the concept of informed consent, long before the rest of the world took the later experimentation of the Nazi regime as a cautionary tale and homed in on medical ethics during the Nuremberg trials. Much of what was established in the 1964 Declaration of Helsinki, the cornerstone of modern research protocol in which the welfare of a patient trumps all, had been discussed in Bergen almost a century previously. It is a doctrine in which patients are not epidemiological statistics, nor political embarrassments, but a people with a proximity to their own destiny, a closeness to their own flesh and blood; in which an individual has the right to be treated humanely, not locked away and forgotten, even in the face of public health calamities. A question of agency might be Norway's greatest contribution to science, established not by Hansen, but by Kari Nielsdatter Spidsøen.

MOLOKAI, HAWAII, USA

Father Damien was a dirty man. Everyone agreed on that. Dirt would accumulate under his fingernails; he rarely washed his hands. His clothes – his habitual cassock and wide-brimmed hat – were worn for days on end; he saw no reason to clean his hut in Kalawao, the leprosy colony on the Hawaiian island of Molokai. His detractors claimed he lacked elegance too: burly with a 'piggish' head, they complained, he squinted from behind a pair of wonky wire-framed circular spectacles. He was eager to learn Hawaiian, it was noted sniffily, but otherwise he had little enthusiasm for languages. His Latin came only by official requirement, his English was sparse; a native Flemish speaker, even his French was stilted. The prose of his letters lacked refinement whatever their language: 'coarse . . . head-strong and bigoted' was one particularly vitriolic posthumous assessment.

None of this worried Damien. Hawaiian did him fine. From that messy home, built in sight of Kalawao's cemetery, Damien wrote to his brother Auguste, also a priest, to say that Molokai was exactly where he wanted to be.

We eat what Providence sends us. The calabash of *poi* is always full; there is also meat; water in quantity, coffee and bread sometimes, wine or beer never. As I have had to work all week and cook on Sunday, you will excuse me if my hands are not as clean as yours, which do nothing, I suppose, but turn the pages of books. Sometimes the plates are not well washed either. But what matter. Hunger and habit make us eat just the same. For dessert, we smoke a pipe. That finished, quickly back on the horse.

In the saddle, Damien would cross Molokai's mountains; his parish over two thousand square kilometres, he rode down the island's valleys beyond Kalawao itself, across water and through fields to find the most remote of his parishioners. Today it is a national park, wild garlic growing in fragrant profusion, its white flowers poking up between ferns, yellow hibiscus and amid the ki-tree, the roots of which were used to brew a potent beer. Across this paradise the finch-like honeycreeper flits, feeding off the red spindly flowers of the evergreen *'ōhi'a lehua* tree. Damien would haul building material and basic medical supplies with him, eager to provide practical as much as spiritual comfort (though he never left without an ad hoc altar of four sticks and a plank). Sometimes he had to abandon the horse and mules to scale by hand and foot the sheer cliff faces which routinely stood between him and his flock. For Damien dirtiness brought him closer to godliness, the grime evidence of his graft.

For his colonial masters, those disdainful of his personal habits, the priest's life was alien at best and an affront to Western order at worst; religion was supposed to be a cleansing antidote to indigenous habits, a washing-away of the idolatry and idleness they projected onto the population, be they sick or healthy. Yet here was Damien, adopting their ways, it would seem, along with their language. His body and the leprous bodies of his parishioners were dangerously entangled even before he himself succumbed to the disease. This was 1872, and the pious (and patronising) commentators of the time muttered that Damien's unvarnished personality was due to his simple farm upbringing in rural Belgium. 'It is absolutely beyond doubt that he contracted the disease through his careless ministrations and uncleanly personal habits,' a representative of the Hawaiian Board of Health tutted, though not without something approaching admiration, noting the priest 'would have leper boys at work in his kitchen so that he could give more time to his ministrations for others, being busy from peep of day until long after dark'. Dirty of body, dirty of mind, would be the eventual assumption: sexual proclivity was whispered. Damien's brother, reading Latin scripture in a clean cassock 12,000 kilometres away, faced no such danger and no such accusations of moral lapse.

———

Damien was never supposed to achieve the fame he did, a symbol of global imperial paranoia and catalyst of religious fetish: a bronze statue, in which he wears his wide-brimmed hat, stick in hand, now represents the state of Hawaii in the US Capitol building's Hall of Columns. He was never supposed to be the subject of culture wars in his lifetime and long after: in 2020, Congresswoman Alexandria Ocasio-Cortez decried the choice of a white man as Washington's symbol of the Polynesian fiftieth state. Damien was supposed to stay working in his parents' fields in Tremelo, a dull village in a duller part of Belgium. The fact that celebrity landed upon him, plucking him from the obscurity of his mission to represent the burgeoning discourse on the disease, says more about the world that orbited him than his actions on the island or his own political nous. There were plenty of other missionaries, in plenty of other colonies, with plenty of other health issues, spreading religion and the soft arm of imperialism. Leprosy, however, had become totemic of a moral depravity or sexual freedom that Europeans had long imagined pervaded the South Seas. The leprous, lascivious body was a perversion that Western proselytising could fix.

Damien was born Jozef, in 1840, the youngest son and seventh child of Frans and Anne-Catherine de Veuster. While Auguste and two of Damien's older sisters, Eugenie and Pauline, were being prepared for religious service by devout Anne-Catherine, Frans wanted Jozef for the farm. The boy was burly and had a remarkable strength and energy that stayed throughout his life, only faltering in the very last throes of death. In Gavan Daws's excellent biography of the priest, written in the 1970s as an academic antidote to both the mass-market hagiographic and poison-pen portraits that came before, the Honolulu-based historian says Jozef was taken out of school by the age of thirteen to harvest crops from the family's fields. The boy had other ideas, however, and on reaching adulthood, having visited his brother at his seminary in Leuven, Jozef broke the festive cheer of Christmas Day in 1858 to tell his parents that he too wanted to join the priesthood, lest he remain 'unhappy forever'. Moreover, in his blunt Flemish, he warned them that 'to forbid your son to follow the will of God . . . would bring down cruel punishments on you'. After the holidays, he packed his bag to join his brother. This obstreperous attitude is one he held to and it became apparent again five years later when Auguste, now ordained, fell ill with typhus and was unable to join a group of six priests and brothers who were due to set sail as missionaries to Hawaii. Jozef, still a seminarian who had entered the congregation and taken the name Damien only three years earlier, bypassed his immediate superiors and petitioned the higher orders in Paris to be allowed to take his place. On 23 October 1863, to his immense excitement, the young man boarded the ship *R. W. Wood* with his seniors from the seminary and a small platoon of nuns for the almost five-month voyage across the world.

———

For indigenous Hawaiians, leprosy arrived as Damien did, an unwanted visitor from across the sea. The disease may have stowed away as early as Captain Cook's colonial voyage, but it only became regarded as a public health issue eighty years later. 'The commander manifested a laudable humanity, in endeavouring to shield the population from the evil effects which so inevitably result from connection between foreign seamen and the native females,' wrote one sympathetic European account of Cook's trip. The evil effects weren't just moral turpitude, but disease too. 'But his efforts were in vain. If the discipline of his own crew could have been strictly enforced, the eagerness of the women was not to be repressed.' Historically, this genesis, regardless of whether the women were actually consenting, inextricably linked sickness with sex in the minds of Hawaiian and colonialist alike, with the former's lack of conformity to Western and Christian mores taking the brunt of the responsibility in the minds of the latter. The *haole* – the white incomers – dodged blame from among Hawaiians for leprosy too. As cases multiplied, the disease became known as *ma'i pake*, the 'Chinese sickness', named after the thousands of Chinese labourers who arrived on the islands at the invitation of American traders endeavouring to create an export market in sandalwood (a precursor to the sugar industry that would dominate the economy in years to come). 'There seems but one way to prevent the whole of Oceania from becoming leprous, and that is the exclusion or the rigid control of all Chinese coolies,' a Scottish physician warned. Wherever it came from, contact was devastating for the indigenous Hawaiian population, which plummeted from the healthy 683,000 people Cook first encountered to just under 40,000 Polynesian islanders left after a century of colonial enterprise and disease.

By the mid-nineteenth century the Hawaiian throne, and the British, were both losing power as the growing cartel of US plantation bosses aggressively sought sway. Under the feudalist system, land was owned by the Hawaiian monarch and controlled by a hierarchy of chiefs, but before long two-thirds of the archipelago had been 'bought' by foreigners, mostly US sugar companies. A newly convened Board of Health, which worked far from the traditions of the medicine chiefs of indigenous Hawaiian society, tackled imported epidemics of smallpox, influenza and cholera; but under pressure from the new business interests, the issue of *ma'i pake* became its most pressing concern. William Hillebrand, German-born and, like six out of seven of the Board of Health officers, white, warned that the disease was 'threatening to become more general'. A few months into 1864, the assessment grew graver, with the English-language *Pacific Commercial Advertiser* thundering, 'It appears that this terrible disease has commenced its slow [but] certain progress', upbraiding the government for its lack of action. 'One year ago there was but one case of *Mai Pake* in this district and that poor native is now in a state shocking to humanity, still no measures have been taken for his removal from amongst the people, but on the contrary, hundreds of natives have been compelled to go or send to the very house he lives in to pay their taxes!'

It was a much remarked-upon puzzle for the white population of Hawaii that the original inhabitants of the islands seemed to have little fear of the disease and suffered none of the reflexive disgust towards patients that the Westerners had internalised. In a journal entry of 22 May 1823, Charles Samuel Stewart, travelling with a group of early English Protestant missionaries, described how he encountered a group of Hawaiians 'seated on the ground, eating *poe* – surrounded by swarms of flies, and sharing their food, with dogs, pigs and ducks, who helped themselves freely, from the dishes of their masters! The *tout ensemble* was almost too disgusting to be witnessed.' Even more distressing for Stewart was that people suffering from what he called the 'most infective, and loathsome cutaneous disease' were sitting within this party 'without reproach except in the eyes of a foreigner'. In disbelief, he reports that he again encountered 'the itch' when shaking hands with a senior member of the Hawaiian court. 'Few seem to regard it as an evil, or take any measure to divest themselves of [this] curse of a God of purity.' It became a chorus call over the ensuing decades: a Californian doctor claimed Hawaiians 'sleep with lepers without any suspicion of results'; an American naval medic complained that the Polynesians displayed none of the 'wholesome horror' of the disease that other ethnicities did. Worse still, a British doctor justified his experimentation on a healthy inmate from Honolulu's prison, inoculating him with leprosy in exchange for the man's freedom, because the 'Hawaiians view with ignorant contempt the fears of the foreigners'.

At the same time as Hansen's segregation policies were coming into force in Norway, in Hawaii, in 1865, American lobbying resulted in a royal charter, signed by the largely compliant monarchy of King Kalākaua, establishing two sites for the segregation of 'any person alleged to be a leper'. These were a hospital near Honolulu that would assess suspected cases, and a colony, Kalawao, on the northern side of Molokai Island in which patients with confirmed leprosy would be marooned. The health authorities complained that many relatives of the patients attempted to shelter their loved ones from both doctors and the police who did their bidding, condemning themselves, they thought – like Verdi's Aida hiding in her beloved Radamès' tomb – to a certain death out of sentimentality. The Hawaiians viewed the new rules as tyrannical; those with the disease were wont to hide in the hills of the islands, forever on the run. In the opera, the lovers die declaiming the 'valley of tears' in which they are imprisoned; the Hawaiian government failed to recognise the similar trauma enforced on the patients. Lifted out of context, Edward Said's damning verdict on *Aida* could be applied to the leprosy colony's role in Hawaiian society: 'an imperial spectacle designed to alienate and impress an almost exclusively European audience'.

On Kalākaua's death in 1891, his sister and successor, Liliuokalani, attempted to restore a degree of indigenous sovereignty, her efforts answered by a US-backed coup d'état in 1893. Championed by the publisher of the *Advertiser*, a newspaper that carried the daily price per ton of sugar on its masthead alongside a weather summary, full annexation of the kingdom followed within five years (and in 1958 Hawaii became the fiftieth US state). It was widely believed, too, that leprosy prevention laws were a useful weapon the settler industrialists could wield against any Polynesian locals who baulked at colonisation. Chris O'Day was an American doctor who had been physician to Liliuokalani. He claimed that dozens were spuriously diagnosed with the disease after they refused to sell up to the sugar farmers. Once they were shipped off to the leprosy colony, the businessmen would seize the land; stuck across the water as a patient on Molokai, the local person had no access to legal remedy. 'The last king of Hawaii stood with the sugar interests,' O'Day said during a series of condemnatory speeches. 'Once the victim was landed on Molokai the world closed its doors against him, and more effectively than in the tomb was he swallowed up.' The *Advertiser* called the claims 'spiteful perversions' – but his accusations chime with other Pacific Island narratives. There is a persistent belief among the indigenous islanders of Rapa Nui (Easter Island) that Chilean colonialists injected them with leprosy in a genocidal act, paving the way for expropriation of the land by business and military directed from Santiago. Though there is no direct evidence to prove the veracity of either claim, O'Day's speeches caused waves in Hawaii and beyond. The case was taken up by *Appeal to Reason*, America's biggest socialist newspaper at the time, in which a correspondent decried that 'the spirit of greed has stifled the white man's conscience . . . Of all the damnable outrages ever inspired by greed for profits, I think this one stands clear and distinct as the most conscienceless.' O'Day was eventually granted access to Kalawao itself and found many perfectly healthy individuals stuck there, seemingly proving his theory. Under pressure, the government agreed to demands from almost two hundred Molokai residents that they be re-examined, with many consequently released. They were returned to their home towns and villages but found, *Appeal to Reason* reported, 'modern commercialism had gripped their islands. They were lost. Their lands were gone. Their families had disappeared.' Dwight Baldwin, a US medical missionary, was among those who championed institutionalisation: 'We have a foul and dangerous disease among us,' Baldwin wrote. 'The native population are not too much alarmed. In this region the healthy are often seen mingling with the leprous, which thing ought not so to be.' His son, Henry, went on to bankroll dormitories on Molokai, using a fortune founded on sugar cane. Today, the company Henry established, the New York Stock Exchange-listed Alexander & Baldwin Inc., is one of the largest landowners in Hawaii.

———

The Board of Health had intended those that it dumped on Molokai to be self-sufficient, but they were soon disappointed in this respect. Ambrose Kanoealii Hutchison, a patient who was employed as the leprosy colony's resident supervisor for thirteen years, recalled that when he first arrived on the steamer, he was left on the rocky shore without food and was forced to stay in a one-room hut with another patient until he could construct his own home. Anarchy all but reigned, with one government health officer reporting: 'so far from aiding their weaker brethren, the strong took possession of everything, devoured and destroyed the large quantity of food on the lands'. For those abandoned in this ghastly paradise, social mores, be they Hawaiian or colonial, became deformed and deranged. In their complaint, though, it was the cost to the public purse and not the well-being of the sick that was the primary concern for the officials in

Honolulu. Nonetheless, they were also troubled by the difficulty in maintaining order. 'Drunkenness, pilferings, immorality and general insubordination were very prevalent: ki-root beer was manufactured and drunk in very large quantities, and great orgies took place.' The patients themselves, cleaved off from the judicious eye of the colonial classes and uprooted from traditional community structures, sometimes proclaimed the maxim *aole kanawai ma keia wahi*: in this place there is no law. It is a textbook self-fulfilling prophecy – the cynic might assume it was done on purpose – to predispose further colonisation. With the indigenous population already perceived as being 'uncivilised' by administrators, in essentially exiling them from all familial and social support, Molokai provided the 'evidence' that without a guiding hand, be it of police or priest, incivility would run riot.

Though improvement was said to have been made in the behaviour and organisation of Molokai in the intervening six years since it was first founded, it was to this environment that the devout Damien came in 1873. His bishop had said he would not order anyone to travel to the settlement on missionary work, but volunteers were sought to do the Church's evangelising. Damien was the first, it seems, to raise his arm.

Damien's departure for the leprosy colony caused a great deal of attention, for reasons that were never clear and which evidently took the Church itself by surprise. Other missionaries – Protestant and Mormon – had been before him, but something about the coarse Belgian Catholic caught local imagination. From the very beginning the Hawaiian press were keen to frame Damien as a heroic figure, a story that would eventually spread across the world, the tragic finale of which would cause a moral panic. A collection was raised among the great and the good of Honolulu after it was reported Damien was sleeping in the open, his only shelter the bushy head of a native screw pine. The Board of Health, under pressure from fiercely rivalrous local Protestants and spooked by the publicity, their own noses out of joint over how the abysmal conditions in Kalawao were being portrayed, intervened to forbid priests from coming and going to their posting. The bishop would therefore either have to recall Damien – a humiliation, given the good publicity he had received – or Damien would have to make his home on Molokai permanently. Under orders, the priest found himself stranded by the Church.

He too found his parishioners 'much addicted to the use of a certain beverage made of sweet potatoes, which they allow to ferment, and thus obtain an obnoxiously intoxicating drink'. His congregation, he lamented, 'were very fond of it, but it makes them excited' – or as the English artist Edward Clifford, who visited to paint Damien early on, put it, they 'forgot all decency and ran about nude, acting as if they were stark mad'. Hutchison gives a similarly forthcoming description of the moral tensions between the patients and their new priest: women were seen 'roariously drunk staggering about the village of Kalawao naked', the supervisor recalled. They were likely patrons of Ka Pa Pupule, the Crazy Pen, a place the people with leprosy had established to drink the homebrew beer and pineapple wine. Damien would try to ruin the party, bursting in and overturning the drinking pots. 'The hilarious feasters abruptly break up, making quick from the place thru the back door to escape his big stick, for he would not hesitate to lay it on good and hard on the poor hapless person who happened to come within reach of his cane.'

These reports inspired the American novelist Jack London, another famed visitor, who opens his heavily-fictionalised tale 'Koolau the Leper' with an erotic orgy being enjoyed by a band of outlaw patients. The writer's sentiment initially seems well-placed, London urging his reader to recognise that they 'in their disintegrating bodies life still loved and longed', but the passage soon descends into pornographic nonsense. 'Love danced in all his movements,' London writes, 'and, next, dancing with him on the mat, was a woman whose heavy hips and generous breast gave the lie to her disease-corroded face . . . With the woman on the mat danced a slender maid whose face was beautiful and unmarred, but whose twisted arms that rose and fell marked the disease's ravage.'

In reality, beyond such slavering prose, much of what was read as sexual activity was mere nudity. As well as the obvious consideration of Hawaii being a hot climate, a person's nakedness had various ceremonial roles, from respect and submissiveness in the presence of authority to being a symbol of grief. Such was the lack of inhibition, a Hawaiian's genitalia was often given an affectionate public name, with a *mele ma'i*, a genital chant, prepared for a newborn child to encourage the perpetuation of the family line. That said, Hawaiian culture *was* more sexually liberal and carried none of the West's nineteenth-century shame on the matter: in a series of articles in which he sought to preserve his own, disappearing indigenous culture, Samuel Kamakau, Hawaii's most famous historian, described how so long as sexual partners were of the same status, little else mattered. Gender, marriage or, for the most senior chiefs, whether one was biologically related, traditionally, were of no concern in choosing a partner. It's little wonder this all caused consternation for the sheltered priest from rural Belgium and his white brethren. That these Hawaiians had leprosy only furthered the crucifix-clutching: the physical illness became expressive of apparent moral sickness. While the government in Honolulu refused Damien's request for the strict separation of the sexes as unworkable and too expensive, the Board of Health agreed: 'The terrible disease which afflicts the Lepers seems to cause among them as great a change in their moral and mental organization as in their physical constitution.'

This colonial projection is analogous to mythologies concerning licentiousness and leprosy, a recurring literary motif since the second century. While the Old Testament heralded the disease – or at least a condition bearing the same name – as a punishment for sin, the Bible was very specific as to what sins these were: slander, gossip, fraud and infringing on the rights of one's neighbour. For a while at least, the sufferer's sexual conduct was in the clear. It was only later that Mishnaic Jewish scholars put a gloss on the Book of Leviticus, with leprosy presented as a mark of various apparent perversions, most notably a sentence passed on to a child if its parents had had intercourse while the mother was ritually impure. Whatever the origin, by the second century – according to the Latin poet Prudentius – Lawrence, a deacon serving Pope Sixtus II, was able to admonish a Roman detractor with the immortal lines that his 'foetid lust has dragged him into the company of whores, staining him with mud and filth as he begs for their foul and disgusting services . . . There is nothing more foul than a sinner, nothing more leprous or putrid. The scars of his sins keep bleeding and they stink like the pit of hell.'

Those with the disease were painted as sexually voracious, with mention of bloated or expanded genitalia, a fear exploited in twelfth-century versions of the Tristan romance by both Eilhart von Oberge and Béroul (though absent from Wagner's much later opera). In these variations of the story, when King Mark discovers his wife, Isolde, is having an affair with Tristan, he considers handing her to a gang of men with leprosy. In Béroul's earlier telling their leader leers: 'Give Isolde to us and she will be held in common. Never will a woman have a worse end. Sire, there is in us such great ardour that there is not a woman on earth who could endure our intercourse for one day.'

Damien's initial disgust towards his parishioners will have been wrapped up in religious dogma – notwithstanding the complexity of historic attitudes to the disease. For the civic authorities, though, the leprous body remained a sexual taboo even when depleted of Christianity. It was instead a motif of what Edward Said called the 'insinuating danger' of the other, the danger being any behavioural challenge to Enlightenment universalism and the supremacy of European culture. With danger, of course, comes also fetishisation (especially as the great edifice of Western cultural hegemony collapsed in the mid-twentieth century).

In Paul Theroux's fictionalised autobiography *My Other Life* ('the story of a life I could have lived if things had been different'), the travel writer describes 'his' stay at a leprosy colony in what is now Malawi (then Nyasaland) in the early 1960s. In the story, the writer finds his English classes unappreciated and falls into a frustrating routine of playing cards with the European missionary priests – anti-Damiens among the smouldering remains of an empire – for whom both enthusiasm and faith have burned out. One night the writer slips away from the table to a drumming circle taking place in the patients' settlement. He finds them writhing in suggestive dance around the fire, dressed in bedsheets to mock the religious orders that run their lives, and among the spectators is Amina, a young woman with leprosy who had brought her blind grandma to his English classes. Standing beside her, Theroux whispers, 'I want to visit you at your hut.' While the tale raises issues of power and consent, there is an empathetic edge to the encounter: 'Her skin has the heavy sensuality of freshly turned earth . . . I stroked her arm and when my fingers touched the leprous patch, the disk of dead skin, I was not alarmed. I had been here long enough to know there was no danger to me.'

The writer knows what he is doing and Amina is afforded more agency than the punchline-treatment Roald Dahl makes of another woman with leprosy in his 'The Visitor', one of the author's short stories for adults. It first appeared in the May 1965 issue of *Playboy* and purports to be an anecdote of a noted lothario, a house guest (when I order up a copy at the British Library, I'm directed to a special section for 'sensitive content' where my reading, having flicked past the topless centrefold, is closely supervised). He flirts with the wife and daughter of his host, a rich Egyptian man living in the Sinai Peninsula, until he believes 'either of the two ladies, should the circumstances permit, was mine for the asking'. Eventually, a figure does creep into his bedroom, but she refuses to illuminate the proceedings, and he remains none the wiser despite their 'extremes of ecstasy'. The 'twist' can be seen from beyond the sand dunes: the man has a second daughter, who has leprosy. Both Theroux and Dahl established themselves amid the permissive counterculture of the 1960s and their sexualisation of the leprosy patient is a symbolic cleansing of the stuffy moral order of the past.

The setting of Dahl's tale is merely expedient – the author knew the region well from his RAF service during the Second World War – but the narrative is almost certainly inspired by the earlier anecdote of a colourful sailor named Dod Orsborne, which saw the salacious story set on a remote chain of islands in the Indian Ocean. In this version the man kills himself in the aftermath of the encounter; western moral order thus restored. The island setting is, in a way, the more clichéd, even if it at least purports to be the more accurate: Orsborne tells of the ruin of the archipelago through trade and alcohol, leprosy symbolic of this societal descent. It is a typical image of the time in which, at best, the Western observer projects onto island culture the pull between innocence and corruption, the 'noble savage' and 'civilisation'. It is unlikely the hard-drinking seafarer and self-publicist was bothered by the art of Paul Gauguin, but the iconic late-nineteenth-century work by the French post-Impressionist

Where Do We Come From? What Are We? Where Are We Going? is a treatise on these dualities. In the centre of the panoramic canvas, on the bank of a stream winding through a typically murky turquoise landscape, a young Tahitian girl, half-naked and barely out of puberty, takes the character of Eve, plucking an apple from a tree. (The artist notoriously engaged in the rape of young girls when living on the Pacific islands.) She is surrounded by a cast of different-aged characters, from the innocent baby on the right to the decayed figure of an old woman on the left. Progress was never positive, for Gauguin, a pessimist, as he was embroiled in poor health, legal and financial trouble, circumstances reflected in his own suicide attempt made shortly before the work was finished.

———

The American writer Charles Warren Stoddard's relationship to Hawaii – which he visited many times, becoming close with Damien – though rooted in the same exoticisation, was determined not on the difference of race but on a shared, or at least perceived, queerness. For a closeted gay man, long before the relative liberation Theroux and Dahl lived through, Hawaii was a place in which 'for the first time I can live as my nature prompts me. It would not answer in America, as a general principle – not even in California, where men are tolerably bold', Stoddard wrote in a letter to the poet Walt Whitman. 'I am numbed with the frigid manners of the Christians; barbarism has given me the fullest joy of my life,' he sighed on his return to San Francisco. (The same may have been true of Edward Clifford, long assumed to be gay from his intense paintings of young men.) His comfort was understandable: in Hawaiian culture the māhū – highly respected figures who occupied a third gender – were integral to rites such as hula dance and chant. The Hawaiian chiefs that Captain Cook encountered were known to have sought *aikane*, young men, as sexual partners. At points in his public writing Stoddard would express his homosexuality openly: there's very little decoding needed in his short story 'Chumming with a Savage', in which he imagines living with a young Hawaiian man on a remote island, who 'would come with a delicious banana to the bed where I was lying and insist upon my gorging myself'. It is an encounter seemingly based on fact, if more of the author's correspondence with Whitman is to be believed.

In his 1885 book *The Lepers of Molokai*, Stoddard sings a hymn to a place even more cut off from the moralising eyes of bourgeois Western life. Like Jack London, his descriptions of the patients linger on their physicality, contrasting the Polynesians 'possessed of much physical beauty' who 'love their friends with a love passing the love of women', with the effect of the disease as it advanced untreated. Stoddard's impressions also chime with earlier reports of the patients' exuberant spirit, though he is evidently sympathetic towards, indeed jealous of, the lack of restraint with which the residents live their lives. 'The lepers, once gathered together, should be forbidden all intercourse with those who are not leprous' – and yet he says, happily, 'they have no fear of contagion: they divide their garments among friends; they pass a pipe from mouth to mouth Indian-fashion; they marry even where one of the other is known to be leprous'. At Kakaako, the Honolulu hospital, 'the lepers are on one side of a high picket-fence; their friends on the other side spend hours daily in affectionate intercourse, passing the pipe back and forth, fondling one another, and even kiss at meeting and parting.'

———

Compare this relaxed attitude among the Hawaiians to Father Damien's initial revulsion, which, though dissipating as the days of his mission turned to years, is common recollection in colonial encounters with Molokai. Damien described how at first he could only tolerate being in the house of a patient for a small amount of time before the 'fetid' atmosphere overwhelmed him. He took up smoking a pipe to counteract a smell of his parishioners 'that poisons the air'. He recalled that he almost had to flee an early mass due to nausea and had trouble swallowing the communion wine. Soon, however, 'all my repugnance toward the lepers has disappeared', and he himself was on the receiving end of disgust, with his own hygiene much discussed.

Charles Darwin placed the sensation of disgust in a cohort of emotions that included loathing and contempt, comparing the shared bodily reactions of a wrinkling of the nose or an aversion of gaze. For the naturalist it was an evolutionary response, a millennia-aged survival instinct to warn the individual away from things that might cause harm: excrement, decomposition and, yes, the physical effects of disease. In this sense the revulsion Damien and others felt so keenly might be understood as a biological alarm bell – a behavioural immune system as some scientists term it – telling them to keep their distance from the infected in order that they might preserve their own health. There are countless examples in the animal kingdom to support the assumption. Yet Damien's experience – and indigenous Hawaiian experience – tells us that this is not true, or at least is not the only story.

Disgust sits as much in the cultural sphere as the biological, and is more often the result of previous experience and socialisation. A group of academics in the 1990s hypothesised that while we might have evolved some 'core disgust', nonetheless, 'like language and sexuality, the adult form of disgust varies in accordance to culture, and children must be "trained up" in the local rules and meanings'. The gay kiss for the homophobe is disgusting, for another it is loving or erotic; the leprous body causes fear for some, for another society it exists entirely without stigma. It is notable how many times in the Western literature I've quoted that the authors patronisingly refer to the Hawaiians as having the temperament of children ('an unreasoning child', according to Stoddard when he wasn't trying to bed them; 'loveable' was London's assessment), as if the Hawaiians had not yet learned the 'right' things to be disgusted by. Nurture as much as nature then, with a massive splash of imperial condescension.

For the anthropologist Mary Douglas, the idea of anything being 'dirty' – unclean! unclean! – was an entirely subjective notion. What was dirt and what was dirty depended on context. We would not, for example, consider a steaming plate of pasta bolognese as dirt, but once, say, the sauce splatters off the plate and lands down our new white shirt, a mess has been caused. Douglas says we might also complain of 'outdoor things indoors, upstairs things, downstairs' – examples of what she terms 'pollution behaviour'. Dirt is essentially anything that sits outside the organising principles that a society has constructed for itself, a mechanism to maintain order, not least within the 'symbolic systems' of religion and ideology. For all their difference in opinion, Darwin foreshadowed Douglas's radical 1960s reassessment when he wrote that 'a person who is scorned is treated like dirt'.

The lack of stigma against leprosy in Hawaiian society presented a challenge to colonial notions of order. The disgust felt towards the patients by white writers and government officials was visceral, but was the 'natural' reaction to a phenomenon that aesthetically, structurally and politically challenged their own sense of supremacy. It was this frisson, too, that appealed to the dirty minds of Dahl's readers in *Playboy*. The messiness of the patient body needed to be cleaned away, tidied up, like a proud houseowner bundling the clutter into a closet before a guest comes round. It was also an expression of power, of ownership: the colonists got to say what goes where. In the formation of a colony there can be no place for deformation; the wrong bodies of the leprous were antithetical to a homogeneity more easily ruled. Let's turn to one other theorist, Georges Bataille, that great proponent of social transgression. It is not Bataille's writing on sex that need concern us, but on aesthetics and his idea of formlessness. For Bataille, like Douglas, society, culture and religion were human-concocted mechanisms used to give form to the world, an illusion that hid the base primal underbelly, which, were one concerned with arriving at any philosophical truth, would need reconnecting to. He was writing in the context of surrealist art, and one might think of the non-heterogeneous form of the disabled body as being similarly confrontational. In this, we might regard the patients of Molokai as queer bodies – inherently political due to their rupture of the norms, their disorder, their revolutionary presence – explaining the empathy, for all his shortcomings, that gay Stoddard had for the island residents.

———

For his detractors, Damien's leprosy was an inevitable consequence of the sympathetic manner in which he lived with his subjects, a belief, in Edward Said's words, that 'going native can only be the result of mutilation, which produces a diseased, ultimately unacceptable loss of identity'. The priest had been out walking, searching for a new water supply for the village in the heat of a summer's day. On his return, throwing off his heavy, sweaty boots, he discovered a huge blister on his foot that had not caused him any pain. Damien knew enough of his parishioner's own stories of diagnosis to understand that this was ominous. Over the following two years that loss of sensitivity spread, until in 1884 leprosy was confirmed. Damien wrote to Stoddard:

'Those microbes have finally settled themselves in my left leg and my ear, and one eyebrow begins to fall. I suspect to have my face soon disfigured.' Damien was 'calm, resigned, and happier among my people', but behind his back, in the world he had left behind, trouble brewed. Rumours began to spread as to how he contracted the disease. The priest's unwitting celebrity had won him enemies both among Catholic peers and Protestant rivals, neither of whom were willing to let such an opportunity go to waste. The gossips in Honolulu's bars were only too happy to spread the idea that Damien was having relations with one or more of his female parishioners. A man among leprosy sufferers was unimpeachably holy in the minds of the public; a holy man who now had leprosy himself suddenly became tainted, his body imbued with a sexual appetite. It was what Molokai medic Arthur Mouritz called the 'Ghost of Immorality' which 'haunts the footsteps of the unfortunate leper'.

Such was the persistence of the rumours, the Board of Health decided it should investigate – but in such a way that it might avoid scandal. When Damien next came for a check-up, Mouritz was ordered to examine him for other diseases that might prove that the priest was sexually active. Recalling the situation thirty years later, the doctor remembered: 'We searched his mouth, throat, cervical glands, also carefully scrutinised his entire person and found absolutely NO TRACE of any other disease.' The doctor did not tell Damien the purpose of this enhanced examination and he 'did not seem to realize the important bearing the discovery of any incriminating evidence might have on his future'. A Board of Health official also dismissed the rumours: 'I never heard from anyone in the settlement that he had been immoral or licentious in any way . . . If there had been anything of the kind hinted at there, it would be commented upon.'

———

Damien's death in April 1889, immobile in bed, white fingers gripping the crucifix that he would be buried with, provoked a firestorm of publicity. There remained naysayers, with a letter sent from one local Protestant missionary to a colleague appearing in an Australian newspaper, its sentiments soon shared round the world: 'We who knew the man are surprised at the extravagant newspaper laudations, as if he was a most saintly philanthropist,' wrote the Reverend Dr Hyde of Honolulu. 'He was not a pure man in his relations with women, and the leprosy of which he died should be attributed to his vices and carelessness.'

It was Robert Louis Stevenson who came to the defence of Damien's reputation. The writer of *Treasure Island* had visited Molokai soon after the priest's death, and paid for his rebuttal to be published internationally. It was, in modern parlance, a spiky takedown of Hyde. Comparing the clean mansion in which Hyde lived, and which Stevenson had also visited, to the dirty conditions that Damien endured, Stevenson wrote: 'It may be news to you that the houses of the missionaries are a cause of mocking on the streets of Honolulu', before speculating that Hyde was embarrassed by how little the Protestant Church, of which Stevenson himself was a member, had done for leprosy patients.

The accusations of immorality provided a sense of immunity to the public: only the dirty became diseased. This lie underscored the avalanche of attention Damien's death received, most of it personally positive, but reflecting a moral panic recharged. His obituaries did more to promote the idea that leprosy was dangerously contagious than a hundred medical reports could support or counter. Leprosy, this disease the Western public had told itself was reserved just for the people it was 'civilising', might *once again* come and corrupt its own: deforming, defaming and queering the political structures they held dear.

YAKUTSK, SAKHA REPUBLIC, RUSSIA

Moscow, early December, fluctuates either side of 0 °C; I slipped on ice in Red Square. Yakutsk, where I arrived earlier this morning after a seven-hour night flight, is an altogether more extreme affair. This is the coldest city on earth, built on permafrost; the oil and gas pipes wind the streets above ground. For five months over winter the temperature never rises above freezing. The -35 °C outside falls a crucial seven degrees colder over the week, each increment of biting frost felt keenly, a cold that sends shooting pains through the hands if I momentarily remove my gloves. Across my bed I lay out the clothes I need. There are two pairs of thermal long johns that I will put on below my thick trousers, two pairs of thick socks, a shirt to go over my T-shirt and a thermal long-sleeved vest I already have on despite the suffocating radiators of the Russian hotel room. A hoodie and a spring jacket fit under a bulkier puffer jacket; a fluorescent fleece work coat I layer over the top. Two pairs of gloves. Under my chin I strap the wool-lined flaps of a hat I bought from an army surplus store in London.

Outside the hotel the snow is half a metre deep, drifting up the city's austere buildings, piling alongside the statue of Lenin that still stands in the central square, his arm outstretched towards, at this time of year, a towering Christmas tree. The Yakutsk population trudge about their lives in the all-day twilight. It is a silent city but for the crunch of snow underfoot; the warm and welcoming rowdy life of its bars and restaurants, casinos and malls, museums and theatres is muffled behind thick window drapes and double-insulated doors. 'Why are you all the way here?' is the refrain of drinkers and taxi drivers, left no less bewildered if I attempt to explain. I have come searching for traces of Kate Marsden, I tell them. Had they heard of her? A British nurse for whom nineteenth-century Yakutsk, and the many leprosy patients that lived across the Sakha Republic, had represented succour and a strange type of salvation.

———

Kate's story does not start in Siberia. She was born on 13 May 1859 in Edmonton, a village and occasional resort which has long been eaten up by the sprawl of London. Her father, Joseph Daniel Marsden, was a partner at a solicitor's practice in the City, and while his career was by no means spectacular, he brought home an income that was enough to keep his large family in comfort. His name appears regularly in legal papers, attached as a facilitator to emotionless announcements of failure and foreclosure: the collapse of a pub empire, the call of creditors to a pair of warehousemen, the bankruptcy of a jewellers. Sophie Matilda, Kate's mother, is more anonymous to the archives, even if her job of looking after eight children was as onerous. Sophie was a strict disciplinarian, in part a product of Victorian convention, but also tragedy. One of Kate's brothers, James, had died of tuberculosis, a disease which lingered across generations of the Marsden family, and which eventually claimed the rest of her siblings, bar one, before adulthood.

Kitty, as Kate was referred to about the house, tested her mother's patience to the extreme. In their lifetime, her sisters, she said, paid heed to the 'usual elementary preparation for taking their place as domesticated daughters in the family circle, and as refined young ladies in polite society'. Kate was as rambunctious and inquisitive as her nickname, a quality she inherited from her late maternal uncle, James Wellsted, an early British colonialist of the Arabian peninsula. Mother would gather Kate's siblings around the garden table on a summer evening, encouraging needlework and reading. At the first opportunity Kate made herself scarce, however, and would be found, broad-shouldered even from a young age and perpetually stern and serious of face, climbing a tree or building hutches and kennels for the veritable menagerie she surrounded herself with. Kate recalled that most of her earliest memories were punctuated by parental rebuke. The consequences she faced after investigating the greenhouse heating system and getting stuck in the flue would have been severe. Such was the frequency of being told that she was 'a very bad girl' that, even prior to entering a hated boarding school in Margate, Kate concluded she was indeed a terrible example of her gender.

When she was fourteen, her father died, an event that had repercussions far beyond the initial mourning. Their finances, it became apparent, were not in the rude health the family's outward trappings suggested. Joseph was just about keeping up appearances. As the year progressed, the servants were dismissed, the carriages disposed of, and the Edmonton estate went on the market. With her widowed mother facing poverty, Kate was pulled from her seaside education, her future uncertain. She was pragmatic and resilient, however, and though she always had an ambivalent attitude to authority, she did have a role model in life. Florence Nightingale was, she said, 'my ideal of an almost perfect Englishwoman'. The Crimean War had ended three years before Kate was born but Florence fever continued in Britain throughout her adolescence; the military nurse remained an unimpeachable national heroine whom Kate could cite if ever chastised that her conduct was unbecoming. The 'Lady with the Lamp' mythology had been forged in breathless news reports from the front and charity campaigns to raise funds for the war wounded, and on Nightingale's return politicians of all hues sought audiences. Prior to this the nursing profession had been regarded as either the preserve of Catholic nuns or a scurrilous one, personified by the drunk and incompetent Mrs Gamp of Dickens's *Martin Chuzzlewit* with her 'dilapidated articles of dress' and 'smell of spirits'. (Indeed, one of Nightingale's initial challenges in Crimea was keeping the young women in her charge sober.)

One institution to form in the wake of Nightingale's fame was the Evangelical Protestant Deaconesses' Institute on Tottenham Green in north London, set up by Michael Laseron, a German Jewish convert, with a syllabus mirroring that being implemented south of the city at the Nightingale Training School at St Thomas's Hospital. The *Daily Telegraph* sniffily referred to the institute as being more akin to 'an Evangelical nunnery', accusing it of 'borrowing from the Church of Rome' customs and expectations for the women in its service. It was anti-Catholicism echoed by Samuel Morley, a Liberal MP who was instrumental in the hospital's fundraising efforts. The eleven nurses were called 'sisters', a term he derided as being 'associated with copes and vestments and things of that kind of which he . . . did not approve'. The sisters were volunteers from the middle classes, women spurred on by Florence's example. Kate looked to nursing both as a vocation, for a sense of direction, but unlike her heroine also as an economic necessity; while her family might have opposed her intention to enrol at Laseron's institution a few years previously, now the provision of bed, board and training was met with pragmatic acceptance.

Dressed in her uniform of a white cap and apron, dark dress and bonnet (laid out on her dormitory bed the day she arrived in 1877), Kate was expected to read the gospel in the wards and offer prayers to those in her care. The patients were, it was understood, a captive audience for conversion if it was deemed necessary. Laseron said he wanted his recruits to 'raise themselves from the indolence of their useless lives and enlist in active, healthy service for Christ'. The German sent Kate and her colleagues out beyond Tottenham Green to administer to those in the slums, areas many would have only previously seen from the vantage point of a carriage. This they would do in regulation long black cloaks, lined with red flannel.

During this time reports about a new war, the Russo–Turkish War then playing out across the Balkans, and of the Ottoman atrocities of the year before, filled the British newspapers. Sitting on a bench under the common lime trees of the green beyond the hospital, Kate would read the articles with a mix of horror and intrigue. The journalists, many embedded within the armies, described the death and disease of the battlefield in the kind of forensic detail that the public had never previously been furnished with. (During the Crimean War, editors had discovered the less they held back, the bigger the daily sales.) For Kate this window to a world far removed from her own fuelled a desire to help, so when a call was made in 1877 for volunteers for a Red Cross nursing platoon to travel to the Balkans, she quickly signed up, aged eighteen and barely experienced in her profession.

———

The Bulgarian town of Svishtov occupies a plateau above the Danube. Today it's hard to imagine anything of much consequence happening there. The shops are practical and entertainment is limited; the cobbled lanes and slate roofs of the nineteenth-century buildings have largely given way to a hodgepodge of architectural styles from the intervening decades. As Kate arrived, the city, then named Sistova, was a pivot point in the war, the armies of the Russian and Turkish empires facing off across the opposing slopes of the river-bank. The town, amid the cannon smoke and gunfire, was also in the depths of a typhoid epidemic. In all, disease killed 81,847 Russian soldiers during the campaign, and though the Red Cross demanded neutrality, the seeds of Kate's lifelong Russophilia were planted as she witnessed their death and injury.

Life was no less dangerous for the medical volunteers, and the nurse did her best within a shambolic operation. Ambulances were prone to get lost, evacuation trains would not turn up when promised and doctors were often sent to the wrong location. The nurses' food rations were spartan and Kate would venture out to capture wildfowl to augment her platoon's dinners. Otherwise, it was a small plate of vegetables, served with bread, cooked in the same pan in which the nurses boiled water for tea. Travelling out of the town to the villages, they slept in huts where they could, though on at least one occasion they were forced to rest in freshly dug graves to escape snowstorms and the bandits who roamed the countryside. Kate's scalp became prone to lice, however much she brushed her hair. To top it off, starving animals, including wild dogs, posed a threat – while sleeping, a colleague was bitten on her cheek by a rat. 'A long, dreary winter passed in the Balkans in the snow and the mud; the army decimated by disease, exposure, and perhaps an epidemic, perhaps the plague,' the correspondent of the *Daily News* wrote. He went on to lament 'weary months of waiting, the expenditure of millions'. Many of Kate's colleagues became ill, two critical with typhoid, and the group's numbers were slowly depleted as comrades were sent back to England to recuperate. Kate, to her justified pride, with her 'strongly-built physique which seemed made for active and laborious work', lasted the full term of her posting.

It was within this environment that the nurse first encountered leprosy. Her medical unit had doubled back along the Bulgarian bank of the Danube to the city of Rustchuk (now Ruse), and their travels took them as far as Vardim, where a Russian assault had been grimly victorious. The bodies of horses and men were seen floating from battles upstream; towns the length of both banks became 'a picture of ruin'. Amid this horror Kate scoured for lost wounded, the landscape still hot from battle. In the decrepit remains of a barn, huddled together and barely visible in the gloom, she came across two local men, unlike those she had treated before. Scaly patches spread across their skin, the infection eating away at the nerves, their eyes bloodshot: the pair warned the young woman against getting too close. These men would have grown up around stories of the cast-out 'leper'; they were under no illusion, in peacetime or war, as to what their status was. They knew the sinful connotations of their condition from sermons they had heard as children; they had seen the depictions of the apparently pitiful medieval figure, wasting away. 'Cut off from their fellow creatures, avoided, despised, and doomed to a living death', as Marsden would later write.

In the Prado Museum in Madrid there is a triptych in oil on oak by Hieronymus Bosch titled the *Adoration of the Magi*. When I read accounts of Kate's encounter with these Bulgarian men – years later she spoke of it reverently, misty-eyed, even, in interviews and profiles – it is this scene, perhaps strangely given it's from another place, another time, that comes to mind. Painted in the closing years of the fifteenth century, the son of God is depicted as a naked babe on Mary's lap; the isolated stable, dilapidated and not unlike a building damaged from battle, stands against a vista as tumultuous and violent as the smoking Balkan fields. The shepherds and magi have the kind of serenity that Kate's breathless descriptions conjure up in those later media portraits. Yet most obviously it is the figure which Bosch painted peering from the dark doorway of the barn that draws me. His skin is 'white as snow', as biblical descriptions of leprosy claimed, and a leprous wound on his left leg is visible through a tight gold bandage. The injury mirrors the injured landscape. The man is dressed in a red cloak and gold chain, both attributes suggesting he is the 'False Messiah', the Antichrist sent to lead the Jewish people. Surrounding him in the shadows are several other ominous figures, the artist similarly using their physical deformations – the snubbed nose and concave eyes of one, the so very pallid skin of another – to signal the supposed sin that lies within.

One of the Bulgarian men had lost his nose, as well as ears and hands. Kate was unperturbed though, and did what she could to help, calling on her stretcher bearers to carry the pair out into the light and up onto a horse-drawn ambulance. The nurse clambered alongside them, pulling shut the curtain over the back of the wooden carriage, and rode to the encampment of tents that made up the field hospital. From there they most likely ended up in the leprosarium in Rustchuk. Kate's closeness as she helped the men onto the ambulance would have come as a shock, her touch an act of transgressive tactility from the teenager.

It is unclear why she was so unencumbered by fear, of the kind that had hindered Father Damien at first. It is unlikely Kate was particularly au fait with the intricacies of the epidemiological debate raging in Bergen at the time or had any great training in the condition. Yet leprosy for Kate would never be the leprosy of the modern age but the supernatural disease of earlier times, a sign of something beyond. It is in the zombie nature of leprosy that, while the perception of most illnesses evolves as science progresses, it seems condemned to its Jekyll and Hyde personality, in which the advances of Hansen inhabit one persona while the religious and quasi-medieval condition live on in another. In the 1970s Susan Sontag wrote of cancer being a disease associated with 'affluence, with excess', but those connotations are long lost in the half-century of medical research that has passed since; even with its millennia-long history, leprosy struggles for such maturity. Kate, despite being a nurse, embraced the leprosy of myth, not medicine. Without ever contracting it herself, the disease would prove a salve to the tribulations that would come, an escape from society as she drew its ire, a comfort against her own self-loathing.

For now she remained clear-headed and selfless, but Kate would later say that it was in Sistova she decided, along this anonymous Bulgarian track, on this bumpy ride across a contested, cannon-damaged country, to dedicate herself to alleviating the suffering of 'Christ's lepers'. 'Before this time the conviction had taken hold upon me that my mission in life was to minister to those who received the smallest attention and care of all God's creatures,' she wrote in her bestselling call-to-arms *On Sledge and Horseback to Outcast Siberian Lepers*. This may have been a bit of revisionist lore-making on her part, but for the nurse, Sistova was her Damascus. Despite the grimness, the insects, and the fear, those four months at war were a glorious release from the expectations of her gender and the claustrophobia of the society she had left behind. To volunteer in battle had social cachet, too. Among the nurses in Bulgaria were members of the aristocratic classes: Princess Golitsyna headed the medical unit; Princess Shakhovskaya, the daughter of a noted general, worked alongside Kate; Baroness Yulia Vrevskaya, previously popular among St Petersburg's bohemian circles, became an expert in dressings and amputations before eventually succumbing to typhus herself. It was a conflict steeped in nationalistic and neo-crusader rhetoric, in which Kate was aiding a humanitarian effort against Ottoman violence (though the Russians were certainly not without fault). Indulging in a heavy bout of patriotism, Dostoevsky wrote how his country's 'self-sacrificing nature and disinterested-ness, . . . its pious religious thirst to suffer for a righteous cause, is almost without precedent among other nations'. Kate fell in love with Russia, but the beginning of an affair with another righteous nation, the Sontagian kingdom of leprosy, was in incubation too.

There was no such halo over the work when Kate returned to England. Earning no more than nine shillings a week – first at the Westminster Hospital before taking a promotion as lady superintendent at a convalescent home in Woolton, now a suburb of Liverpool – she could no longer picture herself the heroine. As it happened, a decision on her future was made for her by a letter that arrived from New Zealand in the autumn of 1884, informing her that her sister Annie Jane was gravely sick. Kate and her mother bought third-class tickets to Wellington, embarking on a monotonous passage of six weeks, broken only as the steamship refuelled at the southern tip of Africa. The passing of her boat might have provided a modicum of distraction for the residents of the leprosarium on Robben Island, twelve kilometres from Cape Town's harbour. Kate merely thought of her sister. She 'hoped and prayed through the anxious journey that she might still be spared and recover' – but it was not to be. Marking up another familial tragedy, Annie Jane died within a week of their arrival. Nonetheless, Kate and Sophie Matilda stayed on in Wellington, the daughter securing a nursing post at the city's hospital.

Kate's life seemed on an upward trajectory. Falling in with a high-society crowd, her status increased through a diary of charitable events and polite salons. An acquaintance even promised to present her at court when back in England. It was during this time, however, 'the period when I took many backward steps and turned away from Christ', that an event happened which would change Kate's life forever and set her on the road to Yakutsk. From her own description, and from the gossip that would be her future undoing, shortly after she had had an accident at work, a fall from a ladder in the hospital laundry room, Kate embarked on a lesbian relationship. The name of her lover, whom Kate met towards the end of her convalescence, was never revealed, but it was, she said, 'a memory ever fraught with keenest regret'.

Such public remorse was the only option of course, but nonetheless the nurse was inhibited enough in character, and certainly closeted enough, for the incident to be a traumatic one. For me, Marsden inhabits the heroine of *The Well of Loneliness*, Radclyffe Hall's semi-autobiographical novel published to much scandal in 1928, three years before Kate's death, who found her sexuality bewildering. 'What am I, in God's name – some kind of abomination?' Stephen – named so by the protagonist's father, who had been expecting a boy – asked herself, as her sexuality awakened an 'impregnable wall of non-comprehension'. Like Stephen, however much she desired it, Kate regarded this sexual relationship – to kiss a woman 'full on the lips as a lover' – as a bewildering moment of madness, a collapse in character that she blamed on the head injury she received during her accident. It was the first of several 'impure relationships' undertaken by Marsden, an American rival would later claim, but Kate said she never took another partner. Yet she certainly had female loves throughout her life, adored, perhaps even lusted after, her story plotted by a series of devoted women whom Kate relied on emotionally and materially.

In what would become an established pattern, in emotional turmoil Kate cast herself out from the moral constraints of the city to seek seclusion. Exploration and travel became an attempt to escape the inescapable, but it was an act of self-preservation that had merit – Kate thrived in her rough self-banishment beyond polite society. That summer she volunteered to lead St John Ambulance expeditions into New Zealand's mining country, where she was tasked with teaching miners rudimentary first aid that might prove vital in what was frequently dangerous pit work. Based for a year out of Nelson, Kate would travel to remote settlements, camping for days at a time. Often she was the only woman among a community of men. Once, a miner, perplexed by the middle-class Englishwoman in their midst, asked if she was afraid. 'I am not in the least afraid of you while you are sober,' was her pithy reply. That night, sleeping on a bed of straw in a makeshift tent created out of the men's clothes, Kate woke to find one of the man's colleagues prowling around. When she raised the alarm, it was explained to her that the second worker meant no harm; he was just after the two dozen cases of brandy the crew had stashed in her encampment thinking it was the safest place to hide it.

Kate had been in New Zealand for around five years when she claimed she encountered leprosy again, this time among Maoris. This assertion made in newspaper interviews brought ridicule back in Wellington from those who either doubted Kate had met indigenous communities or, if she had, that she had mistaken a common type of eczema for the more serious disease. Whether Kate had made a diagnostic mistake or not, or even whether she exaggerated the nature of her fieldwork, was not what was really at play. Before her accident Kate's name appears in various local press cuttings, all positive, noting her good work on the wards. That the tone changed after the gay relationship, knowledge of which must have become widespread if not explicitly discussed, is so marked it cannot be coincidental. This was the double face of a whispering campaign that would spread across the globe from New Zealand to London, New York and St Petersburg, casting Marsden's honesty into doubt, leading to accusations of fabrication regarding her trips, and eventually of gross financial impropriety. Underlying all this, however, was homophobia, rarely put as bluntly as one New Zealand tabloid, which broke ranks and decried Kate's 'immorality of the most shocking kind'. Kate's story is one that runs alongside that of journalism, as the press shed its staid, polite delivery of the early nineteenth century for the more brutal landscape that we are familiar with today. Henry James described the new media that Kate found herself battling, in which 'everything and everyone were everyone's business'. For this modern class of newsmen, 'print meant simply infinite reporting, a promptitude of announcement, abusive if necessary, or even when not, about his fellow-citizens'. Kate was forced to write to one paper to say that her words had been twisted and she had said the disease was 'known amongst the Maoris only very slightly'.

———

Returning to Britain by ship in 1889, with the promise of an audience with Queen Victoria, Kate struck up a brief, intense friendship with a woman named Ellen Hewitt. This time sailing via Rio de Janeiro, and as recounted in private letters later, Kate told Ellen she was interested in converting to Protestantism from Catholicism (though Kate was at least born into the Church of England). The question of her faith will never be truly understood, but certainly Kate's approach to leprosy was more papal than Protestant, with the disease beginning to take on the status of an indulgence, an opportunity, as she saw it, to walk back on those 'steps away from Christ'. Sexuality doesn't work like that, of course, and while we don't know the precise nature of it, her relationship with Ellen would have huge consequences. The women stayed in contact after they had docked in Britain and, while travelling to Berlin together at one point, a violent argument broke out, Ellen accusing Kate of defrauding her. Certainly, Kate possessed the kind of money that was way beyond a nurse's salary. It would leave Ellen bitter for years to come. She was a dangerous enemy to have, given Kate had confided so much in her during the short time they had known each other.

Living in a red-brick semi-detached house in Eastbourne, Kate lapped up coverage of leprosy in the journals of the day, including *The Nineteenth Century*, that periodical so obsessed by the subject in the midst of the British colonial conquests. It was becoming an all-consuming preoccupation, the disease the mark of Kate's sin and, as she saw it, her own redemption. *The Nineteenth Century* followed Agnes Lambert's essay on leprosy in the Middle Ages with a much-discussed article by Sir Morell Mackenzie titled the 'The Dreadful Revival of Leprosy', an unequivocal call for segregation, in which the British doctor exhaustively catalogued cases globally, from leprosy 'extending its ravages' in the West Indies to its spread 'to an alarming degree in Russia'. When news emerged of Father Damien's death, Kate wrote immediately to the authorities in Hawaii to ask if she could join the Molokai mission. Such was the priest's posthumous fame that the Board of Health had been inundated with similar requests, and they politely rebuffed her.

Kate's mother died in 1891, and with all her siblings having succumbed to tuberculosis, she was left alone in the world at the age of thirty-two. Kate responded by setting off for St Petersburg, where she was due to be awarded a medal for her war work, travelling a circuitous route via Alexandria, Jerusalem, Constantinople and Tiflis (now Tbilisi). In grief and in turmoil, leprosy became an all-consuming obsession. This trip, Marsden admitted, was a 'roving commission to hunt up lepers wherever she had an inkling of their existence'. She was mesmerised by the idea, her mission perhaps a kind of therapy. On the road to Bethlehem she visited a leprosy hospital. 'For hundreds of years the poor creatures afflicted with the malady had sat by the wayside close to the [city] gates, outcast and destitute; and dependent on charity,' she recalled. 'Some lived in miserable huts, and others passed the night in holes in rocks.' German patrons had since built a hospital, however. 'All they could do was alleviate suffering, without a hope of effecting a cure. And ministering spiritual consolation, for every inmate there, brooded in the shadow of death.' In Jerusalem she revelled in the idea that 'the Great Healer Himself had been amongst the lepers'. Despite this genuinely felt sympathy she was angered to encounter leprosy sufferers living independently, not confined to the walls of the institution: 'A dreadful sight. The flies swarmed around them, irritating their sores, and perhaps carrying the disease to healthy people.' Sticking with the allegiance of her time in the Russo–Turkish War, when she moved on to Constantinople she found the city 'too awful to describe'. It was 'abominable'; she measured that 'about four hundred lepers were believed to be mingling with other people in the streets and shops'.

Some months later in Krasnoyarsk, the city Chekhov esteemed as the most beautiful in all Siberia, Kate tried to buy a tarantass, a horse-drawn carriage, which without springs was uncomfortable but hardy and reliable enough for the inhospitable journey she had ahead of her. In Constantinople she had heard of a possible cure for leprosy, a herb native to the Russian Far East. In Tbilisi, she met some Russians who had also heard rumour of this remedy, and with this apparent confirmation Kate decided that her calling was to travel to one of the world's most remote regions. The men of Krasnoyarsk crowded around her trying to flog her rickety travel options at inflated prices. She was astute and firm, however, holding out until a better, newer model was offered at a more sensible thirty roubles. She spent days in the vehicle, cramped in the back, shuddering through the Russian landscape, each bump and crater ricocheting through her body. 'Your limbs ache, your muscles ache, your head aches, and worst of all your insides ache,' she recalled. Her journey covered 6,500 kilometres across the country, made by carriage, sleigh, boat, foot and horseback, a route barely mapped.

To invoke her service to God, every discomfort of the journey was laid down in graphic detail for her resulting travelogue. There was also a willingness to take unnecessary risks, safe in the knowledge she was, she said, undertaking a 'Divine summons'. Later biographers have ventured that such rashness might be evidence of an affective disorder: whatever the exact diagnosis, certainly a sense of mania prevailed. At one point her sleigh upturned, her driver 'all but dead, half crushed under a wheel'. She suffered 'torments from mosquitoes' and was stalked by wolves and bears. Her companion, a Russian-speaking lady named Ada Field, was forced to turn back through illness, and as the roads petered out Kate was left in the company of a guard provided to her by the Russian empress. 'For two days I could scarcely walk,' she writes midway through her journey. 'My body ached and smarted as if it had been beaten. As I thanked God with all my heart that he had brought me thus far, I felt that nothing in the world would induce me to undertake the journey again, except spreading, in a humble way, the Gospel of Christ and helping the lepers.' In another moment she asked: 'The lepers in the far-off uncivilised regions of the world – who cared for them? What tender ministration from the gentle hand of a woman soothed their sufferings?' She lamented, contradicting her Constantinople complaints, how they were 'debarred from intercourse with others, except for those who suffered in a similar way'.

Kate slept among fellow travellers on the floor of hot, sweaty shelters with nothing in the way of amenities, sharing food that had 'been fingered and mauled about by dirty peasants'. Often she would arrive in a town and her sense of charitable duty got the better of her – she would take to the poorhouses and grim, violent prisons 'to go amongst the convicts' alone and Christ-like, handing out food and Bibles. 'More struggling and floundering through marshes and bogs, more pitch-dark forests, bear alarms and frightened horses . . . swimming head and exhaustion . . . a plunge into the morass would be the end of me.'

Finally at Yakutsk, the first leprosy sufferer Kate met was a fourteen-year-old Yakut boy, sent away from his neighbours and told to live at least fifteen kilometres away from any other hut or human being. The boy told her how he had lived this solitary life for some time, tortured by the loneliness. Now his mother would sneak him into her rough family home each night after dark, hiding him in a back room. This was no life, though; the boy was in constant anxiety of being discovered. 'I can never forget the terrified appearance of that boy as I went near to touch him; he at first flinched, expecting that I meant to hurt him,' Kate recalled. 'The shrinking of that child would have touched the most callous heart.' Kate imperiously commanded the tribal chief to legitimise this arrangement, and mother and son were reunited.

———

One day in Yakutsk I walk to the River Lena, to the point where Kate first arrived in the city. I move through the snow as swiftly as my layers of clothing allow, passing a street market at which carcasses of reindeer, horse and fish are displayed on bare tables, the -42 °C keeping them icily preserved. There is something about the raw flesh and scales of the produce against the white icy landscape that brings home the gothic danger to this place, a terror conjured in the minds of visitors for centuries. Kate herself had encountered something similar, a dead horse in the woods, describing, with a macabre turn of phrase, 'the blood-stained snow, and the animal's flesh torn off'. But Yakutsk is a modern city – hadn't I sung karaoke in the warmth of a biker bar the night before? 'Sweet Caroline' belted out in the cheery embrace of four oil company workers, beer slipping down the front of their Lacoste polo shirts as we swayed into the early hours. Yet there is a real danger, a possibility that despite its modern trappings, this place could easily consume you, kill the body, destroy the spirit: around town I see foolish young men with raw frostbite burns on their cheeks, having stayed out too long smoking and drinking. One of the oil guys tells me that just weeks after the USSR collapsed, when he himself was a boy, a teenager had hanged himself in the central square, aghast at this great geography left drained of ideology. Leaning back on his stool, pausing over his beer, he describes, with the wicked look of someone telling a tall tale, how the body dangled from Lenin's concrete hand.

The Yakut people, originally a shamanic indigenous tribe of reindeer herders, horse handlers and hunters, established a settlement here in the thirteenth and fourteenth centuries. When Kate visited, they made up almost 90 per cent of the population, with Russians as well as Evenks, Yukaghir and other indigenous groups constituting the remainder. Walking around the Far Eastern city today it is evident that Yakuts are down to just over half the population, with Russians making up the largest minority. In 1631 the Cossack explorer Pyotr Beketov arrived from the west tasked with collecting taxes in the form of animal pelts from the previously free populations along the Lena. The small raiding parties that followed Beketov east did so with terror, burning villages and using torture to enforce their authority. The Yakuts, however, did not succumb easily, and in a series of rebellions lasting a decade they fought against Russian imperialism. It was not military might that beat them in the end, but disease. Smallpox arrived in Siberia contemporaneously to Beketov and over the following twenty years killed approximately 80 per cent of the indigenous population. There is a myth among the Yukaghir that *comóje-yo'u*, 'the great illness', was a Russian spirit, transported to the battlefield in a box which once opened, unleashing a plume of smoke, killed their soldiers in multitude. The Yakut believe the disease arrived in the form of a woman-devil. Next came leprosy, measles, and finally, as more Russians arrived and lived and worked in this burgeoning commercial centre, venereal diseases and alcoholism, previously unheard of, took their toll.

In the nineteenth century, Tsarist Russia's interest in the territory paid for itself as gold and diamonds were discovered, with full-scale mining starting at the beginning of the twentieth century. One night, at a restaurant teetering on the kitsch, the waiters in leather jerkins and with traditional daggers on their belts, I ate local dishes of horse and foal; another time I was served *stroganina*, a kind of Siberian ceviche of diced frozen white fish. While local culture is memorialised, the Sakha Republic's riches flow west.

Continuing my walk to the river, I make my way down a street and then a track; the residential blocks peter out and the weather begins to worsen. After twenty minutes or so electricity pylons loom like mountains out of the cold, markers announcing the end of the city. I continue through a gap in the trees beyond, the snow rising deep to the edge of my ankle boots, heading in the direction I think the riverbank should be. Forty minutes in, I have a daunting quandary as to whether I should take off my gloves to check on my phone that I'm not completely lost, against the resulting drain of all colour and feeling from my uninsulated hands. The tips of my fingers turn yellow then to white as they wrinkle against the icy air, the muscles seizing up to uselessness. The old Yakutian belief was that their settlements – traditionally just a handful of yurts – were islands of *alases*, fertile depressions in the permafrost ripe for farming, places of safety and security beyond which lay the uncontrolled dangers of the forest beyond. An hour or so before the 3 p.m. dusk, an ice fog descends, an extreme condition occurring when the air's moisture begins to freeze. It is disconcerting, a sub-zero dreamscape in which the atmosphere itself seems to solidify. In my own panicked, touristic way, I am outside the safety of tamed land, getting gradually disorientated as the trees become denser. I push on, foolishly determined to find the river's edge.

This was where the leprous were banished, way beyond the lives of their family and friends. Without a bed, often barely dressed in distressed and dirty *soubas* (fur pelts), it was a cosmological as much as medical admonishment. Yakuts suffered leprosy to a much higher percentage than the global average. While all sickness was regarded as the possession of the human body by a malignant spirit, most was treatable by the local shaman. Leprosy, like smallpox, was regarded as an evil too great, however, and in traditional medicine the disease was believed to be beyond redemption. Even after the patient was expelled to the snow beyond the settlement, the not unreasonable superstition was to avoid the place in which they had fallen sick. Kate tells of a leprosy refuge that had been abandoned for lack of funds, and how her guides refused to even go near its ruins. The leprous were seen to live in a dark universe, where soul-eating spirits lay. The lucky ones were sent food parcels tied by a rope to the neck of a dog. The Russian ethnographer Vladimir Jochelson, who was exiled to Yakutsk by order of the tsar in 1887, paints a more sympathetic picture of the care the Yakuts provided for their ill, but by Kate's description most were left to all but starve.

On the road down to the river, outside the nondescript headquarters of a mining company, I had seen a bust of Stalin, erected by subscription of veterans and Communist Party members in 2013. In Soviet times thousands of prisoners followed the expulsions of the tsarist regime, sent to the 105 gulags that would come to cover almost a third of the Sakha Republic: first Poles captured during the war, then Germans, and then political prisoners caught up in the purges. Yakuts, too, were interned, particularly shamans and the other leaders who had led a brutally crushed rebellion against collectivisation in 1921. The bones of the dead have never been found, the location of their mass graves still locked away in state archives, but the remnants of the camps can be discovered if you venture far enough into the wilderness. New Siberian prisons remain, many holding the political foes of Vladimir Putin (including a Yakutian shaman incarcerated in a high-security psychiatric hospital for his opposition to the president). The Yakuts used to call these sites 'deaf places': zones that they did not want to hear of, a horror best left unheard and unspoken.

———

With my head aching and my eyes sore, tears against the cold crystallising to icicles in my lashes, I abandon the hike and turn around. My feet have long become heavy bricks and I fear being lost to the landscape, while chastising myself for probably over-reacting. I have not found the river's edge, though I begin to suspect it might be beneath me, some metres under the snow, unreachable until the warming thaw of April. Geography became a monstrous character within Kate's travels too, as if it itself had caught the disease she had come to cure. Her narrative is plotted with omens. On the way, one of her horses is almost swallowed up in a bog, floundering 'nearly to its neck'; 'every large stump of a fallen tree took the shape of a bear'. She passes 'the unearthly scene' of peat fires: 'flames of many colours – red, gold, blue and purple – darted up on every hand, some forked and jagged, some straight as a javelin, rising here and there above the earth'. At another length of her journey, she travels through a forest in which hundreds of trees have fallen, her horse picking its way through the upended destitute trunks. The Yakut story about the cause of this devastation tells of an argument between witches who met in the forest to fight. The forest spirit became angry at the conflict in its midst and let loose a band of devils who tore through the trees, toppling them on the quarrellers. (The modern scientific reason is perhaps even more extraordinary: released from deep under the frost as it partially thaws in the summer months is carbon. Natural combustion makes the trees weak and vulnerable to the slightest wind.)

During Kate's journey some villagers complained to her that a nearby paper mill had destroyed their source of spring water, reporting that 'cattle refused to drink the water, that men, women and children were ill from it'. This was a forerunner to the damage wrought by the gold, uranium and coal mines that were to come. A 1960s Soviet propaganda poster shows a *choron* (a traditional Yakut goblet) fallen on its side with a bounty of diamonds tumbling out. The aim was to get the locals on side for a mining operation which would leave the Vilyuy, the tributary which runs into the Lena upstream from Yakutsk, all but lifeless from heavy metal and phenol poisoning. In the late twentieth century this environmental fear became an existential threat as the Soviet Union conducted secretive underground nuclear tests in the region. The authorities at first claimed that all these tests took place without incident, but – as long suspected by many locals – they later admitted accidents had occurred. In 1974 and 1978, two detonations resulted in nuclear fallout close to the Vilyuy. The first of the controlled explosions was intended to break up the permafrost to allow the construction of a dam and the second was even more severe and involved a detonation of a similar magnitude as the bomb that fell on Hiroshima. In both cases reactors had been placed too close to the earth's surface and leakages occurred, sickness coming up from the underworld. For a long time, plutonium-239 levels were higher than those in Chernobyl and people who lived by the river became sick with illnesses that could not be identified and which the authorities refused to acknowledge. The nightmare of an infection is that while its havoc is felt within the body, it comes from the outside, unannounced and more often invisible. Even today vestiges of these nuclear accidents can be detected in local lichens and tree bark, flora that go into the food chain. At the National Art Museum of the Republic of Sakha in town I see cosmological paintings by Timofey Stepanov depicting scenes from the Olonkho, a series of epic poems, traditionally imparted orally from memory, that tell of three separate worlds: the upper world of the spirits (those that are good are from the east; the bad ones are from the west); the middle world of the people; and the lower world of devils. This configuration seemed prescient: if beneath the earth lay danger then the heavens too proved as much a threat in the modern era. By the time the Soviet space programme was in operation old Yakutian beliefs had mostly fallen by the wayside, but rumours continued of an extraterrestrial poison. The exact number of rocket components that landed in the area remains unknown, but whenever there was a Soviet rocket launch at the Baikonur Cosmodrome in Kazakhstan, a part of the projectile was jettisoned in Sakha once orbit had been achieved. The debris from space brought toxic gas containing heptyl, triggering cancer cases and, locals report, mass graveyards of great mammals and birds in Siberia's forests. The region, Eurasia's extremity, has long borne the brunt of whatever sickness affected its heart.

———

Kate and her party would discover more leprosy patients in the woods near the town of Vilyuysk: alone, frightened, some had erected crosses to warn others to keep their distance. She met a woman who had been forced to live with a stranger in the same *yourta*, a man also with leprosy but who had been driven insane by his predicament: 'For four years this poor woman had to live with a madman in the depth of the forest away from every human, never sure from one to another of her life.' Each meeting confirmed Kate's divine mission: 'I thanked God for sending me here to these helpless, forsaken ones.' Kate's care alleviated the immediate situation (though the herb turned out to be useless) and the people who suffered from leprosy were hopeful of her promise to build a new hospital, but by now there seems something severely off in her demeanour, something uncomfortable in the excitement she expresses among these people far from her own home. She dwells on their hardship in detail, and in some cases their deformities, writing of 'distorted' faces, of them limping, one using a stool to aid their way through the Siberian mud and cold slush. 'The stench took away my breath,' she says of entering another dwelling. 'One of the women has lived here for twenty years! Her feet had rotted up to the ankles.' There's a dehumanising element to all this, a sense of subjugation: a weird desperation to seek out trauma, a fetishism of healing for absolution. 'It is a mission that only the noblest, bravest and purest in the land should do. And I am so faulty!' she cries. At one point Kate collects the skin of a leprosy victim for medical examination back in London, she says; in another she describes a woman prostrating herself in gratitude, and a man left in earnest prayer to God thanking him for sending Kate.

Simone de Beauvoir, the French feminist, wrote that 'if human love is denied [a woman] by circumstances . . . she may choose to adore divinity in the person of God Himself', warning that erotomania, the assumption that God reciprocates this infatuation, is a risk. 'The erotomaniac feels she is made worthy through the love of a sovereign being; he takes the initiative in the amorous relation, he loves more passionately than he is loved; he makes his sentiments known by visible but secret signs.' In *On Sledge and Horseback to Outcast Siberian Lepers*, Kate makes a subtle visual simile between her being unable to walk from cramp and exhaustion, 'almost powerless', and a couple with leprosy who 'could only crawl on their knees, and they had but a little girl of six to help them'. The reasoning seems to be: if the leprous were worthy of particular heavenly love, each God incarnate, then their saviour is surely close to sainthood. After yet another ecstatic encounter Kate falls into melancholic comedown:

'After wishing the people Good-bye and creeping into my sledge, a sense of misery would come over me.' Her appointments with leprosy patients were no longer that of a professional nurse but quasi-spiritual moments, narcissistic mystical encounters in which these people seemed to represent her own salvation.

———

Kate was by no means unique in experiencing such rapture – remember Queen Matilda of England. Leprophilia, to borrow Graham Greene's turn of phrase, is as old as leprosy itself. In Greene's novel *A Burnt-Out Case*, the medic of a leprosy hospital in Congo asks the mission's priest of Querry, an architect who has turned up in search of seclusion: 'What do you think of Querry, father? Why do you think he's here? . . . Few people would choose a leproserie as a holiday resort . . . I was afraid for a moment that we might have a leprophil on our hands.' Father Thomas replies, '"A leprophil? Am I a leprophil?" "No, father. You are here under obedience. But you know very well that leprophils exist, though I daresay they are more often women than men . . . They would rather wash the feet with their hair like the woman in the gospel than clean them with something more antiseptic."'

Angela de Foligno, an Italian Catholic mystic who was born in 1248, is one of many such characters. To prove her holiness and pure devotion to God she described how she supped on the water she had washed the feet of leprosy patients with. 'The beverage flooded us with such sweetness that the joy followed us home,' de Foligno wrote. 'Never had I drunk with such pleasure. In my throat was lodged a piece of scaly skin from the lepers' sores. Instead of getting rid of it, I made great effort to swallow it and I succeeded. It seemed to me that I had just partaken of communion. I shall never be able to express the delight that inundated me.' Angela's gruesome act was not so much altruism as penance for her own behaviour. Having married into wealth and had children, she committed unspecified 'sins' – most likely adultery – but by 1288 her husband and children had succumbed to a plague. It was then, probably in the midst of grief and moral guilt (the heady mix Kate too suffered), that her visions began and a conversion quickly followed.

It is perhaps telling that on Angela's canonisation in 2013 she was given the patronage of those afflicted by sexual temptation, and it will surprise no one that she became a fascination for a generation of twentieth-century French post-structuralist philosophers. In his book *Guilt*, Georges Bataille dwells on Angela's use of leprosy as a means of sadistic purification, likening the leprosy patients' suffering to that of Christ's, whose destruction and pain on the cross allowed eternal forgiveness. In other lines that might likewise apply to Kate's use of the sick, Bataille writes of a photograph of a torture victim in his possession: 'he communicated his pain to me or perhaps the excessive nature of his pain, and it was precisely that which I was seeking, not so as to take pleasure in it, but in order to ruin in me that which is opposed to ruin'.

Kate's work in Russia, too, seems a kind of Freudian transference, both in terms of the almost erotic thrill she appears to get from her encounters with leprosy patients – encounters which are allowed within the social order, unlike lesbianism – and the manner in which her guilt over her sexuality is projected onto the supposed religious guilt of the ill. That she pivoted between transcendental highs and utmost depression as she ventured across the dark, haunting landscape of Siberia, a place of exile and escape, imprisonment and magic, makes tragic sense.

————

The publicity surrounding Kate's trip was tremendous; she ensured that news of her adventures filtered back to the British press every step of the way. She was a charismatic interviewee and, while women explorers were not unheard-of, this strange lady and her unusual adventure proved hugely intriguing to the public. The image of Kate, in trousers, a long-sleeved jacket and deerstalker hat, with revolver, riding whip and travelling bag to hand, was sensational. Her mental anguish was not made public at this stage and the image of the Christian heroine went unquestioned. She presented her trip as a religious mission but was engaging and funny, often dropping self-deprecating details at odds with her personal turmoil. She told reporters she had packed a staggering forty pounds of plum pudding that 'a dear English lady friend offered and provided'. She happily posed in the thick insulating clothing donated to her by Jaeger, lending her name to a series of adverts the clothing brand took out boasting of the partnership.

Her life in this period was a dizzying mix of psychosexual quasi-religious transcendence and shrewd pragmatism in which Kate, surpassing Father Damien, became one of the most talked-about people in British society. In November 1892, amid much internal discourse around the so-called 'female question', she was among the first women elected as fellows of the Royal Geographical Society, alongside such explorers as Isabella Bishop and May French Sheldon (after the first cohort of twenty-two in 1892–3, no more women would be admitted until 1913). Queen Victoria sought an audience – this time without the formality of the court, but a personal meeting at Balmoral at which the monarch agreed to endorse Kate's book. Before my trip to Yakutsk, though left at home, I bought a first edition of *On Sledge and Horseback Through Siberia*, bound in blue cloth with the title in gold emboss (meanwhile a cheaply reproduced and soon-to-be dog-eared and annotated paperback was thrown in my luggage). Inside, as effusive as I imagine royal protocol allowed, the dedication tells us that the Queen 'has taken a deep interest in the work undertaken by Miss Marsden amongst the lepers and desires to recommend her to the attention and consideration of any persons'. Victoria also gifted Kate an Elkington & Co. gold brooch in the form of an angel.

Before returning to England, Kate raised thousands of roubles, with more funds pouring in once she was home. Both the British and American editions of what some reviewers called her 'thrilling story' – telling of 'a courageous and heroic task' – sold well, profits further boosting the fund for her proposed hospital. Priced at six shillings or one guinea for the 'large, richly-bound' version, five reprints were warranted through a packed year of speaking engagements at various societies, culminating in an address to the Royal Geographical Society on Savile Row.

Her downfall was as swift, however. News of Kate's adventures travelled across the Atlantic. Watching this unfold was an American journalist and translator named Isabel Hapgood – 'a tall fine-looking woman with grey hair and winning smile', one description told, 'a great favourite within the social circles of New York'. Hapgood became infuriated with the publicity afforded Kate, especially regarding her connections within Russia, which the writer, whose translations of Tolstoy and Turgenev are still in print today, regarded as her territory. If Hapgood had channelled her jealousy merely through the bad review of Kate's travelogue she provided for *The Nation* – in which she estimated *On Horseback . . .* to be 'absolutely devoid of literary merit, grammar . . . filled up with piety as little interesting as the "adventures"' – that might have been the end of it. Instead Hapgood's vindictiveness became all-consuming, with happenstance providing further opportunity to persecute a woman she had never met. Through an acquaintance, the American struck up correspondence with a minister's wife named Elizabeth Lovering who happened to have been staying at the same Berlin guesthouse as Kate and Ellen Hewitt, and to whom Ellen had unburdened her grief. Given titbits of the most damaging gossip against Kate, Hapgood started digging, writing to contacts in Wellington and Nelson until she had the ammunition she needed, winging letters across the world, unbeknownst to the subject maligned within.

Promised funding dried up for Kate; the profiles in the press disappeared. The final calamity was a letter in *The Times* from the head of a committee of supporters she had gathered in Russia, claiming that there were inconsistencies with the 'leper fund' accounts. The accounting claim might have been false, but it was made to spare blushes as to the real reason Kate had become *persona non grata*: none but a few of her grand friends wanted to be associated with a gay woman. Kate took legal action nonetheless, much to the astonishment of those who knew the real reason behind her fall from grace. The time it took for Kate to fully comprehend her situation was inverse to how quickly her fame collapsed to infamy. It was only in 1895, anxiously eying the hell Oscar Wilde was being dragged through in his own trial that year, that Kate called off her lawyers and left for the US. There, over several years, she tried to salvage her reputation by founding the St Francis Leper Guild, a Catholic charitable organisation, but her celebrity had become such that there was no hiding. She was often recognised and chastised in public, even stateside, and eventually resigned herself to suburban Philadelphia, where she lived for some time in quiet seclusion.

———

Kate's final years, an old woman now, were spent back in Britain in the company of Emily Norris, a moneyed artist, on whom she deeply relied. Her health was delicate and finances unstable, yet together they lived a genteel life by the sea on England's south coast. Kate made one final attempt at public rehabilitation, seeking to establish a local museum in Bexhill with a few of the resort's other middle-class residents. Kate set about securing funding and exhibits for a natural history institution, the ambition for what was originally a small venture quickly snowballing as she entertained the task with characteristic single-mindedness. Bexhill Museum opened in 1914, but Kate was not there at the inauguration: a few months earlier, word of her apparently scandalous past, otherwise forgotten to the newspaper archives and few memories, reached the rest of the organising committee. Kate was forced to flee once more, this time with Emily, banished from the town and its wagging tongues.

She died in 1931 confined to a psychiatric hospital back in the suburbs of London, a broken outcast like those she had wanted to help. Her grave, for years without a headstone, lies at the end of an overgrown row in a lost corner of a West London cemetery.

On my last day in Yakutsk I come across something that moves me in my travel exhaustion. I'm walking through the reconstructed old town, a series of wooden cabins, many with carved pictorial frontages, the imagery of which is obscured by the snow and ice. The sun glances off the white crisp ground today, but I am still having to find somewhere to warm up at least once every half hour. I dive into what I think could be a shop, though the nature of the buildings are not always evident given the thick drapes over the windows. It's a craft store, each table laid out with an individual maker's wares. There's lace embroidery in one corner, next to some woodwork made by a man who constantly coughs into his scarf. Across the room a woman has laid out dozens of porcelain dolls, each of which she's given a hand-stitched outfit. They're fantastically detailed, more kitsch decorative objects for adults than toys for children, the costumes mimicking those I've seen at the nearby folk museum. Yakutians in winter furs; Yakutians in bright summer shawls and blue embroidered dresses. Among them stands a familiar figure: Kate Marsden in her Red Cross uniform. Reduced to archetype, feminised but remembered. I pick her up, the colour inching back into my hands as the warmth of the shop does its work.

For all her faults, when faced with a foe like Hapgood or the onslaught of moral rectitude against her gender and sexuality, Kate lacked guile or spite. She was prone to proselytising, calculating when it came to spending other peoples' money and guilty of highhandedness and snobbery, but her mission still bore fruit: the leprosy hospital in Siberia was built, serving patients until 1962; the St Francis Leprosy Guild remains in operation internationally. I think about how badly she was treated. Her orchestrated descent into something like madness served a social function, a warning, a method of control, an act of moralistic violence. Execrated and excreted, Kate retreated beyond society, to God, to the other side of the world, to mania, to those who had nothing.

ROBBEN ISLAND, SOUTH AFRICA

I never find out whether you are supposed to wander Robben Island alone. To duck out at the end of the guided tour, to miss your ticketed ferry back, to return on the afternoon crossing to Cape Town instead. It seems harmless enough, just a question of catching up with the later waves of visitors arriving at this rocky outpost with the regularity of the bay's ferocious swell. It is strange to think Kate Marsden came this way, even if she never left her steamship. Table Mountain lurks in the clouds as I scurry at pace past the family steak restaurants and fancy shops of the city's harbourside development. I arrive just in time to cross the metal ramp onto the ferry, catching the tail of the hundred or so sightseers from around the world who have already boarded. Soon the *Krotoa* is reversing out of the harbour, water spraying against the sealed windows. The songs of South African freedom that play over the boat's PA system give way to an introductory video which accompanies the crossing of the bay.

With the journey just twenty minutes, the film covers Robben Island's early history at speed: first landed by the Portuguese in 1498, it was used by the British and Dutch as a refuelling station on their colonial voyages. When the latter established settlements on the Cape in the seventeenth century, they immediately identified these five square kilometres as the ideal place to jettison the troublemakers of their new outpost. Formalised as a prison, the coloniser shipped over former kings, princes and religious leaders of its possessions in the East Indies, abandoning them alongside the homegrown undesirables. The seals that the colonial masters named the island after – the Dutch 'r' rolled to an almost English 'w', the second 'b' hard – soon faced extinction, the prisoners hunting and skinning them as means of survival.

When the British took possession two centuries later the island continued to be used as a dumping ground for anti-colonial insurgents. The rebels of St Helena, Bencoolen, Penang, Singapore, Malacca, Burma, Aden and Mauritius were landed here by the East India Company. One group, banished after the Cape frontier wars, tried to escape. Some drowned, others died as they were recaptured, most were returned before being beheaded and their heads displayed on poles along the shoreline. By the mid-nineteenth century, the prisoners had left and the island's new residents were arriving: the Cape's leprosy patients, who were forced to call this home for almost a century while the mainland was completely reconfigured through waves of colonial management and mismanagement. The *Krotoa* video is in fact skimpier on detail than this expanded telling; for the most part, as we cross the choppy waters, the South Atlantic a bubble bath of foam, the film concerns itself with the outpost's most infamous role: a maximum-security prison to the heroes of South Africa's anti-apartheid struggle. If this boat trip has been made by patients and political prisoners alike, then likewise the laws against leprosy helped navigate South Africa's slide into racialised segregation, the cordon sanitaire providing a blueprint for prejudice.

A concrete harbour arm folds out from beyond the island's rocks like the flexed bicep of a weightlifter, and the boat inches towards the landing area until the engines come to a halt in a roar of backwash. In 1909 a government official noted that the 'low-lying' island was subject to 'sea-fogs and cold, damp north winds' and on this June morning nothing has changed. Robben Island, such a byword of discrimination and resistance that the real place risks all but disappearing – a 'rhetorical space', as the professor of language Richard Marback has called it – materialises just momentarily beneath my trainers. When we disembark the ferry, a dozen or so tour guides in uniform fleece quickly divide us up into groups. It's a kind of efficiency the prisoners themselves were met with. There are some places in the world – not many, perhaps, rarity is integral – that are so charged with expectation and memory that anything mundane or practical feels an affront. I remember feeling the same when visiting Chernobyl, and I am certain it would also be the case at Auschwitz. Places in which each syllable of the name oozes contamination. Black holes of humanity that live beyond their geography and suck in every emotion.

The groups are packed onto minibuses, and as I'm boarding I ask the driver which side I should sit to see the graveyard of the leprosy patients and, as I'm the last on to a full bus, swap with a lady who has brought her grandchildren over to her country of birth for the first time. Her accent twinges South African, while theirs is pure West Coast US. She moves seats with a slight hint of puzzlement, but even so, and though the bus drives slowly, it is hard to see the headstones from a distance.

For most who have paid their 600 rand, this bus trip is mere precursor to the main event: the walking tour of the high-security prison where some 1,500 Black South African political subversives were kept. The prisoners had fallen foul of the litany of laws that paved the way to their oppression: the 1950 Suppression of Communism Act, the 1953 Public Safety Act, the 1953 Criminal Law Amendment Act, the 1956 Riotous Assemblies Act, the 1960 Unlawful Organisations Act, the Sabotage Act of 1962. Each was a tightening screw in the legislation that upheld apartheid between 1948 and the early 1990s and, such was the suffocating management of race and politics, the last of these covered everything from strikes and trade union activity to writing anti-apartheid slogans on walls.

Off the bus a new guide takes over: Dede Ntsoelengoe, or prisoner 38/84 as he was once known. Affable in a puffer jacket and baseball cap, he says that we will come to the cell of Robben Island's 'second most famous prisoner' at the end of the tour. 'First,' he says with a smile, 'you should see where the most famous one was kept: me.' We funnel through the sombre concrete complex, Ntsoelengoe's jokes dissipating as he tells of the cruelties of the regime under which he lived for seven years: officially forty (often more) men crammed into a room all day, unless they were out undertaking forced labour. Ntsoelengoe had been one of the prisoners who built the roads we had driven on. Eventually we are shown, as grimly uniform as all the others – bars on the window, small table, sleeping mat on the floor – the poky cell in which Nelson Mandela slept for eighteen of the twenty-seven years he was incarcerated by the regime.

———

Prior to its 1910 incorporation into the Union of South Africa, a self-governing dominion of the British Empire (which later became the independent, apartheid-riven South Africa), the Cape Colony had a reputation for multiracial liberalism. Racist attitudes were undoubtedly ingrained in colonial administrators, and the poorer schools were filled with the children of Black families, who on a Sunday stuck to the rear pews at church, but the vote was available to white and Black men alike (there was a provision that the voter must own property, but the value was very low). Moreover, a visit to the District 6 Museum in downtown Cape Town, a more ramshackle affair than the Robben Island set-up, shows that for a decade or so from the abolition of slavery a remarkable heterogeneity occurred in the inner city neighbourhood. Established as a 'doorstep dormitory' for harbour workers, it was a place where Black dockers mixed with Malay Muslims and Jewish families from tsarist Russia. They lived among Indian immigrants and working-class white Europeans who had come south to try their luck. Trades began to spring up along the crowded streets: carpenters, bootmakers and dressmakers working from ad hoc wooden terrace houses that were forever being modified to cope with growing and often interracial families. Bars and dancing spots followed. Life was hard and wild by all accounts, but the residents were largely left alone by the apparatus of colonialism – until a series of health scares brought this milieu to an end.

In August 1883, Alexander Abercrombie, a Scottish-born member of the Board of Health and the colony's legislative assembly, appeared before a select committee on the subject of leprosy. He would have sat in the parliament's chambers in a masonic lodge, now on the grounds of the current seat of government, a few minutes' walk from District 6. 'I can speak merely from what I see daily in my rounds about the streets of Cape Town, and I can say that it is rapidly increasing . . . amongst the lower classes; chiefly the coloured races.' Robben Island had been used to house leprosy patients from 1845 when, largely for budgetary reasons, a group of patients were moved from another camp long established in the Hemel En Aarde Valley (all trace of which has disappeared under the pinot noir vineyards that the inclines are now chiefly famed for). Admission to the leprosarium remained voluntary, at least in theory, and the population rarely peaked beyond fifty, confined 'chiefly to the pauper class' who had little other option than to submit themselves to the hands of the state. They could come and go, and frequently hitched lifts with passing fishing fleets to visit family on the mainland. Abercrombie's contribution was part of a debate over changing the law to establish forced segregation. Hansen's discovery loomed large in the evidence the doctor gave. 'A specific bacillus has lately been found in leprosy, and this will, no doubt, in course of time, throw much light on the cause of the disease,' Abercrombie told his political colleagues. 'It would be communicated to a person who came in contact with a leprous person if he had a sore or an abrasion. For instance, if he were to touch a leprous person with sore fingers; use the same knife or fork; or drink out of the same glass.' On questioning, he admitted that he had come across many married couples in which one half had the disease but the other did not, but that was just a matter of 'constitution', therefore, personally, 'I would not like to sleep in the same bed as a leper.'

His testimony came as the Cape had already introduced its first public health act in 1883, in response to a smallpox outbreak, which gave administrators the power to clear areas of the city in case of an epidemic. Following the evidence of Abercrombie and others, the 1884 Leprosy Repression Bill similarly allowed the removal of individuals, but in this case the authorities did not have to declare any mass health emergency. Both were sweeping new powers for the government but neither were put into practice immediately; the former was reserved for the next big calamity, the latter batted between administrators local and in London, again with an eye on the purse strings, knowing that the maintenance of what would surely be a much-enlarged Robben Island operation came at a price.

The hysteria over Father Damien's death in Hawaii, as well as the election of Cecil Rhodes domestically, changed the equation again. With the 'leper scare' in full swing globally, within a year of coming to power Rhodes ratified the leprosy segregation law in 1891: those with signs of the disease were pulled from their homes in the likes of District 6 without warning, often in handcuffs, the authorities worried that otherwise they might go into hiding. 'There is a descent upon the house . . . there is no time to do anything – the ambulance is waiting, therefore the person must go. In many cases it is a removal for life, and it has to be done in five minutes,' one Church of England minister complained, citing a particularly distressing case in which a twenty-year-old woman was taken by a group of plain-clothed men.

'The mother flew into a temper and said she would not let them take her daughter that day. Then they sent for the police and of course there was a disturbance in the street.'

Most doctors went along with this persecution, but not all were convinced and the global debate over contagion and freedom played out through the harried lanes of Cape Town. Robert Forsysth was one such medic who was willing to risk sanctions for failing to report a case if he assessed it to be particularly mild. Admitting such a practice, the local doctor defended himself by saying that though he was bound by the resolutions of the leprosy congresses in Berlin and Bergen that segregation was necessary, in Norway 'even those in asylums are allowed to go about the roads' and 'I think more of the liberty of my patients than of paying a small fine'. His peers were dismissive: 'They deal with a different class of people,' a colleague stationed on Robben Island countered in regard to the Nordic country. The Medical Officer for Health was even more explicit in the racism. 'Here you have a very different population to deal with. A people largely composed of native and coloured, unreliable, indifferent to the dangers of the disease, ignorant and devoid of the simplest knowledge of hygiene.' Within a year the number of those who were interned on the island climbed to 413; by 1915 there were 600 people living there.

The island residents, whose previous neglect might have allowed, in a strange way, for a certain amount of freedom, found themselves living under a whole new regime from which there was no escape. They were no longer allowed to kiss or touch their visitors, they were deprived of their right to vote and the men were barred from prosecuting adulterous wives back on the mainland. The neighbouring colonies of what would become the Union of South Africa followed suit with their own laws (after the union the individual laws were combined and leprosaria across the newly united country likewise expanded to meet the demand). Neither Damien's death, nor indeed the increasing numbers of white South Africans who were sent to Robben Island, did much to dampen the prejudice that leprosy was a disease chiefly of the non-white population. Instead, the white patients were presented as victims of the supposed hygienic dereliction among Black people. Samuel Impey, who was Chief Medical Superintendent of the island colony for four years and had even travelled to Norway to meet Hansen, carefully described how 'Hottentots and Bushmen, who were always a more or less nomadic people, soon settled in Basutoland and with them brought the loathsome disease'. He did acknowledge that 'the reign of the East India Company' and the 'free intercourse between the Cape Colony and the East and West Indies, where the disease was rife' might also be to blame. The latter is an echo of Henry Press Wright, that firebrand rector of Greatham previously encountered, and his description of the disease as an 'imperial danger', a by-product of the global circulation of goods, capital and people that defines empire-building. The danger lay for such commentators, however, not in the people to whom the resources of that network flowed but to the people who were exploited in the process. While white people could get leprosy, in the eyes of the imperial classes of nineteenth-century southern Africa, as much as anywhere across the colonised world, a 'leper' was always Black, and among Black people – or Asians, islanders, indigenous nations – lurked the potential for leprosy.

———

While it haunted colonial psychology, the problem, affecting hundreds but not thousands of individuals, might not have been enough on its own to make disease the overriding political issue of the time. Just as the Black Death had hardened social attitudes to leprosy in the fourteenth century, it was the bubonic plague – on the rise in India as the twentieth century dawned and which would go on to kill an estimated fifteen million people globally – that made disease the number-one catalyst for change in the Cape. Officials were afflicted by 'sanitation syndrome', as the US historian Maynard Swanson has termed it, in which mess and dirt became an existential risk to maintaining order. The plague came to the colony on boats carrying military uniforms from India for the British soldiers fighting the Second Boer War (that imperial danger again). Oversized rats had been spotted for some time on the waterfront, which was as messy and utilitarian then as it is clean and corporate today, before anyone reported it to the medical authorities. By 1901 it had claimed its first victims from among the ship workers, labour that was invariably undertaken by the Black and mixed-race population. The city's Medical Officer of Health warned 'the dreaded bubonic plague – the scourge of India – had at length made its appearance in our midst', and by March that year 130 cases had been confirmed, killing just under half of those infected.

It raged deeply but quickly, yet there were those who guessed which way the wind would blow as the numbers increased. Mahatma Gandhi, his resistance barely seeded, was at the time in the neighbouring Colony of Natal, where racism was more overt. The young lawyer wrote that 'the cup of woe of the Indians in South Africa evidently does not appear to have as yet become full; and the bubonic plague promises to fill that cup well up to the brim'. Natal promptly enacted laws banning entry to Indian South Africans unless they had a special pass, even if they hadn't actually set foot in India for decades. Gandhi took up the cause, complaining about the effect on livelihoods. The rules – which foreshadowed the apartheid pass system – were 'not only most stringent and unreasonable but oppressive and unbusinesslike'. Gandhi, who at the time regarded himself as British first and Indian second, set up a field hospital in which to nurse victims of the pandemic, quarantining them in a vacant house and raising money for basic medical supplies. While he decried the response of the government, he also seems to have internalised the idea that white people were intrinsically cleaner and less likely to be susceptible to disease. In an article titled 'A Lesson from the Plague' he wrote: 'We should set about putting our houses in order as well literally as figuratively . . . We should ingrain into our hearts the English saying that cleanliness is next to godliness.'

The Black population of Cape Colony was in the majority and it was they who suffered the most in the authorities' decidedly ungodly but apparently sanitary response. An area reserved for Black Africans had been mooted previously, but action had been held up by questions both ideological – snagged between the Whiggish liberalism of Cape politics and the more hardline racism of Boer influence – and coldly practical (how would the Black population be able to provide cheap labour to the city if removed to its further limits?). As the deaths mounted up, however, the emergency powers of the Public Health Act were invoked and the first mass urban clearance in the Cape took place in 1902, a practice that would become the defining feature of apartheid. In the name of protecting the white minority from the plague, Black families were forcibly evicted en masse from central Cape Town, marched out by British soldiers and their rifles, to a new settlement on the outskirts of the city near a sewage farm on the Cape Flats. If the desire for such racial segregation had always been latent, now under the auspices of the health emergency, dressed in liberal paternalism, the taboo was broken. Ndabeni, as the suburb is known today, was a Blacks-only field hospital and isolation camp at first, housed in barracks and huts purchased from the military, but it soon became a permanent settlement of thousands living in lean-tos and tents. It was an unprecedented clearance that didn't go unchallenged by the Black population, with a series of street protests and sit-ins taking place in District 6 and community meetings organised on the slopes of Table Mountain, all broken up by the police. They were ultimately to no avail and the zoning was cemented with the 1902 Native Reserve Location Act.

———

On Robben Island, in the glare of the old exercise yard, bare but for gravel and a couple of intrepid yuccas framed by the high walls, people are thanking Ntsoelengoe for his tour. Despite this being the nth time guiding people through a place he never wanted to come back to, he has been charismatic and introspective. Leaving the penal complex, most turn left back towards the gift shop on the harbourside. I ask Ntsoelengoe if he knew about the island's past as a leprosarium when he was imprisoned here, but he says no – denied access to books, they only knew what they could tell each other and few had such details. They had a future to plot, anyway, not a past to worry about. I give him my thanks, too, but turn right, walking back up to the cemetery. It is a scrubby memorial, a small clearing in a clump of trees set back from the road. The grass is long and the few headstones that remain, or were ever erected, appear like clusters of dirty grey stalagmites – scant souvenirs of the many more graves that were crushed beneath the construction of the high-security prison or scattered across the south-east of the island. A sagging mesh fence prohibits closer inspection of the graves, and the names are mostly too obscured by lichen and age to be discernible.

There are trees now, most of which were not here in the island's days as a leprosy colony, though for desperate need of shade the patients themselves planted what they could. In his autobiography, Mandela writes how the glare from the island's white chalky ground damaged his eyes, unremitting even on the frequent days of fog. On the guided tour we had been shown the quarry where the prisoners were made to dig for limestone, out in the elements, denied sunglasses, their labour serving little purpose but to break the spirit. Mandela described how it was difficult for him to cry, even in old age, his tear ducts destroyed. Leprosy is also prone to attack the nerve endings surrounding the eyes, stopping a patient from blinking and causing ocular ulcers. For many, the exposure on this desolate place was torture relieved only by the eventual blindness that occurred in almost all the patients with tubercular leprosy. The issue dominates their testimonies. 'The glare and the dust hurt my eyes; I can hardly see through them,' recalled a patient named Cornelis. 'The sun is very hot and trying to our eyes,' a woman named Kitty complained. 'We get rheumatism, chest complaints and our eyes are injured,' Frederick Lange told a health committee in 1909. 'A short time ago a fog came on suddenly and one of our patients who was outside caught a chill and fourteen days after he was dead.'

———

Introducing his concept of 'total institutions', the sociologist Erving Goffman ran through a few examples of places and communities that are isolated from the outside world to such an extent that the 'three spheres of life' – sleep, play and work – all occur in the same confined space and with the same discrete group of people. 'There are places established to care for persons felt to be both incapable of looking after themselves and a threat to the community, albeit an unintended one.' He mentions tuberculosis sanatoria, mental hospitals and leprosaria. Another type of total institution protects 'the community against what are felt to be intentional dangers to it, thus with the welfare of the sequestered not the immediate issue:

jails, penitentiaries, POW camps and concentration camps'. The leprosarium at Robben Island should have been a model of the first type, but in reality it more resembled the latter.

Giving evidence to the same select committee as Abercrombie, a Dr Parsons, who visited the island many times before compulsory segregation, said that: 'In no sense of the word is there a hospital for lepers, but simply a number of wards set apart for those paupers who are suffering from the disease . . . They undergo no special treatment and the arrangements of their accommodation are very bad.' Across the island the authorities placed seventy-eight people who had been committed to the Cape's mental asylums, who included prostitutes with STDs and alcoholics, as well as ninety-two people deemed chronically sick and poor.

There was supposed to be little interaction between these groups, but certainly in 1887 two blind residents of the latter institutions were found to be ripping off leprosy patients, smuggling substantial quantities of brandy and cannabis in the corsets of visiting women and selling it at inflated profit to their captive market. I feel a pang of happiness that, despite the extortionate prices, they were able to have a good time. (Later island superintendents, like Damien in Molokai, spent a great deal of time breaking up home-brew operations.) Parsons was aware that there was no cure for the disease but believed that the residents would suffer less if the authorities improved their environment. 'They have no baths worth the name, only a few small foot baths (wooden), and a half hogshead or two for use with cold water.' He adds, however, 'The class they belong to are not noted for cleanliness . . . They eat, drink and sleep, and sometimes cook, in the same room all year round, in a low ill-ventilated, badly-lighted build-ing. Their outer clothing is coarse cloth and incapable of being washed and constantly smeared with the discharges from their wounds.' His words are echoed in Goffman's observation that prison staff often see 'inmates as bitter, secretive and untrustworthy, while inmates often see staff as condescending, high-handed and mean. Staff tend to feel superior and righteous; inmates tend, in some ways at least, to feel inferior, weak, blameworthy and guilty.'

The select committee had been called in anticipation of mandatory segregation. The hysteria that the government itself had caused was already proving a headache. Transport companies that had previously boarded people with leprosy quite happily now said they could no longer do so. An exclusive carriage was coupled to trains to bring patients from outside Cape Town, and the mail steamers that had previously made stops at the island on the way out of the bay – like the one Kate Marsden had sailed past on – began to refuse such requests. The extra administrative work was piling up and the sheer expense of removing the patients' liberty was causing consternation. The authorities correctly assumed there would be a huge surge in numbers on the island, and with that number likely including whites, who had rarely been represented above single digits previously, an upgrade in facilities was needed. Most white people with leprosy, richer, had been able to avoid the crossing and had been looked after at home, and the few white patients who did come to the island received preferential treatment, many able to pay their way into private cottages. With a budget of £30,000, accommodation that could house hundreds of patients was built, the women left on the north-east of the island while the men were to live by the sea, midway down the path I'm on now. An old photograph, probably taken to demonstrate the improvements, shows that they were long, shedlike wards housing rows of beds. A few pictures hang on the wall and small screens by each bed provide a whiff of privacy.

New arrivals had always been classified according to race, but little was formally done with the information. After the forced segregation of leprosy patients was waved through parliament, a more systematic racial division was mandated, the feeling being that mixing would be a step too far for the white inmates. Each of the new buildings was therefore allocated according not just to gender but skin colour too. A sign of official priorities can be found in how the beds were allotted, each new arrival being assigned their place by racial classification first and, only if possible, by the stage their medical condition had reached second. One of the few pleasures the men and women had were the occasional seasonal cricket matches. When such a match was played on a Saturday around 300 would gather to watch, but the spectators were still divided by race, 'the Europeans have a stand to themselves, and the coloured have a stand', a resident doctor noted with satisfaction. How the genders mingled was notably different too. Black men and women, including at least one married couple, were banned from each other's quarters and only allowed to meet in the so-called 'neutral' area. If a couple were found, as they occasionally were, down in the cliff nooks that might invite lovers to the seafront, their permission to work was taken away, their pay forfeit. Worse still, the men were banned from the neutral area for a year, the women for life. The white patients had no such area and were free to go back and forth between each other's buildings. 'The whites have really a lot of liberty. They are allowed to walk about and to do practically what they please as they are trusted,' said William Babington Magennis, a much-disliked commissioner of the leprosarium in the first decade of the twentieth century. Some of these measures were made by the authorities on the white patients' behalf, but some of the patients themselves demanded better division. A higher wall between the racialised areas was requested, a monument perhaps to hardening attitudes across the bay, while others believed that the segregation wasn't nuanced enough, with one visitor noting that 'whites mix up freely with the coloured patients and [they] make friends with each other'.

In the Cape Town Archives, a grand building at which I will spend many hours wading through the bureaucratic detritus of an increasingly racist administration, I find an inordinate amount of correspondence that flitted between the desks of various administrators on the subject of corsets. In 1904 a white female patient arriving on the island would be issued with a standard kit that covered everything from two print dresses and two stuff dresses, replaced annually if needed, to their bedstead, mattress and sheets, and dinner plate, soup bowl and tumbler. Cuffs, ribbons and ties were available on request. Black female arrivals got the same, but for a few small but irritating substitutions, the nature of which seem merely to signal inferiority or difference: boots were provided instead of the Oxford shoes that the white patients received, red handkerchiefs instead of white; there were no corsets available or cloth slippers, no bentwood chair or deckchair but a stool instead. The Under Secretary for Cape Colony wrote to Magennis in prim cursive handwriting that a 'request of Female Coloured Leper Patients of corsets' had been received. 'Will you say if these articles were intentionally omitted – there are probably cases where patients have been accustomed but the great majority have never worn them and would commence now if given these things. This hardly seems necessary or advisable.' The reply came, 'I never thought of corsets in connection with kits of coloured patients and it was never suggested to me. I dare say there are a certain number of half-coloured or better class coloured and especially those brought up in towns who have been in the habit of wearing corsets. Personally I see no necessity for them to be provided and consider people are better without them.' A decision was made a week later, formalised on a typewriter: no corsets for the mixed-race patients. Cecil Rhodes himself sowed further division when he personally donated a bath chair for patients' use, and then two horses and a cart, but only for the whites.

In the archives, when I go through the boxes, I find myself following in the track of those that have been here before me. Harriet Deacon, for a long time head of research at the Robben Island Museum, has unearthed mountains of what might today be termed 'microaggressions' against the Black patients, detailed among the musty ribbon-tied files here and elsewhere. The whites got tinned sardines, the Blacks did not; the whites were allowed to come to the jetty to meet visitors and deliveries, the Blacks were not. Even in death the slights continued: the whites were granted name plates on their coffins while the Blacks' went unmarked.

Sixty years later, Ntsoelengoe told us, the guards would play the same psychological games with the political prisoners, none of whom were white: there were small discrepancies in rations doled out to 'Bantus' against those given to the 'Coloured and Asiatics'. The ex-prisoner had shown us the menu from his time here: mixed-race and Asian prisoners received six ounces of meat, while the Black prisoners received five ounces; the former had coffee for both breakfast and supper, the latter only in the morning; the former were given an ounce of jam or syrup, the latter none. 'The aim', Ntsoelengoe said, 'was to sow division.'

The Black leprosy patients on Robben Island did not take their situation lightly and were acutely attuned to the symbolism such measures held. While the women did not get their corsets, they had more success in the issue of payment for work done on the island. Dr Ross, the surgeon superintendent in the late 1880s, might have described his charges as 'sulky idle people' who would not work, but after enforced segregation, with the increase in numbers, patients who were physically capable were expected to help in the operation of the facility. The women baulked, believing such labour was the kind expected of convicts, not patients in a hospital: that fine line of a total institution again. They went on strike, refusing to send their washing to the newly opened laundry at which they were supposed to work, refusing to clean their own dorms or sweep the roads and clean the yards. Patients gradually began to accept employment within the leprosarium complex itself only after being promised remuneration, the government spending around £4,000 a year in wages. There was no option but for the state to comply: with the 'leper scare' forestalling recruitment from outside, without the patients' labour the whole island would have ground to a halt. Many of the men and women had been subsistence farmers on the mainland but, finding it virtually impossible to grow crops among these spartan rocks, some turned instead to fishing off the coast and keeping chickens and other such small livestock on the land. Much to the annoyance of those with an eye on the colony's expenditure, the government was forced to buy from the patients. (In one year an estimated 111,600 eggs were procured.) The cooks were external staff, but the kitchen and scullery maids eventually came from within the patient body (at which point the medical staff refused to eat the food made in that kitchen), as did many of the ward assistants and maintenance workers. A Black patient taught at one of the missionary schools and others wrote letters home on behalf of the illiterate. 'They will never do a single thing unless paid. If you want a man to read for a blind patient he would ask payment for it,' Magennis huffed. 'We feed them and clothe them and pay them in addition.' In reality they were underpaid – the two carpenters on the island earned 3s 6d a day from the government, and their work was deemed a very high standard, but they would have earned around 15s to £1 a day on the mainland. It was a point of principle, among a generation for whom slavery was still in living memory, as much as economic necessity. Their demand was simple: to be 'treated as . . . free British Subject[s]', as one letter of complaint to the authorities pleaded.

Franz Jacobs was a former teacher of mixed ethnicity, who, before enforced segregation, had relished his trips home to see his wife, children and stepchildren in Woodstock. When these rights were revoked, he sent a plea directly to Queen Victoria, invoking emancipation and abolition. 'Our request and entreaty to the Queen of this Empire is let us poor sick ones have our freedom. We are imprisoned and shut up on Robben Island for it is prohibited to go away. We live as if we were dead. It is so dark here. We are taken from our homes, that is worse than slaves. There should be a time for coming out, but we might stay here forever. What she does for the slaves, will our Queen do for us and free us from slavery?' Jacobs' appeal to the Crown came only after his letters to the Cape government and the Attorney General went ignored. On silence too from the palace – Queen Victoria happy to hear from the likes of Kate Marsden about the plight of patients, but not the patients themselves, it would seem – in 1892 Jacobs, like the women on the island had previously, decided to take matters into his own hands, threatening 'war and riot' among those he was sequestered with. While imprisonment in general was the chief complaint, the demands Jacobs zoned in on in his petitions to the authorities are interesting. Yes, he wished to see his wife, but he also wished, at least according to Chief Medical Superintendent Impey, that Black patients have access to cruet stands, finger glasses, table napkins 'and delicacies of all kinds'. Jacobs' revolt was not just over basic human rights but an appeal for equal rights and the accoutrements of civilised life, the small vestiges of which were disappearing on both island and mainland for Black people, healthy and otherwise. 'For us, such struggles – for sunglasses, long trousers, study privileges, equalised food – were corollaries to the struggle we waged outside prison,' Mandela writes in *Long Walk to Freedom*. 'The campaign to improve conditions in prison was part of the apartheid struggle. It was, in that sense, all the same; we fought injustice wherever we found it, no matter how large, or how small, and we fought injustice to preserve our own humanity.' The same might be said of Jacobs' demands.

Fearing the worst, Impey requested a platoon of armed police, duly sent, to crush this nascent revolution. Jacobs was put in solitary confinement, before being removed temporarily to a hospital on the mainland. He was returned briefly, an apology forced out of him and his demands 'recanted', but died a year later.

There were other agitators in the island's history as a leprosarium. Twenty years later, the directorship of Magennis, 'in whom all sympathy for us patients is dead', according to one of his charges, caused much consternation among both the white and Black patients. Rankles ranged from the lack of trained nurses to the erection of fences that obscured the view to the mainland. Magennis and the Union authorities identified a man they referred to as 'Leper Williams' as the ringleader. Like Jacobs before him, they sought to remove James Williams before his insurrection could spread. Being white, however, he proved trickier to dispose of. He would have to be found a cottage 'round which a good corrugated iron fence could be cheaply erected', because the only other option, removal to Emjanyana, a colony elsewhere in the Union exclusively populated by Black leprosy patients, was out of the question, nor could they run the risk that he might 'promptly repeat his proceedings at that place'. While his punishment was severe, Williams' character was left intact – indeed he is described respectfully, noted as a former sergeant of the Lancers and 'of considerable education and possessing financial means'.

Compare this to Jacobs, who acted as a catechist at the island's Dutch Reformed Church: first denounced by Impey as 'a religious lunatic' before a more serious accusation, of making rape threats against the nurses, was reported by Henry Loch, the high commissioner for Southern Africa. The accusation has been repeated at face value by historians, but it seems odd that Impey, who was actually witness to the revolt, had only previously written in the correspondence that Jacobs 'threatened to strike them with crutches'. Maybe Jacobs did make the rape threat, maybe he didn't, but it is symbolic of the fear and loathing colonial administrators held for both leprosy patients and the rebellious Black or mixed-race man. It fitted to a moral panic dubbed 'the Black peril' emerging in this period across southern Africa, in which Black masculinity was presented in the language of contagion, in which the sexualised Black man might infect and destroy white female 'purity'.

The Ghanaian literary critic Ato Quayson has written of Robben Island as a place 'where the social boundaries of embodied otherness (in terms of race, gender, class, and disability) were set out and sometimes contested'. In this sense, Jacobs, and the accusation levelled at him, become totemic of the colonial administration's 'aesthetic nervousness', to use Quayson's term, the fear of losing control of the narrative, a fear of defilement in which the white nurses can be read as stand-ins for European moral power. The Black Peril, the Leper Scare; Jacobs never stood a chance. More would suffer as Jacobs suffered. It might signal the strength of the empire, but I think perhaps the opposite could be true: the assumption of imperial superiority was threatened and with that came the acknowledgement that Britain had become so consumed by the empire that its loss would be irreparably catastrophic to the national psyche. I think of the Fox News report on those migrant caravans that had led me here: perhaps the migrant fear is the embodiment of dying US hegemony too, a reckoning Europeans have already gone through.

———

As I tramp back from the edge of the island, the view to Table Mountain is restored, Magennis's fences long gone; the fog has cleared but the wind bites harder. I spot one of the rabbits that were introduced by the Dutch, invasive and all too destructive, as it bounds through the bushes. There are snakes and tortoises as well apparently, a colony of endangered African penguins, and the seals are back, too. More obviously, as I take the path up around the edge of the island, black oystercatchers launch themselves from the white rocks to feed from the turbulent surf beyond. It was in this raw environment that those with leprosy had to survive, living in the most basic of conditions. Other than the land itself, undulating but unremarkable, there's little to show for the decades they spent here. By the time the last of the patients were removed in 1931, transported back to the mainland to a colony in Pretoria as the union became fully sovereign from London, a small town, albeit 'old and dilapidated', had taken hold, with a dairy, a piggery, bakery, library and space for recreation. In the exodus, however, all that was burned to the ground, ostensibly for sanitary reasons. In reality such traces hindered the government's initial plan to sell the island, which the *Cape Times* suggested was the perfect 'first prize in a state lottery', or had potential to host an amusement park, reformatory or health resort.

Only the modest church, a mosaic of pale and dark bricks with arched windows and a corrugated roof and porch, remains. Built by the patients themselves, it wasn't government property then and still isn't now, and so was spared the flames. I try the door, but this sole architectural trace of the colony is locked.

Instead, back at the harbour at last, I kill time in the gift shop. I have a little laugh at the Nelson Mandela products on offer. There's the biography, some serious history books and decent enough souvenir guides, but racks too of aprons, babygrows and suchlike, all bearing the great man's face. It's easy to be cynical about this Mandela industry, but the more I think, as I await the ferry, the more I recognise the power in this ubiquity. The Black man who is not meek, who does not bow to colonialism, who is very present, who isn't apart, is a helpful danger. Apartheid inferred that it was not just ideas and actions that might enfeeble the white supremacist system but the proximity of non-subservient Black bodies. Better to make them 'lepers' than to allow such a contagion to spread, to hide the revolution away like the patients who had gone before, to leave the colonised body to wither here on this cold grey rock. It didn't work: there are always a brave few, be they Ntsoelengoe, Mandela and their colleagues, or Jacobs before them, who refuse to disappear.

PART TWO

We are phoenixes. When we have new ideas or gain new insights, when we obtain the life of a leper, this is when we are resurrected as humans.

Hōjō Tamio, *The First Night of Life*, 1936.
Trans. Michio Miyasaka

TICHILEŞTI, ROMANIA

O ff a road that skirts the Romanian–Ukrainian border, down a track long omitted from maps, is a collection of squat one-storey houses. Two white-painted terraces face each other over a dusty yard in which a couple of dogs laze. Further along, more ramshackle homes with roofs of corrugated iron hide amid a hill of thick woods. This quiet community is Tichileşti, Europe's last leprosarium, a hangover from the nineteenth-century leprosy scare, a fervour that became mutated by the revolutions and revulsions of the early twentieth century but never quite disappeared. The eight patients remaining are all over the age of sixty, and most arrived decades ago from across Romania and beyond. They are living testaments to the gross acceleration in the eugenicist model, pioneered during the colonisation projects of the Western powers, reaching its zenith in the Nazi Party and the most intolerant strains of communism.

Maria sits in the hospital's spartan common room, her small frame eaten up by the large sofa. Above her hang half a dozen flower paintings in cheap gold-spray frames. They were painted by a former patient. A soap opera plays silently on the television to an otherwise empty room. It is supposed to be summer and the wood burner in the corner sits cold, but outside, caught on my tape recorder when I listen back, is the odd rumble of thunder. It is a place that feels out of time, or in which time has stopped. Maria is eighty-three, with brown eyes and a shy smile, her hair hidden under a pale headscarf – she asks that I don't include her surname. She wears a floral dress buttoned at the front with a striped, maroon tunic over the top, black socks and black Crocs. In a low, raspy voice, a common symptom of leprosy, she is emotionless but resilient, pausing only to remember details of the past.

Maria grew up in rural Olt, a county in the south of Romania, a five-hour drive west of here. She first experienced a loss of sensitivity in her legs aged fifteen. 'Prick me with a needle,' she says, fiddling with her necklace. 'Nothing.' Over the next five years further problems arose: dry patches began to appear on her skin, brown, hard, spreading like an infection. The local doctor drew a blank. Maria struggled through. A quiet girl whose world was the village she lived in, she had no plans to leave, and right into her late teens she had not found cause to. She would marry a local boy and watch her four sisters do the same. Her family worried, though. The muscles in her hands were becoming stiff. When she was twenty, her only brother, older than she, began working as a truck driver, transporting the harvest of Olt's vineyards to Bucharest. It was he who suggested to their parents that he take his sister to a hospital in the capital.

The doctors in Bucharest were quick with Maria's diagnosis, and with it the young woman's anxiety turned to dread. From then, things moved even faster. She was marched from the hospital to an ambulance, the medics not bothering to wait for her brother's return from his delivery rounds. 'I asked them where they were taking me; they would not tell me.' Locked in the back of the vehicle, she was headed across the country. At the city of Brăila, the ambulance boarded a barge to transport Maria across the Danube. I used it myself to get here, the flat boat gently gliding across the river, while van drivers and foot passengers broke up the ten-minute crossing with cigarettes smoked hanging over the waist-height railings. Maria panicked and attempted an escape. Forcing open the back doors of the vehicle and rushing to the side of the barge, she planned to jump into the cold water. She tells me she can't swim. 'I was just a baby without a mother and father, it's better to die.' Her caretakers were too quick, however, grabbing hold of her, pulling her back inside the ambulance. 'Thank God,' she says.

Maria arrived at Tichileşti in 1960, joining 160 patients, including children, who slept up to six to a dorm. She was given a room with just one other woman, though; she stayed here for three years, receiving a treatment of Promin, the precursor to the more effective multidrug therapy. For a further two years she was remanded in the hospital for observation, as nurses tracked the slow improvement to her skin and the gradual return of movement in her hands and feet. All this time her family remained in the dark as to what had become of her. She married a fellow patient, her roommate's brother, and was eventually allowed to leave the hospital.

The young couple made their home in the man's village, him taking a job with the railways. She was able to get a letter to her parents: she told them she was safe, but didn't go into details. They were simple people, she says, they would not have understood. In 1972, her husband developed a problem with his lungs. Medics said it was the work he was doing – the coal, the dust, the smoke – and that he needed fresh air. A return to Tichileşti was mooted. The couple settled. They had their own room, with a door that opened onto the yard; this is where Maria still lives, alone, as a widow.

As she comes to the end of her story Maria trains her eyes on the television. I think she is staring beyond the on-screen drama. Neither of us say anything for a few seconds. 'Tichileşti and what I see on the television has been my world for a long time now,' she says with a shrug. I say nothing. Glancing back at me, suddenly smiling, she pours more of the strong black tea that has been sitting out, slowly cooling.

———

Leprosy patients have lived along the Danube since 1877 when, as the Kingdom of Romania was formed out of the ashes of the

Russo–Turkish War, an informal community gathered in the wilds of the country's marshlands some forty kilometres away. They settled in the grounds of an old monastery across the river from Tichileşti in present-day Ukraine; there were no staff to look after them; it was just a place to hide away from ashamed families and judgemental neighbours. Shelter was perfunctory among the ecclesiastical ruins. At the start of the First World War, Romania remained neutral before it joined the allies of Britain, France and Russia in 1916. Two years later, however, the Central Powers had overrun the country and, swept up in the Balkans theatre, many of the patients perished or fled, their makeshift home ransacked by the Bulgarian army as it marched towards Russia.

In 1927, Filip Brunea-Fox, a journalist who had found fame in his pioneering literary approach to reporting, sought out this site. Living among the survivors for five days, he was shocked by the continuing deprivation, and his subsequent reporting led to a public outcry. 'The building looks like an old mansion or an abandoned inn after a dark drama. But what obscure disease withered its appearance, peeled its walls, whitewashed its fortifications? Mimicry? Can things adapt to man?' the reporter wrote. Inside, sheltering in the squalor, with no medicine and a well that was prone to drying up, were people of 'swollen cheekbones, nose reduced to a navel of flesh, small eyes without eyelashes, without eyebrows'. Whether Brunea-Fox's audience was concerned as to the welfare of the patients or in horror at the idea that people with leprosy were free to wander among them is open to debate. Brunea-Fox had received the tip-off for his story from a resident of a nearby town, who was outraged about the occasional appearance of the sick near his home.

Either way, within two years, the pavilions were built on the present site, with high walls cut through a lime grove to keep the 200 relocated patients away from the rest of society. The authorities issued a statement assuring Brunea-Fox's readers that these new premises were isolated, had drinking water, with land to grow produce. More doctors were hired to look after the residents too, a role that proved surprisingly popular – 600 physicians applied for one vacancy, lured by a decent salary. While comfort was promised, with food supposedly provided, conditions remained grim. It seems Brunea-Fox's suggestion that the leprosarium be a welcoming place, with the entertainments of a gramophone and dominoes on hand, was not heeded – frustration among the patients remained.

This came to a head on the morning of 9 June 1932, when a twenty-five-strong group of residents escaped the hospital in starving desperation and marched on the town of Isaccea. News of their arrival that morning sent a wave of panic from door to door, shop to shop, the townsfolk rushing inside and barricading themselves against the apparently infectious invasion. The group, clad in rags, thin and drawn, shouted and cried that they needed food: some of Isaccea's residents threw what they had from the windows in an attempt to placate the protesters. The patients had not eaten properly for months, and no funds had arrived from Bucharest for over a week. Some of the shopkeepers and local farmers were familiar with the situation; they had stopped sending their regular orders to the hospital after bills had gone unpaid by the government. When the group threatened to 'march on Bucharest' – albeit an unlikely scenario, given the distance – a battalion of gendarmes was called. Arriving on horseback, they rounded up the patients and by the evening the police had successfully driven the protesters back to the confines of the hospital with promises that the authorities would rectify their appalling situation. Patients from Tichileşti would escape and 'terrorise' Isaccea, as one newspaper put it, on subsequent occasions, though often with less noble or desperate intent. A year later, a party of seven were apprehended looking for booze. Returning them to the hospital, the correspondent noted, was a 'tedious job' for the police.

———

If the inhabitants of Tichileşti felt forgotten, by the time fascism spread through Europe they were invisible no longer. The Kingdom of Romania was initially neutral as the continent divided, but as France fell to the Nazis in June 1940, King Carol II was under increasing pressure from far-right factions to throw in his lot with the Axis powers. A coup deposed Carol in September, and Ion Antonescu was installed as the country's military dictator. Antonescu immediately set up an alliance with Hitler. That lasted until the monarchy regained power in 1944 and Romania swapped sides once again.

For the four years under Antonescu, the country kept a significant degree of independence from Germany, yet the Romanian dictator's thinking was unified with the Nazi regime: Antonescu initiated his own holocaust, which saw an estimated 380,000 Jews and Roma systematically murdered. In old Romania, Jews were harassed and persecuted, the Iron Guard meting out violence and seizing businesses arbitrarily, but most of the deaths occurred in Northern Bukovina (a region now partly within Ukrainian territory), Transnistria (now a breakaway state of Moldova) and Bessarabia, the westernmost border of which Tichileşti abuts. This has allowed successive Romanian governments – until the early 2000s – to minimise responsibility for the deaths of Jews and others that occurred in the country.

Among the tens of thousands of documents held by the United States Holocaust Memorial Museum, each telling their own horror story, is a single sheet of paper, undated, filed among hundreds of others pertaining to the deportation of Roma to Transnistria in 1942. In fading type it is headed *Bolnavi de lepră ce urmează a fi trimişi la*

146

Leprozerie: 'Leprosy Patients to be Sent to the Leper Colony'. Underneath are sixteen names:

Nicolae Gh. Serban, 48

Ion Gh. Serban, 44

Gheorghe Gh. Serban, 32

Dumitru Gh. Serban, 42

Maria Gh. Serban, 65

Ion David Lera, 43

Crisante V. Alexe, 40

Gologan Cristescu, 46

Gheorman Cristescu, 51

Emil Gh. Cristescu, 14

Eremia Gherman Cristescu, 15

Gheorghe Chitan, 39

Gheorghe Munteanu, 40

Maria I. Păunescu, 63

Gheorghiţa Const. Sandu, 61

Stefan S. Frângu Daneş, 20

Against each name, as if keeping tally on who had been pulled from their homes, or perhaps who had been pushed onto a train to travel the hundreds of kilometres east, is a handwritten tick. The bureaucratic pragmatism of the whole thing is chilling. An indecipherable signature acknowledges a job completed. The fate of fourteen-year-old Emil and fifteen-year-old Eremia when they arrived in Transnistria is unknown, but leprosy patients were harassed and exterminated under the Nazi regime. In Germany the sick fell foul of Hitler's law for the 'Prevention of Offspring with Hereditary Diseases', which mandated the forced sterilisation of those with physical disability and mental illness. There was no such thing as a sick individual in Nazi Germany: one person's sickness was the sickness of the nation. A rallying call, used to extol the virtues of a good diet, decreed: 'Your body belongs to the nation! Your body belongs to the Führer! You have a duty to be healthy! Food is not a private matter!' Jews and other 'undesirables' under National Socialism would often be analogised and pathologised as a cancer that must be cut from society; the biological body and the body politic intermingled.

At a Nuremberg speech Hitler presented Nazism as a 'cure for the people' – but this cure had to be collective. The Third Reich initiated a crackdown on individual and unsupervised sports which were demonised as wanton, privileged pastimes. Instead, activities such as hiking and hostelling were encouraged via the Hitler Youth, which organised group marches through the German hills. The movement also took control of youth football leagues and, for girls, organised collective athletics tournaments, such as rhythmic gymnastics. The policy was pragmatic, of course: groups of youth were easier to indoctrinate, and a physically fit nation was needed to fight on behalf of the Führer and his plans for Germany's expansion. It was also ideological, however. Foucault would later write how 'all the problems of healthcare and public hygiene must, or any rate can, be rethought as elements which may or may not improve human capital'. This was Hitler's aim, and has always been the aim of those tackling leprosy, regardless of which side of the war they stood on. 'Every sick man is a bad workman and therefore a loss to society,' Hansen had told the Berlin conference half a century earlier. For Hitler, team sports were in pursuit of 'strength through joy', toning up the Aryan race in a racialised bastardisation of Nietzsche's Übermensch, in which supreme beings could materialise on earth through the Führer's plans. Leprosy provided no strength, no joy, to those in power; it was an embarrassment that had to be vanquished.

If Jews were demonised as being susceptible to disease, it became a self-fulfilling prophecy given the unsanitary conditions, from ghettos to the camps, in which the Nazis forced them to live and die. When Germany invaded Poland in 1939, the sewage system of Warsaw was severely damaged. It led to a massive typhus epidemic in a city that was home to the largest Jewish population in Europe, and the first twentieth-century ghettoisation of Jewish areas happened a year later under the auspices of public health, with a neighbourhood in the north of the capital labelled *Seuchensperrgebiet,* a restricted epidemic area. The signs warning residents of possible contagion carried by their Jewish neighbours – which were erected in smaller cities too – were soon followed by brick walls and guard houses, effectively imprisoning a population of 40,000 within a few square kilometres. Once the Warsaw ghetto was enclosed, running water became even more limited and access to sanitary products rare, the resulting conditions further justifying the oppressive 'health measures' in the eyes of the Germans.

The situation was as grim in the two ghettos of Kovno, an area in Kaunas established by the Nazis in 1941 to hold 29,000 Lithuanian Jews. There was no bathhouse and no running water, only wells and cesspits, the latter left unclosed after residents had been forced to burn the fences to keep warm during the winter. Such was the prevalence of serious disease that one Lithuanian Jew, Moses Brauns, a noted epidemiologist before the war, set up a small hospital for contagious patients; other medical personnel were recruited from among the community.

In both ghettos, separated by a single street, most of the residents were forced into labour. Each morning hundreds were transported to build military facilities and other such infrastructure beyond the barbed wire strung across the streets of their cramped neighbourhoods. In the early hours of 4 October 1941, however, the labour transportation trucks didn't arrive at the smaller of the two ghettos; the SS troops instead ordered the whole population to assemble on the cobbles of the main square. An officer walked the lines, weeding out individuals identified as being unfit for work: older residents, the disabled, the children of the orphanage. This 'audit' sealed their fate. Then, in horror, the ghetto watched as the Germans boarded up and barricaded Brauns' medical centre, the sick and nurses still inside, and the strongest among the Jewish population were ordered to dig deep trenches around the hospital. In the confusion the bespectacled Brauns tried to intervene, but he was prevented by the soldiers.

One survivor recalled, 'The Germans found a leper in the Kovno ghetto infectious disease hospital. The Hitlerites had an obsession that there was leprosy in the ghetto. There was no leprosy. Typhus was in the ghetto but it was underground and not registered.' The Nazis were virulently prejudiced against any form of disability, but tarring the Jews as 'lepers', with the mass extermination programme just months away, would only help demonise and dehumanise them in the eyes of the German public; it played into historic prejudices that both groups were dirty and a corrosive influence, an iteration of the 1321 'lepers' plot'. With Brauns accused of harbouring such patients, at midday the building was doused in fuel and the SS chucked a match into his life-saving clinic. The smoke billowed out thick into the evening.

Brauns vowed to continue his care, hiding subsequent patients, treating them each personally in secret. Another survivor wrote in his diary, 'We are not allowed to be sick. We must be healthy . . . If one is sick with typhoid or typhus, the Germans would use it to justify wiping out an entire district or maybe even the whole ghetto.' There was a sickness in Kovno, but it wasn't leprosy or typhoid, and it wasn't the Jewish people that harboured it.

'[The State] must see to it that only the healthy beget children; that there is only one disgrace: despite one's own sickness and deficiencies, to bring children into the world . . . Here the state must act as the guardian of a millennial future in the face of which the wishes and the selfishness of the individual must appear as nothing and submit.' Hitler wrote this in *Mein Kampf* and in regard to public policy on leprosy internationally, he was not stating anything new or anything that would be considered particularly controversial prior to the war. In policies enacted by governments both Allied and Axis, leprosy patients had long been discouraged or outright banned from having children. As the Cameroonian historian Achille Mbembe has pointed out, 'Nazism and Stalinism did no more than amplify a series of mechanisms that already existed in Western European social and political formations (subjugation of the body, health regulations, social Darwinism, eugenics, medico-legal theories on heredity, degeneration, and race)'. The biopolitical imperative dictates that one person's health will always be of lesser value than social health, the terms of that health dictated by those in power. Indeed, there were figures within the Nazi medical establishment who had cut their teeth on the nineteenth-century anti-leprosy programmes. Erich Martini, a doctor and friend of Heinrich Himmler, the SS commander, had previously been hired by the Colombian government to head its programme against the disease. In line with the approach of British, US, Spanish, Dutch and imperial powers previously, he mandated that babies be forcibly removed from the parents if either were diagnosed with leprosy. Manfred Oberdörffer was a regular at the international leprosy conferences before the war and worked in Nigeria with the British Empire Leprosy Relief Association. Back in Nazi Germany he continued his medical research with feeding experiments on Black French prisoners of war.

The idea of biopolitics and the body politic go far back: 'The Belly and the Members', one of Aesop's fables, tells the growing resentment of the hands and legs, who felt they did all the work to feed the body while the stomach sat idle, receiving the food and getting fat. The limbs decide to go on strike, but without food the hands soon become weak and the legs ache. The moral, quoted by self-serving senators of Ancient Rome onwards, was that every part of society was interconnected and had its task (and that the public should overlook the widening waistlines of their political leaders). By the twelfth century, the English writer John of Salisbury, while philosophising on fealty to an absolute monarch (total, he decreed, unless the monarch went against God), noted 'an injury to the head, as we have said above, is brought home to all the members, and that a wound unjustly inflicted on any member tends to the injury of the head'. Leprosy was a festering injury to the body politic, the Nazis enacting a total war against this apparent attack, a battle in which governance and extermination of life are indistinguishable – a revenge Mbembe would characterise as 'necropolitics'.

———

This persecution resonates with Domnica Mişcov, who was born in Tichileşti in 1945, though for most of her adult life she has come and gone from the hospital grounds. She received treatment here and she regularly returned to look after her mother, keeping a small apartment in the nearby city of Tulcea where she could find work. Her parents, Călin and Ioana, now both dead, met at the hospital as teenagers. Călin built the tiny house in which Domnica still lives, the only private property on the Ministry of Health site: a two-room cottage with a corrugated roof at the top of the yard, just to the right of the Baptist chapel, itself a simple pebble-dashed building with a white porch. A rusted mesh wire fence divides the two. Blind, her father enlisted the help of the other patients in his endeavour. Walking the short path to her front door, Domnica, in leather sandals and blue checked smock-dress, first shows off her garden as the sun comes out, a wild profusion of pink, puce and orange gerbera among which an orchestra of crickets plays. The front door opens with a slight creak. Inside, Domnica has hung embroidered textiles on the wall and family portraits dot every surface. She sits on her single bed, back perfectly straight, while her story continues to unfold.

It is a history that has proved impossible to verify but she tells how her Russian-speaking father, who grew up near Odessa, began to show symptoms of leprosy as a young boy. As the only child in a brood of twelve to do so, he was sent to a hospital in what is, today, Moldova. Domnica points in the direction of the Danube that flows just a kilometre or so beyond the trees. 'He had been desperate to go to school,' she says. As the Axis powers advanced across the Soviet front in 1941, her father knew that the patients and the Jewish doctors who cared for them were in danger. In November that year, a Nazi propaganda sheet made their shared peril clear with a headline that ran 'Finally the city of Chișinău got rid of Jewish leprosy'. The boy and a few others fled just in time: two days later, Domnica says, German soldiers arrived and those patients that had hesitated were lined up and slaughtered, along with the medical staff who were forced to remain. 'He survived. He fled into the forest on foot and somehow made his way here.' She goes on to tell how the residents of Tichilești almost suffered the same fate, when a horse-backed battalion of German soldiers set up camp outside in August 1944. 'My father said they used to take chickens and supplies from the colony, because they themselves weren't getting enough rations.' They were surely going to kill the patients at some point, but, just in time, Romania's pact with Hitler broke and the troops rode off.

With the full extent of Nazi atrocities uncovered in the aftermath of the war, anything that remotely smacked of eugenics fell dramatically out of favour among the Western nations. The coercive laws they had pioneered, once regarded as mainstream disease prevention procedure, were measured against the extreme medicalised barbarity of the German concentration camps. It was the beginning of the end of the leprosy colony – these spaces of purgatorial living death – but the end still had to be fought for. If the residents of Tichileşti imagined that communism would bring a more equitable ethos to the social fabric, they were disappointed with the successive nationalist regimes of Gheorghe Gheorghiu-Dej and Nicolae Ceauşescu. Both leaders presented themselves as paternalistic autocrats; Ceauşescu saw Romania as a single organism, an extension of his own self. Tichileşti demonstrates that leprosy and nationalism can never sit together comfortably: the patriotic body is too sensitive to the attacking microbacteria. In 1905, the Swedish political scientist Rudolf Kjellén, the man who first used the term 'biopolitics' (and indeed 'geopolitics'), described a country as something like a biological organism, a 'super-individual creature'. Ceauşescu even went so far as to appoint his personal doctor, a man with no major administrative or political experience, as Minister of Health. The megalomaniacal reasoning went that if the doctor was able to look after Ceauşescu's body, then he was able to look after the country's, too. The head of society therefore has both responsibility and domination over the rest of the social body. Ceauşescu's health was the country's health.

This brand of biopolitical communism, most obviously, led to devastating consequences in terms of reproductive rights. Before Ceauşescu came to power abortion was readily available in Romania, one of the few areas in which the country followed the progressive line of the pre-Stalinised Soviet Union. Yet within a year of Ceauşescu assuming the position of General Secretary from Gheorghiu-Dej in 1965, the new leader, worried about the falling population and determined to make Romania a great power, criminalised abortion in all but the rarest circumstances and removed all contraceptives from pharmacy shelves. Abortion was available only to women who had borne five children, and carrot-and-stick policies were introduced, including financial benefits. Neighbours were encouraged to report suspected back-street terminations to the secret police; women who managed to give birth to ten or more children were celebrated as 'heroine mothers'. These highly restrictive policies are often credited to Elena Ceauşescu, Nicolae's wife, herself bestowed with the title 'The Best Mother Romania Could Have'. By 1970 the birth rate had doubled and hundreds of new nurseries and schools were built to cope with this baby boom. There were schemes to recognise the most intelligent children and place them in advanced programmes, and sport became key to the health of the nation. All this was necessary to achieve Ceauşescu's 'New Man', a mythological superman, attainable, in another Nietzschean twist, by everyone under his benevolent leadership.

The real result of these natalist policies was millions of unwanted children who, their parents unable to cope, were given over to the state to raise. These children would be first sorted into one of two groups: those who looked strong and might be good for labour were sent to *case de copii*, children's homes; any child – and given they were often born into the malnourished poverty of an outsized family, this was many of them – that showed signs of disease, disability or weakness were dumped in a *cămine spitale*. These were hospitals in name only: there was no treatment, barely any food and little human contact. After the Ceauşescus were deposed, the world discovered an approximate 170,000 abandoned youngsters, from babies to teenagers, many suffering severe developmental and physical problems.

The living conditions of the residents of Tichileşti were better than those of the abandoned children – but likewise their existence was excised from public consciousness. Their bodies were not the bodies of the New Man. Unlike many types of cancer, for example, hidden away, an internal evil, its harm below the skin, leprosy has a public face, its visible besmirchment becomes a blemish on society – one that in the eyes of the powerful, of varied political hue, of capital too, needs to be concealed. This is the cause of leprosy's outsized reputation. The leprosarium was removed from all maps: the battered sign stating 'Spitalul Tichileşti' that I pass as I turn in from the main road is a later addition. If individual patients were seen as an obscenity against the idea of Romanian perfection, then to achieve that nationalist 'superman' there must be a black hole in which anyone who did not fit could be disappeared, a zone of contagion that must not be breached, operating semi-autonomously beyond society. Foucault describes leprosaria (and mental asylums) not just as places to contain a possibly dangerous disease but as a walled site in which demons might live and multiply, in which the 'territory of confinement had taken on powers of its own, and had become in its turn a breeding ground of evil'. This is how Tichileşti was viewed by the Romanian state, and how the stigma of leprosy was maintained into the twentieth century, a biopolitical hell beyond consciousness.

———

Aurelian Tuta was brought here as an adult, aged thirty-six. For most of his life he had been a model figure of Ceauşescu's Romania. He wasn't educated but had fathered five boys and worked as a tractor driver and mechanic in the south of the country. One harvest, out threshing corn, he burned himself on the machinery and yet, like Maria, he too felt no pain. The local physician recognised this loss of feeling as leprosy immediately and ordered him to leave the village. Later he learned that a team from the government was sent to disinfect his house. No mere public health measure, it was a ritualistic erasing: Aurelian's neighbours turned against him and his family broke contact. He arrived, alone, to a place that officially did not exist. Now, in his mid-seventies, he is remarkably sanguine about his fate. His one regret is not seeing his grandchildren grow up, he says.

Despite a generation gap, his partner in crime at Tichilești is Grigore Grigorov, who arrived during communist times too, but as a child, aged thirteen. They ask to be interviewed together, poking and prodding each other and laughing at jokes that go over my head. Known as Grișa, Grigore is still the baby of the community. Without a speck of grey in his hair, in an orange T-shirt and black trousers, he is stout but clearly still strong. For him, it was his grandfather who first noticed the sores. It was the summer of 1976, the school holidays, and he was playing out in the yard at his grandparents' home in the Black Sea port of Sulina. Perplexed at these spreading blemishes, they took him to the family doctor, then the hospital in Tulcea, before ending up in Bucharest. He was kept there for three weeks under observation until his fate was sealed. Led out to an ambulance and unloaded at Tichilești, he was the only child among eighty patients. His family were also not told where he was being kept. A day or so after he arrived an older man, a patient, asked Grișa: 'You know why you are here?' No, Grișa answered. 'Come on, don't lie,' the man said, jabbing his finger. 'You are a leper.'

On hearing his new name, othered as 'a leper', Grișa was emptied of his old life, of the possibilities and aspirations the child may have had – psychological rupture, in essence. In his diaries, the Russian film director Andrey Tarkovsky describes a film he wished to make, one that never made it beyond his jottings from 12 February 1979. In the kernel of a script, a novelist, 'a man of great spiritual depths . . .

honest, virtuous', glances in the mirror one day and notices the first signs of leprosy. He is sent away to some unmentioned place and monitored for a year, yet the disease develops no further. Eventually the doctors allow him to go back home, which is now desolate and covered in dust. He tries to write, but his notepaper has become damp in his prolonged absence and his pen spears through the surface. 'He is empty,' Tarkovsky concludes. 'As empty as a chrysalis from which a butterfly has emerged.' This is what the label of 'leper' does, it empties the subject: they are no longer human, but a reflection of all that society fears. The writer cannot write, Tarkovsky seems to be saying, because in the eyes of the world, there is nothing human left in this husk of a body; the body becomes a black hole like the dark geography of the hospital that envelops it.

Faced with this great existential void, thirteen-year-old Grişa started to cry. And yet, the man shushed him: 'Don't be a baby. It is OK. We are all lepers here.' Slowly losing sensitivity in the tips of his hand, at one point Grişa tried to cut his finger off, an attempt, perhaps, like Tarkovsky's writer, to at least feel something, to regain the self. Of course Grişa remained human, and in time responded well to treatment. He took to climbing the trees, making camps in the wood, enjoying life in this strange new home. The lesions on his skin cleared up; some of his sense of touch returned. He even left Tichileşti for a few years, though that was not a success. As a wayward young man he would often abandon his prescription, eat poorly and go out drinking. It had a permanent physical effect: on his left hand the fingers are truncated. He prefers living back here, he tells me, now older and healthier. There's a typically pessimistic and aphoristic line from the Romanian philosopher Emil Cioran, who writes of how the 'smiling leper' found happiness: 'The truly solitary being is not the man who is abandoned by men, but the man who suffers in their midst, who drags his desert through the marketplace.' Here, the patients, now free to leave, are lonely among friends. Grișa still ventures out regularly, not least to earn a bit of cash doing handiwork in a nearby village. With a grin he also tells me about the various women there he is currently romancing, the backgammon games he plays and the beer he drinks. Aurelian rolls his eyes, giggling, slapping his friend's shoulder in encouragement.

Domnica too recalls living well under Communist rule, telling how she never went hungry – nostalgia for the dictatorship is high in Romania as the promises of neoliberalism and prosperity have fizzled out – but contemporary accounts report buildings crumbling from years of neglect. Their seclusion also sheltered them from the worst excesses of the regime. The chapel next to Domnica's house, with its visiting pastor, remained open and largely free of interference, and Tichilești was possibly one of the few places in Romania not to have state informants: by the 1980s the paranoia of Ceaușescu had led to around half a million of the population, not least thousands of children, working clandestinely for the Securitate, the state security agency. Threatened and blackmailed, or through fealty to the leader, kids would spy on parents, teachers on pupils, neighbours and colleagues on each other. On the rare occasions that Tichilești did receive a visitor, patients and doctors alike were required to report their names and write up their conversations. The state police did visit on at least one occasion, in the 1970s, after anonymous letters containing Bible passages were sent to top Communist officials. They were traced back to a patient, a religious man who had replaced the colony's long-standing Baptist preacher.

In 1989 most in the community supported the ousting of Nicolae and Elena Ceaușescu, even if they were suspicious of their executors' motives and worried about what was to come. They had watched the crowds on television boo the leader's last speech in the snow on what has been renamed Revolution Square; they had seen the dictator become confused and heard Elena imperiously demanding silence from the protesters. The residents of Tichileşti would have read of the subsequent trial and, on Christmas Day, of the couple's death in a hail of bullets. That night, after Nicolae and Elena's bodies had been left slumped on the ground in the yard of a military base outside Bucharest, many of the patients even celebrated with the radio on, dancing, those that could, in the communal lounge of the hospital late into the early hours of St Stephen's Day.

———

Today, the residents of Tichileşti are more comfortable than many in rural Romania. With their food and clothes provided by the government, nurses in attendance, they live a pleasant retirement. Before I arrive, Cristina, the director here, says I can bring cigarettes and chocolates as gifts for the residents: 'It is still a hospital,' she reminds me. 'Cigarettes and alcohol are the only things we can't provide.' There are beehives just beyond the gates that some of the patients collect honey from; plum and lime trees are in profusion, fruiting so generously that some of the paths have been made slippery with fallen produce. Brunea-Fox's vision of a welcoming place for patients has largely come to pass: by way of marking the end of my visit Cristina sweetly orders a dozen pizzas which we eat at a trestle table set up for the occasion outside, the residents on either side gossiping and joking. Yet it remains a self-contained community, an enclave torn from the rest of the country – to such an extent that one could be born here, like Domnica, and be buried, like her parents, in the cemetery just up the steep track, just a little way from where the fizzy pop is opened and these margarita and pepperoni slices are shared.

CABO DELGADO, MOZAMBIQUE

Pemba comes into view through the window of the forty-four-seater plane, one of the biggest that will land at the airport this week. As we descend, the town's bay spreads out in a grimace below; the sea is dotted with fishing boats, the coastline bordered by one of the few surfaced roads. A haphazard map of dirt brick homes and red dusty streets and passageways becomes clearer as we descend. The sun winks back off the corrugated iron roofs.

The capital of Cabo Delgado, Mozambique's most northern province, should be home to a little over 200,000 people. Since the beginning of the Islamist insurgency in 2017, however, a conflict that has made the region highly unstable and taken the lives of thousands, that number has swelled; by 2022 the population had almost doubled with people fleeing for their lives, arriving on foot, bike, boat and truck. People are crammed into the often one-room homes of aunties and uncles, distant cousins, in-laws; there they have been welcomed, more often despite their host's own precarious economic means. The worst of circumstances can bring out the best of solidarity. The runway on which I land has served yet more incomers of late, but in the guise of military from Rwanda, Tanzania, South Africa, the USA and Portugal. Alongside Mozambique's own army, the soldiers have formed an often fractured international response that has made some headway in wresting back control from the insurgents. Shortly after Mozambique's president visited Vladimir Putin in Moscow in 2019, mercenaries from Russia's Wagner Group arrived here too.

Pemba Airport comprises a single building, painted cream against the heat. We squat on the tarmac to fill in our landing slips, waiting to funnel through a single swing door to security. But for a nun, Italian and in her seventies, every passenger on my flight from South Africa is male. They use their passports – a mixture of African, Middle Eastern and Chinese – to lean against as they scrawl their details on a border declaration in tiny block capitals. I get ready to pay my visa fee and with a sceptical raised eyebrow the immigration officer asks, 'Turista?' I had decided not to risk applying for a journalist visa, or even the work permit required for volunteer aid trips. Instead, I mutter something about scuba diving, a detail I had picked up from an overly optimistic – or at least out-of-date – travel website. Bored, the man lands his ink stamp on an empty page of my passport and with relief I head through to the exit.

There are two sides to Pemba. One has the informal market selling fish from the boats, fruits and vegetables carried in by hand from nearby villages, old clothes and pay-as-you-go SIM cards. There are churches and mosques there, and the children play tag and football in the dust. The other side, the side with the airport, is more integrated into the state, boasting a couple of banks, a single large supermarket, and a few offices – buildings that stretch three or four storeys above their neighbours. Neither has any street lighting or universal rubbish collection. Along the beach are a handful of hotels built with the idea they would play host to rich holiday-makers from Maputo, the Mozambique capital, or South Africa, those who at one point might really have come to dive the underwater reefs. Six years of war has ended any such hope. Now these resorts can set their price points even higher, their customers the accounts departments of the oil and mining companies and their security personnel, who I assume are footing the bills for my fellow plane passengers' trips here. It is on this side of town, too, that most of the NGOs and relief agencies are based, their staff highly educated, fashionably dressed and easily sliding from Portuguese to

English and, less frequently, the local languages. They are almost entirely from the capital or the richer south of the country. Toyotas with their employers' insignia rattle along the bumpy streets, the logos discreetly posted at the entrances of the villas in which they've set up field offices. Save the Children, Médecins Sans Frontières, Norwegian Refugee Council, Doctors with Africa CUAMM, UNICEF, UNOPS, UNHRC, World Food Programme, the WHO, the Leprosy Mission. Outside some stand guards with guns.

The Leprosy Mission is here because Mozambique has one of the highest instances of the disease in the world. If history has witnessed government or coloniser intervention to the detriment of the lives of those with leprosy, Mozambique is a country in which basic state provision has all but disappeared in some areas of the country.

Just before dawn on the first Thursday of October 2017, a group of around thirty young men stormed three police stations in the town of Mocímboa da Praia, a coastal city in the north of Cabo Delgado. They killed seventeen people, including two policemen and a community leader. They looted weapons and hoisted a black-and-white flag of radical Islam over the town, calling themselves Ansar al-Sunna. They told residents that they were there to liberate them from the 'degraded' teachings of the town's mosques; that it was haram to pay taxes to the secular state. They rallied against the supposed corrupting influence of public schools and the health system. If the attack caught the rest of Mozambique – and the world – by surprise, locals knew trouble had been brewing. Young men had already begun to be radicalised over the preceding two years, small factions from within the poorest pockets of the town manipulated by a couple of richer traders in the informal market. By word of mouth, the teachings of the late Aboud Rogo Mohammed, a Kenyan preacher with links to the Somali terror network Al-Shabaab, started to spread. Ansar al-Sunna would later take the more famous terrorist group's name, though there's little evidence of international co-ordination. The men would meet in an unfinished building, which they later declared a mosque; they wore black gowns, short trousers and white turbans over their shaven heads, and grew long beards. They would watch Aboud's lectures together, and some even travelled to Somalia, a welcome expenses-paid adventure for a youth with little prospects. They began to carry machetes and knives to represent their jihad. Religious leaders went to the local government with their fears, but they say they were ignored. The police were able to rebuff the first attack, but it was just the start of a sustained campaign. A couple of days later, the fishing village of Maluku was overrun and the inhabitants fled, the first of many displaced people. The terrorists marched on to another village, Columbe, capturing it on 22 October, spooking not just locals but also an American oil company that was operating nearby and which started to pull its staff out. As time passed, the attacks became more vicious and more victorious for the insurgents, the chaos spreading south; Muslims were targeted as much as Christians and Western companies. Beyond the murders and instability, the crisis was brutal for the health of ordinary people: 2017 saw a huge jump in new leprosy cases: 1,926, up from 1,289 the previous year; 2,442 additional cases reported by 2018. The following year, fate, or climate change, threw two cyclones, Idai and Kenneth, into this brewing catastrophe. By June 2020 the armed gangs had completely taken over Mocímboa da Praia and in the spring of the new year the town of Palma fell. Reported new leprosy cases were at 2,639, but the north of Cabo Delgado had all but disappeared to the outside world.

———

Extreme poverty and divisions riven through a country constructed by colonialism are the background to this slide into extremism.

Mozambique is long and thin, over 2,500 kilometres end to end; most in the rural areas don't speak Portuguese, and for those it is easy to believe the government in the far southern capital of Maputo has forgotten them. When it gained independence in 1975 after the collapse of Portugal's dictatorship, the country descended into a civil war instigated by Resistência Nacional Moçambicana (RENAMO), a right-wing movement backed by Rhodesia and South Africa which rebelled against the Marxist one-party government. Though the conflict was bloody and protracted, the end of the Cold War in 1992, and the collapse of apartheid next door, allowed multiparty elections and something like peace. Violence still flared intermittently, with armed clashes between security forces and militant splinter groups, but as the ruling Frente de Libertação de Moçambique (FRELIMO) swapped its insignia from a crossed golden hammer and hoe against Marxist red to one featuring a drum and a cob of corn, capitalism moved in. The resorts were built; geologists found the first signs of natural gas off the coast of Cabo Delgado. Sensing that the oceans – previously only populated by turtles, dolphins and fishermen – might prove profitable, multinational companies commissioned further exploration. In 2018, a consortium led by Italian oil company Eni started to build a rig, and it is partnering with Exxon on a second development. Two years later, the French company Total signed off on its own $20 billion project, the largest single foreign investment in Africa, with the company trumpeting how the deal would provide jobs and massive social development, lifting the region out of decades of neglect.

The people of Cabo Delgado have seen this story play out before. Plans to build shipyards and develop tuna fishing stalled when it was discovered that national politicians had conspired with bankers from Credit Suisse and Russia's VTB on over $2 billion of secret, undeclared loans to fund the plans ($200 million went on bribes and kickbacks to individuals on either side of the odious deal). The inland areas of the province instead became rife with illegal logging, including in the Quirimbas National Park, home to elephants, lions and leopards, where Chinese companies have spirited away at least half a billion dollars' worth of wood annually. Small-scale ruby miners – *garimpeiros* – were violently cleared from their prospecting near Montepuez, Cabo Delgado's next biggest city after Pemba, to allow a British mining company to move in. Gemfields, the corporation that counts Fabergé among its brands, admitted no liability but eventually paid out a £5.8 million settlement over human rights abuses claimed to have been committed on land it licences. Videos were shared on social media which allegedly show local miners beaten, tied to trees and forced into stress position by armed, uniformed men, and human rights lawyers have argued that people were killed in the clearances. The miners that escaped were scattered across the region, angry with the state and the West; a few more young, fit men that were made easy to exploit and available for armed insurrection. Total has better PR, but gas deals have seen 550 families displaced by an onshore treatment facility, and 3,000 fishermen have lost access to waters. Many have had to wait years for the compensation that was outlined in the contracts they signed with Anadarko, Total's predecessor on the project, with some claiming their consent was provided only under pressure. The cynicism about the benefits of the liquid gas industry is therefore understandable.

———

A few days later I am sitting in the front of the Leprosy Mission's four-by-four, its white exterior already splattered with dirt of deep ochre from our short journey out of Pemba. The NGO's driver is extremely skilled in navigating the potholes strewn across the roads, swerving this way and that to avoid the craters, at times crossing the verge completely to keep us on time.

Though the disease was officially declared 'eliminated' over a decade ago – based on case numbers dropping below one patient per 10,000 nationally – here in Cabo Delgado it is anything but a thing of the past. On the country's northern tip, at least where the health authorities maintain operations, there were a reported 745 new cases in 2023, more than three times the threshold for a community to be thought 'leprosy free'. No one really believes these are the true numbers, however – statistics mean nothing when so much of the province is closed to the outside. How do those with the disease cope when all-out anarchy reigns? After the collapse of empires, the disasters of neocolonialism, these are the people who get buried.

The road soon crosses into parched open countryside, great craggy tombstone mountains breaking up the horizon – but we never leave the people. Along the road they walk, alone, in pairs, in groups, children and the elderly carrying fruit or great bags of charcoal to sell in towns or at crossroads, or balancing huge bundles of grasses on heads, materials to repair and replace roofs and walls of homes. Concrete and glass as a construction material soon become the exception in the villages we pass; homes and shops are now more likely built from mud and iron, mud and straw, brick and straw or brick and iron. We are waved through a couple of police checkpoints, but in the high morning sun that burns fiercer as we get further from the coast, the likelihood of trouble seems remote. A month or two before my journey, I'd been in touch with a British journalist for whom Mozambique had been home for many years, until his visa was unceremoniously cancelled by the government in a fit of pique over his coverage. He'd been hesitant about wholeheartedly encouraging my trip. Up to the Tanzanian border, Al-Shabaab control much of the land north of Chiúre, the district through which we are driving, and it is impossible for me to reach; around here, where the government retains control or has taken it back, pockets of resistance remain. The journalist had said he'd be worried about me travelling through the village of Ancuabe and, despite Justin Timberlake playing on the radio, and the light chat between the driver and Ana, my security co-ordinator, I feel myself tense as the blue cursor of Google Maps inches towards it. Several villages around here have been attacked in the last twelve months, the insurgents killing indiscriminately and causing almost 10,000 people to flee, many of them already displaced from other areas. (This same particular group of men went on to target the Gemfields mining site.)

'Are you nervous?' I had been asked by someone at the Leprosy Mission a few days earlier. It's fine, I reasoned, people walk these roads everyday – I'm not sure I have a right to be scared taking the trip once. Ana tells me how her parents in the south had been horrified when she got the job, worried for her, but that she and they now just park that anxiety in a box at the back of their mind. Serious and professional, even though she says she misses the nightlife and restaurants of Maputo, Ana explains how the team meticulously plan every trip, relying on local knowledge by always ringing ahead up to the morning of departure to check there are no signs of the insurgents. What are the signs? 'Burning,' she says. 'They burn down people's houses.' This is not an insurgency that is looking to win hearts and minds but an angry, nihilistic explosion: economic estrangement wearing the mask of religious fundamentalism.

We arrive in Mucacata, the commercial centre of Chiúre district, on Mozambique's Independence Day. It is hard to tally the obvious dangers with everyday life, which continues as usual by desire as much as necessity. The departure of the Portuguese is being celebrated by a group of young men playing Afrobeats and R&B at awesome volume on the veranda of a concrete bar. Their younger siblings can be found grouped around an old computer screen hooked up to a portable solar panel, each kid jostling to take turns on the first-person-shooter game. A market continues its business despite the holiday: potatoes brim to the top of rubble sacks and huge piles of red onions and dried beans are piled on blankets. Textiles and building materials are for sale, fake top-tier football shirts (Neymar the inevitable favourite) and cheap plastic kitchenware. Having a beer in a dimly lit bar after dinner that night, we watch a group of women get up from the next table to dance exuberantly as Zouk and Venda pop tracks by the likes of Button Rose and Makhadzi play out. The women are all in dresses made of the same blue and shimmering silver wide-checked lamé cloth and Ana tells me they would have met up to sew them collectively in preparation for this party, each session a party before the party.

If it weren't Independence Day, our hotel would be lively too, with every room taken. The lone accommodation for kilometres, it is used by myriad NGOs, but we are the only ones who check in that night. The light in the room is harsh, the furnishing brutally sparse. The wood ceiling is splintering in places and a fridge on a fruit crate hums. The wires to a TV hang limply without a plug; a pamphlet on HIV prevention lies by the bed. But we are half a day closer to our destination. The Portuguese-speaking aid workers might be absent, but it means the town's motoboys get the pool table outside my window to themselves. I drift off to the sound of their laughter and conversation as ball hits against pocket.

———

The next morning, the route provides the driver with greater challenges, the car often tilting forty degrees as he navigates roads eroded into near-ravines. We're joined on the journey by Gabriel Barbosa, the district nurse, though all his training on leprosy came from the Leprosy Mission and they are paying for his time today. Soon we're off any mapped path, slowly making our way through mud tracks cut into high grass. Gabriel says he normally travels by motorbike, that this is no terrain for a car. As stones thrown up by the tyres hit the metal bodywork with a smack and branches whip the windows, I understand where the crack along the windscreen has come from. There are hours of this until the undergrowth clears and we reach the edge of a large village.

Namogelia is just north of the Lúrio river and grows outwards from a central sandy square. It's alive with children who dawdle, clutching exercise books, awaiting a teacher who should have travelled in but hasn't turned up. Built in the centre of the square, in sight of the kids' straw-roofed classroom, is a corrugated structure with open sides, used to shelter village meetings from the sun. A couple of wooden benches are lined up which gradually fill with the village elders, and some plastic chairs are found for us. In turn the president, the secretary, the residents' leader and the pastor introduce themselves, all men who help organise the community. Gabriel is the most familiar face of our group and he introduces me in Makhuwa. It is imperative we have the elders' permission before we walk around (though given they're expecting us, it was never likely to be refused). Not only is it polite, but people have grown wary of strangers over the past few years.

The final person to introduce himself is Manuel dos Santos, who wears a white kufi cap, jeans and a fading T-shirt bearing the logo of the Leprosy Mission. He is one of the charity's network of village volunteers and a rare local Portuguese speaker. It is fair to say, twinkly-eyed in his sixties, he represents the best of humanity. Manuel has had the disease himself but was lucky enough to receive an early diagnosis and relatively easy access to drugs. In an agreement that runs to 2025, these are provided free via the WHO by the Swiss manufacturer, but given how remote the communities are and how stretched the health service is at the best of times, ensuring the uninterrupted flow of the combination therapy drugs is often impossible. In Pemba I had visited a small community operated by ALEMO, a patients' rights group, some of its residents even from around Chiúre, others from districts to the north who found it safer to relocate. Leaving husbands, wives and families, they voluntarily live in the shared compound for the six- or twelve-month duration of their treatment, knowing that it is the only sure-fire way to complete the course; some, the most vulnerable, in whom the disease has left permanent damage, elect to remain there even afterwards.

In Namogelia, now healthy, Manuel's days are full with his volunteer role. He takes Gabriel and me to a building just off the square, repurposed today as an ad hoc clinic. It is empty but for a wooden table, and sun cuts sharply into the cool gloom through gaps in the straw roof. Manuel has organised a short queue of suspected leprosy cases, all children today, who nervously hover outside. Dozens more kids crowd round inquisitively to see what's going on until he shoos them away to give the patients their privacy. The first of them Gabriel dismisses immediately: a baby boy, under a year old and barely walking, could not have leprosy, he hasn't lived the minimum incubation period of the disease. Gabriel asks the mother various questions and reassures her that the child is OK, though he does have a skin condition, a result of unhygienic conditions. He makes some gentle suggestions for improvement. The next to come is an older girl, nine years old. Her mother lifts her up off the dusty floor to sit on the table, feet dangling down, and then pulls the Peppa Pig T-shirt from over the child's head. The nurse begins his examination, holding up the torch of his phone to illuminate each area of skin while running his plastic-gloved fingers over every centimetre. The girl has a white patch on her cheek, the mark that during Manuel's regular door-to-door visits made him suggest the mother bring the child today. Gabriel identifies five further patches but explains how these alone can't prove a positive diagnosis, and that he is looking for a loss of sensitivity in other parts of the body. He massages the girl's elbow, tracing the ulnar nerve down past the plastic bracelets she is wearing to the palm of her hand and her fingertips. The girl shyly nods or shakes her head in response to Gabriel's questions. Gently directing her to turn and face one way and then the other, the nurse now traces the nerve on either side of the neck, testing by touch to see if it's enlarged in any way. After a thorough ten minutes, Gabriel says it is a positive case, quite advanced.

He starts filling out the paperwork. He enters his new patient's details into a notebook, which will later get transferred onto a computer, and then he fills out a slip of paper that includes a diagrammatic figure on which he marks the location of the girl's skin marks. He will aim to return to Namogelia in three months to check if they've grown or, hopefully, contracted. When he does, he will need to see all the girl's immediate family – her parents and any of the four siblings who are over two years of age – who will each be similarly examined. If they seem OK, they will be put on a preventative course of single-dose rifampicin; otherwise, they too will start full treatment. Gabriel hands over a month's worth of the multidrug therapy that he has with him. Each foil-covered sheet contains all the different pills, demarcated in a maze of different colours. The girl will have to take six pills in succession today, then embark on a sequence of one pill tomorrow, two the next, which in her case, given the substantial amount of the bacteria present, will last a year. Her mother is warned that it might cause nausea, that her daughter's urine may change colour. From here, Manuel takes over. Each element of the combination therapy needs to be taken with different intervals and it can be pretty confusing at first. Manuel will visit the girl's mother each day for the first week to help her get it right, and before the month is out he will take the child's ID on his bike to the nearest health centre to get more drugs. He will also invite her to take part in what is probably the Leprosy Mission's most important initiative, given Cabo Delgado's political situation and other challenges: the weekly self-care group.

We walk around the village, the mud-brick houses and their small-holdings backed up against the occasional baobab tree and thoroughfares of free-ranging goats and chickens. Gabriel and Manuel are doing their rounds. There are a pair of boys, goofy and shy in equal measure, and their older brother, who speaks to me on their behalf; both are under-going the same treatment the girl we just met is about to embark on. Then I meet Maria, whose life story unfolds slowly but who does not know her age. Does she remember the Portuguese leaving, I ask? Yes, she says, 'I was pregnant with my first child.' 'I think you are probably in your late sixties,' I say. She seems pleased. She made the long journey to hospital twice, knowing that something was wrong with her, but each time the symptoms weren't recognised as leprosy. It was only after the district nurse happened to pass by, and from a distance identified a possible case, that she started to receive the right treatment. By that time she had suffered irreversible disabilities in her hands and feet. 'I'm happy to feel better now,' she says when I ask if she's angry. It's a differ-ent story when I ask what she thinks the government could do better. My translator struggles to keep up in his note-taking of her Makhuwa, given how detailed the response is.

We move on to Feliciano, who tells me that while he himself is Muslim – in Islam the disease was never regarded as ritually unclean – he knows leprosy was stigmatised in the Bible. Here, however, he says, its prevalence means there is little discrimination. He gets up to show me his sparse one-room home, empty except for a fire in the middle and a bed of knotted palm. Francisco 'O Cavalo', his nick-name meaning 'the horse', is a flashy, charismatic guy, donning blue jeans and a T-shirt bedecked with palm trees and the face of an Afrobeats star. He first recognised the symptoms of leprosy while off working as a *garimpeiro*, part of a small group mining for graphite. He ignored them for as long as he could but eventually he returned to the village, annoyed that his dream of buying a motorbike had been curtailed. What did he want the motorbike for? My pen hovers above my notepad ready to report something inspirational. 'To show off to the neighbours,' he laughs.

They don't all go to the self-care group – O Cavalo has other priorities – but most are keen to take part. Sitting on a criss-cross woven bench in the shade of a tree, Manuel tells me that around twenty-five people – most with leprosy themselves, some family members – meet once a week with roughly the same agenda. First each washes anywhere that the disease has affected, those patches we'd seen, a gentle fight against infection. They will apply oil, too, which prevents the dry hardening of the flesh, each member of the group then helping others to apply the ointment in parts unreachable on their own, the more able-bodied members of the groups helping the elderly or the disabled and supervising the children among them. What is remarkable, as I had noted before on witnessing the friendly bonhomie of the residents of the ALEMO community in Pemba, is that the disease inspires a sense of community. The self-care groups provide some of the few moments in which the likes of Maria or Feliciano aren't struggling against a day-to-day grind, eking out a meagre sustenance, hiking the long paths to the market. The way people joke and touch each other affectionately reminds me of the women in the bar the night before – no dancing or matching outfits, but the same close empathy.

Manuel might deliver a lecture, too, on the causes of leprosy, on its prevention, on signs to look out for among family members or neighbours. It's a lot of work for him, who, unlike everyone else from the NGO or from the health department – or any of us sitting under this tree – is not paid for his time. He is happy to do it, he says; he feels great sympathy for his neighbours and wants to help them. There are undoubtedly budgetary reasons behind the Leprosy Mission's decision, but it also envisages its own institutional retreat from the village. The organisation is self-reflective enough to understand that charity is not a long-term solution, that such work has its roots in the old colonist and missionary interventions in Africa, and that ideally there will be a time when they are not needed. It is also hard enough to get here regularly with the state of the roads, even in the best of times, so self-help groups fulfil an immediate need, though there is also a darker scenario envisaged: the largely unspoken acknowledgement that, given the instability, there may come a time when communities are entirely cut off from even this slight outside provision. This comes to pass in February 2024, a few months later, with a huge resurgence in violence across the Chiúre district in particular. The Rwandan army, drafted alongside Mozambique forces, fails to stop the insurgents and, for the first time, the unrest spreads across the river to the neighbouring province. It's clear my trip to Cabo Delgado – through luck for me, but not for those I met and left behind – is during a tiny window of calm. This war is not over.

———

We spend a couple of days driving through villages, each with its own character, meeting patients. The road into Meequia is no less bumpy than all the rest. On arrival I walk across the square as, again, the elders assemble, the message passed to the further reaches of the settlement that the car they were expecting has arrived. A school borders one side of the square here too; the lessons are finished for the day, the sunlight breaking through small gaps in the roof and lighting up rows of empty wooden desks and chairs, and the blackboard that stands at the head of the classroom is brushed clean. This one is run by the villagers themselves, with no professional teachers. Amid the violence, education is as precarious as healthcare: forty schools in Chiúre district are forced to temporarily close when the violence flares again.

On the other side of the square is the remains of a barber's, destroyed in a storm and since relocated further among the houses. In the distance men shape mud into sharp, perfectly formed bricks, ready to bake in the sun; they are midway through building what will be quite a large house. The Leprosy Mission driver is talking to a man holding a brace of chickens by their legs – I'm wondering if he's planning on buying one and whether it will still be alive when it's put in the car. My attention is caught by a giant pig snuffling away. A stately beast, the pride, I assume, of its owner. It glances in my direction before continuing the never-ending appeasement of its appetite, slowly vacuuming through the trees. There are kids popping corn over a fire, a woman bundling building grasses; a general air of great industry pervades. We go through the same routine with the elders, but at the end, one, the magistrate, peels off and suggests we visit him in his compound.

Jorge Laide explains he has leprosy. On the top of his balding head a crochet cap perches, and the wrinkles on his face are only beginning to reveal that he has reached his mid-seventies. His home is a sprawling, multigenerational abode of several buildings: his wife hovers nearby cooking and a daughter breastfeeds her newborn. He has pens for his goats and a couple of solar panels for electricity. On my tape recording, Jorge's deep Makhuwa is spoken somewhere between the back of the mouth and nose, in which the vowels have no desire to be hurried; I can sometimes hear the child's happy gurgling among the cheerful soundtrack of clucking chickens. I ask Jorge how he is and he unbuttons the top of his white shirt to show me a mark on his chest, a small off-colour mountain range rising up from his skin. He shrugs it off: 'I took it to the supervisor when he visited last and I'm taking the drugs, it is improving.' Does he have any other symptoms? He smiles. 'My eyesight is bad, but I'm old so who knows, it's probably just that.' It is not leprosy he really wants to talk about though, but the village. As we chat he chops and peels a cassava root he'd like me to eat.

He has lived here his whole life and his role is an important one, arbitrating small disputes over property and suchlike, helping settle arguments between neighbours. While the position of village magistrate has its roots in the constitutionally mandated 'community courts', in this community adrift it feels like everything else, cleaved off from the state, operating largely autonomously. Medicine, education – why not the judiciary? When I ask Jorge what he'd like to see improve in his village, his list is not extraordinary but consists of the basic tenets of government provision: 'I'd like to see a school, a paramedic on a motorbike that can come here or the roads improved so an ambulance is able to drive down. Perhaps a milling machine for the community, that would help us a lot.'

Sitting in Europe, reading the history books of the modern Portuguese Empire fracturing after the Carnation Revolution, as a teenager who had devoured Ryszard Kapuściński's memoirs of the Angolan civil war, I had naively regarded Mozambique as a place in which left-wing ideals still held sway. Much has changed since those days. 'I'm an old man, I'm going blind,' Jorge continues, 'but I hope in the ten or so years I have I will see improvement here. The village only grows, people come but people don't have the opportunity to leave. When the government arrives to set up the polling booths during the elections, every time I tell them I want to vote them out four times.' He is joking of course, but in November 2023, the ruling FRELIMO party, once a standard-bearer for socialism in its post-democratic era, but since, in the ironic words of one longtime Mozambique-watcher, 'the star pupil for Western capitalism', violently quashed a series of protests contesting the outcome of the municipal elections. A sixteen-year-old boy in this district died at the hands of the police.

I had been beginning to think of these villages as islands from the state, but now I understand that the state, the oligarchs who run it, the Western companies, have islanded themselves from the people. They have been abandoned, like those who were abandoned on Molokai or Robben Island: the population of Cabo Delgado, likewise an economic inconvenience in the exploitation of their land. The insurrection is an awful side product of the great gulf between the elite in their guarded compounds, and people such as the residents of Meequia, who get on with the business of building lives and livelihoods as best they can. Misguided and broken, others turn to senseless violence to save themselves. 'In this village it has been peaceful, *mashallah*,' Jorge says. 'But we have heard about attacks in neighbouring villages, and I know the community is afraid. They are scared to go to the market or to farm along the tracks.' Since the communities nearby were ransacked, some of the population has fled south on foot, crossing the river to Nampula province, while others have gone to the relative safety of the district headquarters. 'We know there aren't many men in these militia groups, and for now here is safer than the north, but they have created an atmosphere in which the fear is always present. We don't know when, and don't know where, they might attack.' The dispersed are more numbers to add to the nearly one million people already displaced. I remember a damning line from an article about the aftermath of Hurricane Idai in Mozambique: 'the vast majority of survivors ultimately saved themselves'.

———

A few days later I take a chair in the office of Dr Alfonso Nicolaus, the health supervisor of Metuge, a neighbouring district. Perspiration assembles across his forehead despite the fan whirling in the corner. His eyes are tired and bloodshot. Behind him stand several shelves of binders and medical books, his desk piled with paperwork and a phone which I imagine to be equally hot from its constant shrill ring. Interrupting our conversation with matters certainly more urgent than my visit are his staff, too, popping their heads around the office door, peppering him with questions. Dr Nicolaus is in a wide-checked grey jacket, white shirt, black trousers and wears a wedding ring. I wonder if his wife has seen him much of late. Before the conflict he was charged with the health of around 86,000 people, but then more than 125,000 displaced people came into his responsibility and the existing hospitals were often overwhelmed. 'The kind of diseases we were treating didn't change, but cases of malaria, tuberculosis and diphtheria exploded,' he says with a sigh. A cholera outbreak is raging on my visit, the patients quarantined in a special facility outside Pemba. In the middle of all this came the cyclones and the Covid-19 pandemic, which, while it was the major story across most of the world, seems to have faded into the background here with everything else going on. While the International Monetary Fund extended Mozambique's credit to fight coronavirus, Dr Nicolaus says they have not seen an increase in their funding from central government to tackle the fallout of conflict. Nonetheless, miraculously, he was able to implement sixteen additional temporary health posts, including mobile units, both in resettlement villages and pre-existing populations, many of whom are hosting friends and relatives.

The violence has laid the perfect conditions for the incubation of leprosy: increasing poverty, a plummet in hygiene levels as people are forced to leave their homes, and a mass mixing of people from outside the province. 'Ideally I would implement a triage system for leprosy,' Dr Nicolaus says, talking specifically of the area he oversees. 'Our official statistics say that the prevalence is quite low, so we aren't given a budget to tackle it, but I think if we were actually able to go out and look for patients, we would find a lot of people suffering.' That's the purpose of the Leprosy Mission volunteers' door-to-door visits in the places it is able to reach safely. Dr Nicolaus says the greater presence of the relief agencies is a grim blessing which fills the gap, the public health system now an extraordinary mesh of NGO acronyms that spread across the region. It's difficult to see an exit strategy for this mini-industry of branded Land Cruisers.

The yard outside is full of staff walking from office to office, surgery to ward, clutching paperwork and thick files; patients mill around waiting to be seen while relatives sit outside under tiny pockets of shade that shrink as the sun climbs higher in the sky. Trucks and pick-ups come and go. Stepping out into this fray, from the hospital I catch a lift with a WHO team who are heading to one of the largest settlements for displaced people. Ntocota was a small village that has grown exponentially since the conflict. Relief agencies first identified its potential for expansion in 2020, analysing the water supply and the viability of the land, eventually moving vast numbers from temporary camps to a set number of plots. Those official spaces have long since multiplied, and when the attacks on Ancuabe and other existing refugee settlements occurred, more families arrived on foot. The WHO team turn off the main road to a track which leads to the original settlement, a reasonably developed village with a few concrete buildings. Beyond, a construction boom churns through the scrubby agricultural land: Save the Children is building a school, the WHO have installed a water collection and treatment facility. Many have sought the services of psychiatrists and psychologists employed by Doctors with Africa CUAMM. They are tasked with helping people process the trauma of the things they witnessed back in their home villages, of the journey and the precarity of their situation now, people alienated from what they know and forced to live among strangers. Female mental health workers will also go door-to-door, helping women come to terms with the epidemic of gender-based violence the conflict has seen.

Joining these new facilities will soon be a medical centre located around a kilometre away, but for now Domingas Nunes's clinic is two white tents that stand in a small fenced off enclosure. One is for ante- and neonatal care and female health, the other for everything else. Printed on the outside is the WHO logo; on the inside fabric of each tent are instructions on how to adapt the structure in case of a drop in temperature, severe rain or a sandstorm. Domingas seems impossibly young: aged twenty-three, this is her first job after finishing nursing college a year ago, but alone she and a medical technician ably serve the approximately 11,000 people who now live here. Her colleague is sick with malaria today, but like every morning around 150 patients still line up outside. That number has reached 400 some days, with parents bringing in multiple children, themselves seeking advice or treatment too.

Unless it is an emergency, in which case the patient will be dispatched to a larger clinic some distance away, Domingas will first stand in front of them in her white coat, her braided hair tied up in a bun, to deliver a lecture on some aspect of public health or personal care. It's a common practice in Mozambique and during the start of the Covid-19 pandemic she might have spoken of hand-washing and the like, at other times the subject could be HIV awareness. The lectures also serve a more urgent purpose. While the public are well versed in many health matters, the lessons are an attempt to ward off the conspiracy theories and fake news that spread across WhatsApp and the marketplace. A few months after my trip, mobs targeted health facilities and health workers, whipped up by false rumours that strategies to prevent cholera – the addition of chlorine to water supplies, the distribution of water purifiers – were spreading the disease. In Namogelia, which became the epicentre of this explosion, four local authority employees were killed. (When I read about the attack back home, I realise it must have happened around the time Gabriel should have been returning to check on the health of the young girl he had diagnosed in front of me.) Such violence is nothing new, mirroring similar attacks coinciding with cholera outbreaks across Chiúre and elsewhere for decades. Again it seems no coincidence that the organs of the state, however distant, are the targets of ire, a logical if ill-informed protest for frustrated people. With such polarisation only widening, it is clear the same alienation that drives today's cholera riots goes hand in hand with the wider Islamist insurgency. In the face of this, someone local like Domingas, taking the role of teacher as well as medic, is probably this country's best hope.

The field hospital has never held a session on leprosy. When I ask Domingas if she was taught anything about the disease at college, she echoes the experience of Gabriel in saying that it was never covered. This is one of the great frustrations for professionals working in the field. While those in the villages know it exists, it has disappeared from the purview of the political establishment. It is an invisibility echoed globally – staff at the Leprosy Mission tell me that one of the hardest things for them is fundraising in a world that thinks the disease is long gone; nor does it have the cachet of the huge celebrity-endorsed charity campaigns that have successfully bank-rolled dramatic drops in HIV prevalence. It is not for nothing that leprosy is classed as a 'neglected tropical disease'. One activist I spoke to put it more bluntly than the charity could: 'We can't compete with the glamour of diseases that also affect rich white people in the West.'

Domingas does recall that she recently had a patient, a displaced person who knew he had leprosy and was searching for a top-up to his supply of drugs. Divorced from the volunteer network, he was forced into a seemingly never-ending hunt to continue his treatment. Domingas regretfully referred the man to a clinic in another town that she thought might be large enough to help, but she could not be certain. (On the other hand, medicine to treat HIV is stocked locally as a matter of course.) We walk through the village to see if we can find this particular patient, but no one is sure if he's still here. With some areas returning to state control, 300,000 people have been able to make the journey home, though the population in Ntocota is said to be relatively stable. Dr Nicolaus had said this presents its own problems: people often don't mention they are moving on, leaving without paperwork relating to their treatment. Any interruption will not only cause the progression of the disease to recommence but it also undermines the kind of contact-tracing Gabriel was undertaking in Namogelia. The consequences for other diseases are similarly dire: medics are supposed to actively observe tuberculosis patients taking their drugs as any disruption can cause resistance, a growing problem even in a country new to such therapies. The health service is not perfect, but there is a path in place for diagnosis and treatment if a villager can find their way into the system and remain there. The returnees are also likely to find the infrastructure in their villages and towns decimated, and while the terrorists may have melted into the shadows momentarily, there is no guarantee that among the people returning are the many thousands of health workers who also fled.

Giving up on locating Domingas's patient, the WHO team and I stop at one home, outside which Angerina Atanasia is playing with her toddling niece as her sister does the washing-up from lunch. New residents should be given a starter kit from which they build their own shelter, but Angerina – aged twenty-eight and 'without a husband', she says emphatically – constructed the one-room home from sticks she gathered from the scrappy surrounding trees, relieved when she was donated the plastic sheeting that serves as the roof. We sit on a couple of woven stools, ours borrowed from a neighbour. A tiny solar panel provides enough electricity to charge a phone. I ask her if she minds me switching my tape recorder on, if I can ask her some questions beyond the initial chit-chat. I'm hesitant as to where our conversation will go, but she is not.

A lot of the people on this journey have been willing to relive traumatic events for me, and while age has not softened the memories – sadness only accumulates – they have at least had time to become familiar with the narrative of what they have lived through. Angerina does not have leprosy, but through the conflict she too has suffered equivalent levels of violence, estrangement and dislocation. She has nothing, she says. Not since running away from her village one night. She had just her flip-flops on her feet when the men came. Shuffling the dirt floor, each sandal strap bears an icon of the Mozambique flag with its AK-47 against the red, green, black and yellow. The village is very close to Ancuabe, the town I'd navigated around last week. The fires, as I've been told time and again, were the first sign. Then the men started their killing. Others, they kidnapped. I don't ask her to dwell on the details, I can't put her through that, but she refuses to be bowed and describes how the village was destroyed; in my mind I see those flip-flops pounding through the night. Angerina answers my questions slowly, unflinching in detail: she can't go back, she says, 'my mind will never let me'

– the name of the place she lived her whole life is now bloodstained beyond redemption. Her whole family, along with their neighbours, were running by her side.

Angerina first travelled to Pemba, but there was nothing for her there, and so she went to Metuge, the town in which Dr Nicolaus's hospital is located. She was picked up by an NGO and brought here. The first days, she and her children slept under the trees, but then another displaced person took them in until she could start building. Many of the people she came with have returned, her own two children included – they couldn't settle in, they were hungry. They are with her grandparents now, whom she phones on the old Nokia, one of her and her sister's few belongings. They are able to provide for them better there.

Her niece, timid, pulled from behind the grown-ups' backs to say hello to this foreign stranger with his notebook and voice recorder, has been given lunch, a salty porridge of beans and wheat made using the few plants that grow up against the mud and bamboo walls of the house. This is what the adults eat too. Would I like some? Obviously I can't take this food, I say. Yet a plastic plate is produced and her sister spoons out a portion. A cup of water is given to wash my hands. I take a little. Starch and beans. It's what they've eaten for weeks, months. It is filling, it is even not bad, but Angerina smiles as I compliment the cooking, aware of the absurdity that surrounds the exchange.

It seems impossible to describe Angerina as lucky. Yet the masses who travelled by foot or, if they had the money and were further north, who paid for passage from cities such as Palma and Mocímboa da Praia, boat to boat along the coast to Pemba Port, are the 'lucky' ones. It's a terribly cruel word for someone fleeing with nothing, people who have seen what Angerina has seen, the fire, the killings, but the journey is arduous and can only be done by the healthy and mobile. Young and fit, she and her sister were able to build this perfunctory shelter and grow their crops, and because of their perseverance, a superhuman one it seems to me, Angerina's niece is well and looked after. For anyone with the kind of disabilities that leprosy can cause, such a perilous flight to even notional safety is impossible. There had been 1,800 people with active leprosy known by the health authorities in the province, but now 400 of those have disappeared off the radar. They are the hidden people. This time what holds them in isn't the boundary of a colony, biopolitics or the law, but a ring of violence and danger built by fear and greed: the majority of fatalities in war are never from the bullets, bombs or burning fires, but disease and neglect, those left in the prison of ill-health.

———

Some towns and villages north of here are too dangerous to enter, others can only be reached by air. These are the places for which the entry roads are too perilous, the attacks from the long grass too frequent. To these places, the WHO staff I am travelling with will be taken by UN planes and helicopters, the air above an oasis of calm and liberty – like every car journey I've undertaken over the past few days, however, their agenda is also set by the sun. They will fly in at dawn and are out by the first inkling of dusk. The WHO doctor shows me a map of the region marking out the airstrips and landing patches of the region. To those sick within their vicinity, each aeroplane symbol represents the chance to keep on living.

A global online database, HeRAMS, updated by multiple relief agencies, keeps track of how operative medical facilities are in the world's conflict zones. Zoom over Cabo Delgado and a topography of red and yellow dots appear, spores across the map, indicating health centres and hospitals fully or partially destroyed by fighting and looting. Twenty-six out of a total of thirty-nine were shut the last time

I checked. Left behind as the medics fly to safety, somewhere inside this closed-off world, are the people war could not displace. The people trapped by disease, by their own bodies, by history, for whom no medicine is available. The people forgotten after the Western oil companies have airlifted out their personnel and the mining companies of the old colonial powers have paused their operations. The people left as the country further fragments between rich and poor.

As the WHO car bumps its way back to Pemba, back to the moribund resort in which the military commanders in fatigues will be picking over tomorrow's breakfast buffet, it strikes me how much the fate of the ordinary people here is decided by entities so far away. In the parliament in Maputo, of course, but further still. It's impossible to delineate clear lines of consequence and cause, but when I think about the little girl Gabriel diagnosed, or hundreds like her in the remote villages of Cabo Delgado, it's strange to realise that Novartis, the drug company that provides a lifeline in free supplies, has its gleaming Basel headquarters just an efficient train ride from Credit Suisse, the bank at the centre of the loans scandal. Or, given their locations, how fundraisers from the Leprosy Mission International might rush past the staff of Gemfields at London's Waterloo Station.

The long aftermath of colonisation, this neocolonisation of the poor for their land, takes the formula of the clean and the unclean; those of society and those shut out. Cabo Delgado has become a leprosy colony of a grand scale, a people torn from their roots, fragmented and trapped, the walls of precarity and fear as strong as any nineteenth-century hospital.

RIO DE JANEIRO, BRAZIL

How do you make an outsider? You destroy their home. Crouched alongside the mountainous favelas of Jacarepaguá, Hospital Curupaiti is an hour inland from the famous beaches of Rio de Janeiro. A couple of security guards sit at a plastic table outside the gatehouse and don't look up from their card game as I walk past. I had read that while Curupaiti might be long closed as a medical facility, I would not find the place empty. Its relative proximity to the Olympic park was a story too tempting for journalists in the lead-up of the 2016 games. 'The Shame of Rio de Janeiro' read a headline in the *Daily Mirror*, a British tabloid, a couple of months before the sports jamboree began. 'Snarling dogs roam freely, rats infest the corridors and prostitutes ply their trade in Curupaiti Hospital . . . The patients at this former leper colony have been left to fend for themselves. Many are amputees. Some have rotting, reeking wounds, but bandages and painkillers are in short supply.' I was primed to witness a society at its very edge, vandalised and in disarray, but on first appearances, this was not so.

The road from the entrance slopes gently upwards through woods of stately mature trees. They lead me into a narrow street of squat houses, outside which people go about their daily business. A woman tends the plants she is growing on her veranda, a man paints the outside of his cottage; another, with newspaper thrown aside, sits scratching a dog who pants contentedly by his side. At the top, a small square, in which concrete street tables with embedded chequers boards grow out from a mosaic of chipped paving stones and wisps of sprouting weeds. The porch of a closed, weatherbeaten church, its green paint stained and peeling, affords a view of the forested valley below. There used to be a six-cell prison, punishment for patients who tried to escape or who missed their medical appointments, and an imported incinerator, a twin of that designed for Carville, the leprosy colony in Louisiana, USA, ensuring nothing left the site. There is now a basketball court where old photos show a formal garden once stood; there is a second church, two small bars, a shop. It is peaceful, a rare adjective to summon in describing any Rio neighbourhood. It's a fragile happiness, though, hard fought for by the residents.

At the far end of Curupaiti, the old wall that otherwise stretches along the perimeter, encasing forty-five hectares of hospital land, has been demolished, the hospital slowly blending with the favela beyond. Morro do Jordão is smaller than the more famous informal neighbourhoods of Jacarepaguá, not least Cidade de Deus, the community painted as a war zone in *City of God*, the 2002 film. Here the cottages of the colony give way to more densely packed streets of bare, unrendered and sometimes unfinished houses, the exposed brickwork quick and unfussy, mortar bursting out like cream from a cake. With the streets garlanded by washing lines and pirated electricity cables, the favela creeps up the mountain. It carries with it more life and music; teenagers hang out on the street, a family says goodbye to visiting relatives, the mother with a baby on each arm. One cries, one sleeps. On numerous lampposts are taped the same flyers I've seen pasted to a wall in the hospital: loan sharks offering their services via a WhatsApp number.

———

I've lived in Brazil, in São Paulo, on and off for the past five years. The country has the second-highest number of leprosy cases annually after India, with 22,773 new diagnoses made in 2023. The history of leprosy control here is one of the darkest in the world. Yet it is countered by a more recent narrative of remarkable solidarity and activism in the face of social brutality, a dichotomy that has surfaced in so many of the stories I've reported since arriving here. Violence and perseverance: these are the rivers that seem to flow through this beautiful and extraordinary country. The fourth-biggest democracy in the world is an upper-middle-income country, and while leprosy is not simply a disease of poverty, the generic assumption is often borne out. (Even in 1923, a medic in the British Army, William MacArthur, was scrawling handwritten notes to his colleague, warning that for all their work on a cure, he knew 'that leprosy is mixed up inter alia with a people's social condition, and that if the inhabitants of a leprosy-infected country could "get rich" the disease would very soon disappear itself'.) Brazil is one of the most unequal societies in the world and the bacillus is most prevalent in the country's poorer north and north-east, as well as the central farming states, while the far richer south records limited cases. Many communities in the north of the country are remote but the Brazilian healthcare system is free, universal and widespread. Individual circumstances appear to be the greatest determining factor. A Brazilian study on tuberculosis provocatively titled 'Is It Better to be Rich in a Poor Area or Poor in a Rich Area?' demonstrated that 'being male, being illiterate, not working in the previous seven days and possessing few goods' were strong indicators whatever the available medical care might be locally. A second study focusing on young people specifically named homelessness, HIV and drug use as explaining the link between poverty and lack of recovery.

Tuberculosis shares many transmission traits with leprosy, and the findings above chime with a third research paper from the country, this time on leprosy, which shows how cash payments from the state facilitate faster recovery rates (and therefore a lower spread). Those who had been diagnosed with leprosy and received Bolsa Familia, a government scheme providing direct economic relief to the poorest Brazilians, were 22 per cent more likely to stick with their medication plan against those outside the programme. One patients' rights activist summarised it to me: 'In Brazil, leprosy has a colour, a class and a gender; it is Black, poor and male.'

The decisive factor for Bolsa Familia, introduced during the first and most radically left-wing term of President Luiz Inácio Lula da Silva, was that the benefits are conditional – and in some ways conditioning – requiring recipients to ensure their children attend school a minimum number of days and undergo a standard vaccination programme (including shots against tuberculosis and yellow fever). After the eugenicist models of the past, this is social engineering applied positively, in which the rights of the individual walk hand in hand with public health. Those diagnosed with leprosy who fail to show up to doctors' appointments are not similarly penalised, but a culture of engagement, as well as obvious factors such as the money enabling patients to take time off work and meet the costs of travel for treatment, have borne fruit. Without it, a depressing fact holds true: if the poor are more likely to get leprosy, then once they have it they are only likely to get poorer.

I meet Nivaldo Farías at the outdoor gym of Curupaiti. He experienced such loss of earnings first-hand. At seventy-seven, and the oldest ex-patient here, he's had his nickname Lobo, 'Wolf', for years, but he seems to have grown into it latterly with his white hair and white beard and strong, stout frame. In old photos he looks a bit like a young Mark Hamill. He waves off my suggestion we sit down somewhere. 'I was nineteen and I was studying at a federal school and found a white spot on my belly,' he recalls, propping himself up against an exercise bike. 'I already had a military career: I was about to become a sergeant, an aeronautical specialist. I was doing a course in the Air Force and I was forced to leave it behind.

They paid really well at the time; it would have been a good career. I didn't want to come but I was given no choice. I was devastated.' The mistreatment – the alienation – he suffered is familiar by now; it's a story that crosses borders. 'The isolation wasn't about stopping infection, it wasn't about science, it was because the public were scared of us. We weren't allowed on buses, we didn't get served in bars. Students from the university would visit us here and they'd look at us like animals in the zoo.' It was 1965 when Lobo first arrived from the town of Pedra de Guaratiba along the coast, and though he finished his treatment within eighteen months, Brazil was one of the last countries in the world to end compulsory segregation. He remained behind the walls for a further twenty years, only allowed out on occasion if he tested negative to a series of medical tests.

———

The bacillus was introduced by European colonisers at the end of the sixteenth century. Alongside the other major ports of Salvador and Recife, also centres of the slave trade, Rio was among the first places in Brazil to be hit. These ground-zero cities soon built hospitals. In Brazil's National Archives there is a twenty-three-page royal charter from 1759, blotchily handwritten and signed by King José I of Portugal, establishing a leprosarium near Salvador. Yet Brazil was oddly behind the curve in making segregation mandatory, waiting until 1923 to mass-imprison its patients, by which point those with leprosy in the hospitals of Robben Island and Tichileşti had been locked out of the wider world for four decades.

There were dissenting voices in Brazil, too: Eduardo Rabelo, a dermatologist, wrote sympathetically in 1926 that 'these patients need isolation, but most of all, a place to live, sleep, and eat'. In other words, they needed a place to call home, with all the freedom and comfort that come with such a word. 'There is no doubt that we should isolate lepers, but we do not have the right to practise strict isolation with a slightly contagious malady, such as leprosy, without being able to even guarantee a cure. We would be behaving anti-scientifically, against all the international decrees, and it would be absurd to move back at this moment.' Despite the failure of similarly authoritarian top-down health policies – in 1904 Rio had seen shops looted and tramcars burned in the so-called 'Vaccine Revolt', an uprising against doctors going door-to-door to administer the small-pox vaccine by force – Rabelo's words were lost in the incoming gale. The *sanitarista* movement, a group of scientists for whom health policy and economic progress were inextricably linked, was gaining political influence. There were commendable elements to their philo-sophy. They planted seeds for preventative health policies and began the social and financial case for universal free healthcare. The doctors went to battle with the Church over who was best placed to care for the sick. They also, however, promoted a racialised form of eugenics. One of their number, Belisário Penna, on being appointed head of Propaganda and Sanitary Education by newly elected president Washington Luís, explained:

Leprosy, Mr. President, is not a disease of civilized countries, nor of savages. There is no leprosy among savages. It is characteristic and symbolic of countries in a state of semi-civilization. Now, Brazil claims to be a civilized country . . . Therefore, it needs to show that it is in fact one. Brazil is really revealing itself to be a semi-civilized country, with this formidable stain.

Persuaded by such rhetoric – Penna also relayed his disgust at seeing a person with leprosy bathing in the sea off Copacabana beach – Luís went on to support the creation of colonies and a huge building project was undertaken under his leadership, yet segregation was still not compulsory.

This was to change after the global economic repercussions of the Wall Street Crash in 1929 saw the Brazilian president deposed by a military junta. Getúlio Vargas came in as a head of the post-revolution provisional government. He was briefly democratically elected before seizing autocratic control (the cliché that Brazil isn't for beginners has never been truer for this period of its history). For their part, the *sanitaristas* supported the new government. For this they were awarded with influential political positions, and the road to forced internment was all but inevitable. When Vargas turned dictator in 1937 under the pretext of a faked communist insurrection, the eight-year 'Estado Novo' regime permeating every pore of society, the *sanitarista* policies went unquestioned. As with Norway half a century earlier, Brazilian policy was driven by what the presence of the bacillus on the country's soil signalled internationally; and like the Cape Colony, political decisions ran on a mixture of hard economics and racism. Vargas continued the policy of *branqueamento*, an immigration drive that, since the end of slavery, aimed at 'whitening' the population by allowing and at times subsidising the passage of Europeans who were 'healthy and able to work'. Under Vargas, immigration was capped at 2 per cent of the numbers that had previously arrived from any particular nation in the last fifty years, a period in which Black immigration was outlawed. This highly racist form of social engineering was well-established in Argentina, Uruguay, pre-revolutionary Cuba and elsewhere, and its 'success' proposed the exact opposite of the 'one-drop' rule in the USA: the 'dilution' of the population. Following a post-presidential trip to Brazil, Theodore Roosevelt wrote, 'It is the Negro who is being absorbed and not the Negro who is absorbing the white man.' Leprosy, a bad advert for the would-be 'good' immigrant, was just another obstacle in the Europeanising of Brazil.

Penna complained: 'It is a tremendous calamity that the politicians of Brazil have not wanted or even known how to confront [leprosy], unaware of its evils and the demoralisation that it causes a country of immense territory, whose exploration and peopling needs to be achieved, in large part, by the importation of effectual foreign workers.' The *effectual* is doing a lot of dog-whistling here. As part of a far-right Catholic integralist movement, Penna would later take part in an attempted coup against Vargas. Heráclides César de Souza Araújo, head of leprosy research at the state Oswaldo Cruz Institute, pitched in: 'That our government imitate the example of the small and prudent Norway is what we desire. The result will be identical.' Though the Bergen model remained an outsized influence on leprosy policy globally, the colonisation projects of the nineteenth century had succeeded in fully racialising the disease.

The *sanitarista* doctors seeded a number of stories in the foreign press about the problem, none more obvious in intention than a *Washington Times* report that the disease was 'alarming sanitary experts', editorialising that 'it should receive the immediate attention of the government'. Whipped up by lobbying and faced with such foreign chiding, Vargas provided funding for the creation of even more colonies, with thirty-three new hospitals in total established in the twentieth century, which from the 1930s onwards would manage the mandatory segregation of an estimated 24,000 people. Each state also boasted a powerful leprosy inspectorate which acted autonomously from the federal health department, itself purged of anyone who didn't sign up to a vehemently pro-segregationist agenda. The imprisonment of patients was not a case of following a scientific consensus that was later proved wrong, but a propaganda decision undertaken with the knowledge that it would largely affect the poorest and, because of their condition, least economically 'useful' Brazilians. Federally enforced segregation was cut from the statute books in 1964 but local health authorities were given freedom over their own policies – for two further decades, as the country's military dictatorship ruled, Rio de Janeiro and the other states continued to remove the diagnosed from their families.

———

In the centre of Curupaiti stand a pair of faded single-storey buildings, each with a central corridor, the walls an institutional mustard, gloomy when coming in from the bright sunlight. Off the side are a series of tiny rooms with uniform brown-checked floors. This is the block that housed the single male patients, and where former patients still remain – some even arrived after the end of the internment policy in 1986, disowned by friends and family and with little other option. They have for the most part made their living quarters homely – the resident of one room has created a spectacular display of magazine cuttings in homage to his two passions, ornithology and Botafogo football club – but the neglect is clear. The pavement outside is cracked and inside the lights flicker occasionally. Lobo tells me this is where he lived when he first arrived, sleeping four patients to a cell. Back then unmarried men and women were separated, but if patients were to couple up, and if one of the small cottages down the lane was available, they were allowed to move in together. Often newlyweds had to wait for at least one half of another couple to die, at which point, with dizzying pragmatism, the deceased's widow or widower was forced out of the property and back into the dorms. Either way, any children would be removed from them and sent to live in a state-run facility.

And yet, despite this, despite it all, Lobo and others at Curupaiti built a community. Before his diagnosis, Lobo had hoped to enrol in a military band. Instead, he staged a music festival in the colony, a riotous, boisterous four-day party that took place annually for almost thirty years. 'We had to create our own social life here, we created everything,' he says. 'I played the trombone – well, I played everything. I don't do false modesty. The trumpet, the saxophone. With music I can do anything, if there's an instrument, I can learn it.' An old photograph from 1965 shows a trio of musicians, each wearing impressively jaunty white bicorn hats, one playing an accordion while his bandmates are on drums and guitar, entertaining an audience during Festa Junina, the holiday marking southern mid-winter. 'I started a carnival *bloco* in 1969, then we had a samba festival and people from Rio's samba schools came here to judge,' Lobo continues. It's a strange illogical anomaly that while patients were only allowed to leave the facilities in exceptional circumstances, outsiders would come and go – more commonly health workers and the like, but sometimes celebrities, generous with their time and lack of prejudice. In the archives of Colônia Antônio Aleixo, Manaus, is a photograph of the footballer Pelé, who visited in 1970 to watch a match between the colony's two resident teams. He stands, smiling and handsome in a tight pull-string shirt and snug trousers, alongside two clearly awed nuns. That the national team was happy to put their greatest asset – that year Pelé had won his third World Cup for the Canarinhos – at such apparent 'risk' seems ironic. Even more dedicated was the enigmatic figure of Malba Tahan, the pen name of Júlio César de Mello e Souza, a wildly popular writer of mathematics puzzles who for a long time claimed to be an Arabic scholar born in Mecca (but actually grew up in a Brazilian coffee-growing village). With his identity revealed, and while his books remained in demand, he took up the cause of the Curupaiti residents, launching a magazine titled *Damiao* (after Father Damien), protesting against the discrimination. He visited the hospital a number of times, and Lobo later sends me a picture of the writer watching Acapulco play. There was also a ten-piece jazz band going by the name Jazz Hands!, as well as film screenings and tug-of-war tournaments.

Lobo waves to the bar close by. A couple of guys are letting the day play out by racking up bottles of Brahma. 'In the 1970s this place opened, not to sell beer but ice cream.' It was established by the Church and was just a hatch then. 'There was a floral arch outside that couples could sit under on a date.' He says there was even an illegal casino for a bit, too, not an uncommon feature in a country where games of chance are banned. Gesticulating again, he explains, 'The hospital food was made in the kitchen over there. It was awful, but a few people in the cottages used to make food themselves and it was much better, and if you had money you could go there and buy it from them.'

In 1986, however, this blossoming community came to an abrupt end as the authorities in Rio revoked the internment policy. As quickly as each of them had had their lives turned upside down on diagnosis, overnight the residents discovered they were free. It was no less traumatic. 'They just opened the gates and suddenly we were allowed to go. They didn't tell us anything, just suddenly people could come and go. It was so strange,' Lobo recalls. 'I found it really hard, I couldn't just leave. I had no life out there, I didn't know what I could do. I had no motive to leave. I had lost my schooling. I regret it now, though, that I didn't just go, but I was impregnated with all these bad feelings about myself, about my life.' He says they were promised social help, assistance with mental health, but nothing came. 'The government wanted us out. But we resisted, we refused. I had suffered so much because of the politicians and the health service, and then they thought they could just get rid of me.' Lobo bitterly adds a classic Brazilian phrase: 'I ate the bread that the devil kneaded. Now they can't even handle it.'

It might be easy to put Lobo's decision to stay down to

institutionalisation, stripped of his self-reliance by the Brazilian state, but to me it feels like his reaction was entirely natural. The land on which he had lived, emotionally at least, no longer belonged to the health department but the residents themselves. So much of the infrastructure had been built or initiated by them, and that is before considering the less tangible assets of friendships, shared histories, clubs, support networks, sports teams and rivalries that make up a community. To describe something as 'medieval' has been conditioned as pejorative, but the atmosphere the patients managed to engineer recalls more the proto-democratic leprosaria of the Middle Ages than the colonial prisons of recent history: it was far from a utopia, but here was a space that was allowed to operate beyond the production of capital and extraction of labour. Even the medicalised aspect of life in Curupaiti was often patient-led: many of the nursing assistants, hospital workers and low-level administrators came from within the patient body, and there were two patients' groups in operation, the Caixa Beneficente, founded in the 1940s, and the later Sociedade Amigos de Curupaiti – the former of which led a campaign for the drug Promin, then being tested in other leprosy colonies internationally, to be brought to Brazil. That Lobo calls Curupaiti home is entirely rational. Emotional ties hold no legal standing, however, and Lobo's battle against the state, and the battle of those like him in leprosaria across Brazil, really began the day the gates were thrown open.

At Curupaiti, instead of evicting the former patients, the government tacitly approved a reverse migration by allowing anyone to come and occupy the land. Amid a civic cash crisis, the last of the medical services dried up and the pharmacy in the former hospital closed; the hospital buildings were left to go derelict. The situation reached its nadir as journalists descended on the city for the Olympics. In 2007, the former patients had started to receive reparations from the government for the way they had been treated historically, which, equalling one and a half times the minimum wage, on top of any other pensions, made them better off than many of those living the other side of the wall (though by no means wealthy). They became sitting targets for lucrative exploitation – many older patients, unaware of outside prices, given they had rarely ventured out of the hospital, were routinely taken advantage of when buying alcohol and the like.

This was a period of intense fluctuation in the community: as part of the renovations of the Maracanã stadium in the lead-up to the 2014 World Cup, police had raided the former Museu do Índio, long squatted by people from various indigenous groups, evicting them with plans to develop the building (plans which never came to fruition). For want of anywhere else to house those displaced, the city authorities installed temporary container houses in the grounds of Curupaiti where Pataxós, Tukanos, Guajajaras and Apurinã lived in claustrophobic conditions for over a year, far from the area in which they had also built a life. The hospital was soon at risk of overcrowding with this mix of ex-patients, *favelados* and displaced indigenous people, and once again it seemed a dumping ground for the authorities.

This destruction of the homeliness of the hospital – whether intentional or not – has a political dimension in that it undermined the community's embryonic solidarity. Where before the message was 'you are not allowed to be part of us', the message became 'you are not allowed to be different'. While the patients never wanted to be segregated, their rapid reintegration seemed just another form of disappearance, hidden not behind walls but within the crowd, any protest to their treatment drowned out among the noise.

———

The dogs make themselves known when I stray further into the favela beyond. One comes nipping the air a metre away from me, its barks alerting its friends who come out for the party, never close enough to land an attack and probably with little inclination either (but intimidating nonetheless). More to the point, they draw attention to this stranger nosing around. Favelas are not the lawless 'slums' painted by sensationalist media but varied communities, with as many bars, churches, sports clubs and neighbourly connections as any other place. Almost a quarter of Cariocas – Rio's residents – live in their midst. It is affordable housing in a city with no other affordable housing. There are *baile* funk parties, where drugs are dealt openly, the dealers with guns, but you are as likely to be invited to an art exhibition or see a community gardening project in the favelas. As the sociologist Janice Perlman wrote in 1976:

> The evidence strongly indicates that the favelados are not *marginal*, but in fact *integrated* into the society, albeit in a manner detrimental to their own interests. They are certainly not separate from, or on the margin of the system, but are tightly bound into it in a severely asymmetrical form. They contribute their hard work, their high hopes, and their loyalties, but they do not benefit from the goods and services of the system.

It's an inequality that makes such settlements the natural neighbour to the old leprosy settlements; and the antipathy of the patients to reintegrate into such an extractivist system understandable.

The people of the favela continue to be used as cheap and easily jettisoned labour – in the bakeries and supermarkets, in factories, whizzing around on mopeds, following the pings of exploitative food delivery apps – while the place they live is characterised as a no-go zone. When Perlman continues, 'they are not socially and culturally marginal, but are stigmatised and excluded from a closed social system', I think of the life inside Curupaiti that blossomed as a town in microcosm, one that sat in isolation. The half-century since Perlman wrote her seminal work *The Myth of Marginality* has seen a major sea change in the organisation of both these communities, though; they became more interlaced, infiltrated by an economic system that runs in parallel to the official one, a place in which loyalties are strictly enforced.

Organised crime began to envelop the poorest districts of Rio at the end of the 1970s with the founding of Comando Vermelho, a drug gang which now operates nationally and internationally. Originally established as a prison crew of leftist guerrillas and ordinary criminals who banded together to protect themselves against guard violence and the brutality of the penal system, the dealers usually do not pose a threat to ordinary residents, but many have died in the crossfire of their battles with Brazil's heavily armed military police, both sides displaying little regard for life. In 2023 police in Rio killed 1,330 people, the majority in operations against the drug gangs, and the security services were described in one NGO report as 'a public health hazard'. In the 2000s a new type of organisation began to arise, the *milícia*, ostensibly vigilante groups, invariably staffed by off-duty civil and military cops as well as serving members of Brazil's armed forces. These groups were often welcomed by inept or corrupt politicians and, initially, some local populations, who praised them for undertaking extrajudicial raids and killings against Comando Vermelho and others. The *milícia*, however, aided by their entanglement with law enforcement and City Hall, soon found means to exploit the territories they gained, infiltrating and commandeering residents' associations and, with favelas largely unsupported by municipal utility infrastructure, overseeing the supply of electricity and water. For this they charged a premium, money that in turn helped fund expansion into property development, loan-sharking and protection rackets. The drug trade, the very thing the *milícia* were founded against, has also proved too lucrative a temptation. In Rio the favelas spread west, on to ground previously beyond the city limits, eating up the forested periphery in which Curupaiti was situated. Modelling themselves on the *bandeirantes*, the old colonial explorers who stole territory from the indigenous inhabitants, the *milícia* are now less likely to take over established neighbourhoods than to develop new favelas on supposedly virgin territory, the land of former leprosaria proving ripe such fruit.

———

Colônia Antônio Justa, on the outskirts of Fortaleza in the northeastern state of Ceará, is in even greater flux than Curupaiti. Where the Rio hospital has roughly retained its shape, this vast former colony, built on boggy ground and opened in 1941, is rapidly being repurposed and transformed. Some fear that the history of what happened here will be lost under a stampede of real-estate speculation, legal and otherwise. Among the few locals who remain oblivious to the rapid changes are the four patients who live in the last few buildings still controlled by the state health authority. All with visible signs of leprosy and all of an advanced age, none have ventured beyond the walls of their accommodation and the former central administrative block of the hospital in a very long time.

The public payphone in the main corridor sits unused and unconnected. My footsteps on the tiles, in the rooms where old photos show Christmas concerts and parties were once held, are a deafening incursion to the silence. The immediate landscape beyond is a bucolic wilderness, a monastic retreat in which palms hang low over the roof of the block and wildflowers spread across former lawns. A stone bust of a doctor stands weatherbeaten off a path cracked with grass. Aside from a skeleton nursing staff, crickets are the patients' most steadfast companions. When I visit, two nurses are brushing the hair of one resident; another sits happily staring out to the garden. On being introduced, she just smiles and waves without a word.

This small area is a holdout. The rest of the colony has been taken over, some cottages occupied by former patients and their children legally, many more by outsiders who squat in the former buildings or have built their own simple homes. The last count formally placed 930 families as living on the land of Antônio Justa, though local health workers estimate that it is triple that. It takes twenty minutes from the remaining medical buildings to pass the old gateposts on the red dust road which marked the end of the 'infected' area, and the same distance again to find the former staff village built around a lagoon. The old colony has become a no-man's-land, a precarious hinterland in which the population have been left to fend for themselves; it has proved, in the words of one local blogger, a haven for 'those who have brute strength, money and friends in municipal management'. There's graffiti daubed on some of the walls and gateposts, demarcating the territory of a local drug gang; as I leave the hospital one of the nurses warns me to be careful, to be discreet. For newcomers or former patients alike, it's hard to make a home here when faced with such fear and corruption.

In the last five years an even stranger sight is to be seen across the territory of the former colony: 'Cave Park', a Stone Age-themed water park, rises up from the landscape, the ticket office housed in an arch of faux rock alongside a big green fibreglass dinosaur. Beyond the turnstiles, where I don't venture, the screams of children going down slides and whizzing around the rides are the only noise to be heard in this otherwise desolate place. As with the other new developments, questions were raised as to whether the park had the right planning permission, but it was hailed by local politicians as a sign of progress nonetheless. A community activist who runs a nearby library and social centre lamented that those getting wet and wild under the prehistoric kitsch are likely oblivious to the land's real but more recent history. This erasure contributes to the disintegration of the community. Here were a people who were disappeared first by Brazil's economic imperative to modernise and now their history is being erased by black market speculation. One can be outcast by being removed from one's home, but it also works the other way – to have your home, your history, your memories, removed from under you will leave you just as alienated.

———

At Antônio Justa, age and ill-health have muted opposition. At another former hospital, this time in the far south of Brazil, patients and their advocates have fought back. In 2023 activists working on behalf of residents at Colônia de Itapuã managed to secure a court injunction against the state government of Rio Grande do Sul, stopping further evictions of the elderly patients from the hospital. By the time the law intervened, only three people remained. The former colony once boasted 600 residents, who were by all accounts incredibly industrious. There was a vigorous internal market in operation, trading goods as varied as handmade clothes and prosthetics as well as homegrown vegetables and even meat, the animals taken to a slaughterhouse operated within the confines of the walls. When the doors were thrown open in the 1980s, many, like Lobo in Curupaiti, elected to stay, making this place a home.

By 2021, however, with the industriousness lost to old age, the government decided the residents would have to move. It was announced under the auspices of reintegration, but former patients and their supporters soon discovered a more pressing reason for their removal. The colony is surrounded by the environmentally protected forests of the Itapuã State Park, and the land of the leprosarium amounts to around 10 per cent of this area of the Atlantic Forest. The aim of the local government had been to incorporate the colony into the rest of the park and seek private tender for its exploitation. The state government admitted when pressed that without the hospital land, which is the only space that can be built on, the deal is not very attractive to investors. In echoes of the fate that could have befallen Robben Island, a resort has been mooted, or exclusive housing, with views of the lush green canopy beyond.

For now, the legal notice allows for the patients to remain in their homes; those who were forced out are able to return if they wish. More than that, getting their case taken up by a local politician from the Workers' Party, they managed to have both the buildings and, probably most symbolically, the 'intangible heritage' of the hospital's history protected as part of state culture.

———

The fight to gain land titles in Curupaiti was just as protracted and bureaucratic, and has left a bitter taste. 'We are all old,' Lobo says. 'They were hoping we would just die.' Nonetheless, each former patient, if they had arrived before the gates were unlocked, won not outright ownership of their property but a lease of ninety-nine years – this can be renewed once and passed down to their children (but is not supposed to be sold). I'd heard, however, that all this was threatened by a struggle between the criminal enterprises over territorial control of Curupaiti. When it comes up in conversation, the residents in Rio are understandably wary of discussing it. Lobo says there was 'some trouble a few years back'. What kind of trouble? 'Brazilian problems.' He means – stereotyping – drugs and violence. There are those who acknowledge that such issues continue to be a concern, though only after carefully lowering their voice, the whisper common to many Brazilians when discussing such matters.

When I find Curupaiti on the Map of Armed Groups in Rio de Janeiro, a landmark interactive database geolocating the control of the city between different criminal enterprises, the trend becomes clear. Its records go back to 2006 and, bar the odd shocking incident – a hold-up, the disposal of a body – the hospital seems to have enjoyed relative peace until 2008, when a *milícia* infiltrated favela Morro do Jordão. Then the patients had Comando Vermelho plying their trade across the eastern border wall until 2016, when the *milícia*, at least according to the data collected, crossed into the hospital grounds itself. Teresa (not her real name), whose mother used to be a patient here, tells me that when the *milícia* were here she and her neighbours were charged a R$50 (around £8) fortnightly 'security' fee. 'They were robbing and stealing things from the Catholic Church, from the alcoholics association. There was robbery all around.' The *milícias* are subject to less police repression because there are so many police officers and other government officials, including public servants and elected representatives, who are among their number or who have a financial stake in their corrupt enterprises. 'They had put up signs offering bits of the hospital for sale; there were stretches of cord pegged along the ground in the woods to divide it up into square pockets,' Teresa recalls. Given the struggle to remain in the place so many had eventually come to regard their own, it was galling to see the ease with which the *milícia* moved in to parcel up great swathes of the lush, wooded grounds.

Anarchy did not totally take over, but the story brings to mind Mozambique and the insurgency spiralling out of control. In Brazil, the former patients again got organised and initiated a plan to defend their community with the help of a national patients' rights group, Morhan, which Lobo and others are members of. United, they bravely confronted the criminals themselves. 'We talked to them and said to them, "You want the feds on your back?" And they eventually left. They would have lost their other businesses.'

How to square all this with the pleasant, quiet place I encountered? 'About five months ago Comando Vermelho took the *milícia* out and took over the colony. They don't charge us [any fees] and it's peaceful,' Teresa says. On the wall surrounding the bar, the colony's old ice-cream parlour, the initials cv are sprayed with fresh black paint, a symbol of ownership and reassurance, it seems. 'The drug dealers say that no one can mess with anyone here, mess with any of us in the community. If someone tried to steal a phone here, they would come and find who was responsible.' It is a typical scenario. The guys who sell drugs are mostly local to the neighbourhood, and though their industry can obviously be ruinous to individual lives – both users and the young men caught up in the business – residents as a whole are invariably better off. Without the protection rackets and utility premiums, the general atmosphere of the community often improves if an area is under the jurisdiction of drug gangs rather than the *milícia* or even the state police.

With the state either absent or actively working against them, those in leprosaria must find alternative routes to financial and literal security, even if that security is reliant on criminal enterprise. 'It's a simple life, but I'm at peace here,' Teresa says. 'I help the older residents, I volunteer, I feed the dogs, I love seeing the children out playing, and if they are playing up I tell them to go home.' It is understandable that she, from a family whose life had been wrecked by the government once already, should throw in her lot with such an extrajudicial network. Lobo, who remembers life before, sees it differently. 'The colony has no future. The favelaisation is almost complete.' He sighs, and before stomping off across the cracked square with a grumpy wave, ends our conversation: 'Our home has been invaded by the so-called healthy.'

JUAZEIRO DO NORTE, BRAZIL

The Brazilian president, Luiz Inácio Lula da Silva, stands at a lectern in the Noble Room of the Palácio do Planalto, the country's seat of government. The crowd in front of him is full of excitement and joy for the occasion. A few hundred have travelled from various corners of the country by coach and plane, most of them wearing T-shirts that proclaim *Fomos Separados*: 'we were separated'. Some have little badges bearing the flag of their home state pinned to the cotton: Maranhão, Pará, Piauí, Ceará. They're singing and chanting; they're seated but barely so, and not at all when the selfies start. '*Olê, olê, olê, olá, Lu-la, Lu-la.*' Whistles and rambunctious whoops resound up the building's Oscar Niemeyer-designed ramps and around the government art collection. The fervent joy and noise feel at odds with the institutional gleam of the pristine white modernism, the sleek architecture; it's as though a family picnic has been set up at the seat of power. There are some tears. If the bricks and mortar of the old leprosy colony system is crumbling, here at least, a community still exists.

Some of the people present – the oldest ones, using wheelchairs or with sticks, in their seventies and eighties – have had leprosy. Most are the children of those who were segregated, taken away from their parents on diagnosis or at birth in the leprosaria themselves, placed in the children's homes built especially to house them – designed, apparently, for their own benefit, to stop them getting sick. Other children were put up for adoption, often used as domestic workers, their whereabouts still unknown, their histories untraceable. The president starts his state apology with a personal one. 'I'm sorry, I will read, because if I speak offhand today, I'm going to tell a lot of stories and I'm going to start crying,' he says in his hoarse, gruff voice. There follows a typical Lula speech, his indignant, personable style honed from years of trade unionism, social campaigning, and now in November 2023, three presidential terms.

'They were deprived of the care and affection of their parents,' he says. 'Abandoned children, forced to grow up in segregated places, often victims of prejudice and mistreatment. Deprived of love and opportunities.' He is warming to his theme. His voice grows louder. 'The fight against prejudice is a historic fight. It is prejudice that is the disease. It is prejudice that is the serious illness. And many people need prejudice to survive, because they need hate to survive, and we need to do exactly the opposite of what these people do. No amount of money in the world is capable of compensating or paying for the scars that segregation caused in the souls and hearts of people with leprosy and their families.'

Money will come, however. With a little ceremony, surrounded by his ministers of health and of social inclusion, Lula signs a law into being that will provide the children separated from patients a compensatory pension, similar to the one he introduced for the patients themselves in 2007 during his second term in office. It is small reward for the devastation of losing a loved one, but perhaps as important was the fight to achieve it, opening up a culture of militancy among ex-residents of the leprosaria and their offspring.

———

Rita Cássia Barbosa, now sixty-nine, was diagnosed after a routine hospital visit when she was eight months pregnant. The maternity staff didn't tell her what was wrong. 'I just heard one of the nurses telling another that she must burn the bedsheets and anything I'd touched. I knew it must be serious. I arrived at the colony two days after that.' Rita's father was in a psychiatric hospital and her oldest brother was in jail. 'Our life was so chaotic already, my mother worked so much and she had so much to do with my brothers and sisters, so I came alone.' She was sent to Curupaiti. 'When I arrived I told the man at the gates that I had been sent, that I had this letter, but he didn't believe me. I didn't look like I had leprosy. I was twenty, I was beautiful, a size 10 before I became pregnant. I wore short skirts and had long hair. I didn't fit.' The full implications of her diagnosis still had not been explained to her even by the time she gave birth two weeks later. 'I had told myself I would learn everything there was to know about this disease, that I would have really bad days but I have something good with this baby inside me . . . It was only after I had given birth that I fully realised what I was going to go through.' Her labour was difficult, Rita alone with the medical staff. 'When Geovana was born I asked to see her, and the doctor and nurse said I wasn't allowed. I only found out then that I wouldn't be able to keep her. They wouldn't let me hold her, feed her.' There was one nurse that felt sorry for her, a mother too, who said she would get the baby and hold her up from afar. 'I remember really trying to take in all the details of that moment. To try to remember everything about the child. She had these big eyes, like my own mother.' With her immediate family unable to look after her daughter and the father out of the equation, Rita was told the baby would be well cared for in a children's home, that this was the solution that had been found for many of her fellow patients. Rita and others who went through similar experiences often use the term *orfanato* when they refer to the place – but of course the children weren't orphans.

———

The official term for the children's homes was a *preventório*, or pre-ventorium in English, an institution pioneered by Father Damien in Hawaii. Understanding that leprosy was not hereditary, the priest had removed children from the patients in his care, sending their healthy offspring to Honolulu. Doctors found that Damien's inter-vention seemed to work: of the hundreds of children born on the island settlement, none showed any signs of the disease. More such homes were opened in the Philippines, India and elsewhere. Convinced of their usefulness, Eunice Weaver, the president of Brazil's charitable Society for Assistance to Lazaros, wrote in 1940: 'At present we have in operation eight preventoria, five of which are on an "emergency" basis. More than a thousand children are cared for in them.' Under Weaver's enthusiastic encouragement, that number increased to fifteen and more were under construction.

Weaver, who was bestowed with government commendations in her lifetime and appeared on Brazilian postage stamps in the 1970s, was perhaps well-meaning; the worst of the institutionalised abuse happened after her death. She and her American husband, a mission-ary named Charles, led enigmatic lives: she had first encountered leprosy after she recognised a former schoolfriend among a group of homeless travellers, all of whom had the disease and had been forced out of their communities, banding together for survival. Charles had been Eunice's teacher and they married when they met again as adults, he now a widower. He ended up with a curious job lecturing on the 'Floating University', a school aboard a cruise liner that set sail across the world in 1929, its students on board. Accompanying her husband at sea, Eunice visited leprosaria in Asia, particularly the Philippines, and met with others in the field. She gained an audience with Gandhi, now famous and back in India.

While Weaver described these preventoria in purely beneficial terms – the purpose is 'not merely to rehabilitate the child of the leper physically, mentally and spiritually, but also socially' – like their parents, the children were regarded as a problem that needed to be solved. 'The child, because of its susceptibility to the infection, is regarded with respect to the dissemination of leprosy like resinous lightwood, laid in readiness for burning,' Weaver thought.

Marli da Silva would have been regarded as such tinder. She explains the legacy of Weaver's building spree. Any care or love that babies such as Rita's daughter Geovana received at the home came only from the older children that they lived alongside, a perversion of Weaver's claim that 'twenty or thirty children can live under the direct care of a competent couple, thus enjoying the social environment of a family'. Marli's mother had leprosy, as did her father, a grandmother and a grandfather. She was born in a colony in 1959, the largest in the country, amid the mining operations of Minas Gerais state. The family were moved from hospital to hospital like prisoners in a penal system. The generations became separated until Marli's father died and her mother was also sent to Curupaiti. Marli was five at that point and entered the same preventorium that Rita's newborn would be placed in a few years later. There was a black book in the children's home that had all the names of the people who were in the colony: the parents of the children incarcerated. Anyone in that book could not visit. 'They were blacklisted from meeting us,' Marli says. She looks younger than her sixty-five years and her dark hair is tied back; she pauses occasionally to tuck stray strands away. Visits were allowed on occasion to the colony, but strictly no physical contact was tolerated. 'When you entered there was a room with a glass screen, with a hole in it so we could speak, but when I visited as a child we weren't able to touch each other. I used to escape and run to my mother, grab her legs to give her a hug. The people from the orphanage would drag me off, hit me.'

Weaver had pleaded that a child should be 'removed from its original environment, where there was a lack of hygiene and inadequate nutrition', so that 'under the care of the physicians who watch the child's development and defend him from other diseases, even where there is a predisposition for leprosy, the child may, with careful diet and hygiene, pass safely the years of childhood and adolescence'. Her vision is reflected in one of several films on the subject produced by the Vargas dictatorship's Department of Press and Propaganda. One sings the praises of Educandário Santa Maria, the institution that Marli was kept in, produced a year after it first opened in 1942. The two-minute motion picture opens with a doctor carefully examining a young girl, assisted by a nun. 'The school takes care of the children by providing them with medical care and dental services and offering technical instruction until adulthood', a voiceover enthuses, before the images cut to children tending a garden, undertaking art classes and sitting for story time. 'Wonderful stories always constitute a source of enchantment for the children,' the narrator continues. This fairy tale is far from the reality Marli and others encountered decades later. The facility, a sprawling boxy building on the western outskirts of Rio de Janeiro, immaculate in its modern architecture when it opened, was grim by the time she arrived (just as the country entered its later right-wing military dictatorship). 'The place was infested with rats, cockroaches and bats – it was awful. The bread was mouldy,' she says.

By the time of our conversation, I'd read the reports and heard the testimonies of others from around the country as to what they too had suffered. Somehow, even though I knew how my conversation with Marli might go, where we might find ourselves – in the mind of a child, fighting awful memories – her words creep up on me. The punishment she would receive for running to her mother was the least of the violence. She unfolds her story slowly, stating the allegations calmly until a calm tone would be misplaced. 'I was locked in a room without food, but some of the other kids – we looked out for each other – made a hole to pass me rations. I had no water so they gave me bits of a plant from the garden, which I was able to suck the liquid from.' Her shoulders crumple slightly and I find myself gripping the phone I'm recording the interview on, holding on tight. 'It was like a cactus in the desert.' It is painful for her, but she is telling me this for a reason. 'I wasn't a naughty child, but all the kids were beaten. They forced us to kneel on grains of corn for hours, they had this big paddle to beat us with. I would speak up to them, speak out at them, and they didn't like that so they used to hit me in the mouth. I lost all my teeth because of that.' Other children were the victims of sexual abuse. Marli breaks off, her breath heavier now. A sob. We pause the interview.

———

Those memories account for the euphoria in the hall as Lula inks some sense of justice into Brazilian law. For Morhan, the group of leprosy patients and former patients who were the driving force behind this victory (as well as in the battle for the property rights the likes of Lobo enjoy), these are the latest wins in a decades-long fight for justice. To make its voice heard in Brasília, Morhan first had to build a new network, one that would replace those ties that had been systematically torn apart; a home constructed through slogans and logos, T-shirts and protests, rallies and petitions. With Lula's re-election over his far-right predecessor, Jair Bolsonaro, the political will was there and so was the ammunition, an overwhelming body of witness statements and historic evidence.

Marli recalls the time when she joined the campaign. 'They brought the lawyers to the colony so that they could start to build a case, but no one wanted to tell the story because it's so hard to relive. We sat there with them in silence for so long, until eventually I thought it had to start with me.' Marli says it was awful – she fainted at one point – but others took courage and followed her, their testimonies not just invaluable to the political victory but a sense of healing.

———

Having held up the statute books for the mass of camera phones, the president hugs those surrounding him, starting with a man named Faustino Pinto who had been one of the first to speak at the signing event. Pinto, as national co-ordinator of Morhan, is the successor to Francisco Augusto Vieira Nunes, a patient who took the nickname 'Bacurau' (Nightjar), when he founded the organisation in 1981. When Bacurau contracted leprosy as a child, Amazonas state authorities placed him in a canoe and towed him by motorboat up the rainforest's river to a colony. Bacurau had been expelled from school because of the disease; he had witnessed his father lose his bakery business because of the association and his baby sisters die in poverty. He had been harassed and mistreated throughout his life, but, the legend goes, the final straw was a seemingly minor disagreement with a nurse over whether patients had to wear shirts in the stifling tropical heat. He organised a protest, offended with this petty removal of his rights, which turned into a movement and then became a crusade and a national tour of colonies to raise awareness. It's a beautifully Brazilian start to a revolution: the right to sit and have a beer in the sun with your shirt off.

Faustino's own story is no less dramatic. He has been involved in activism since 1988, a few months after his diagnosis and just a few years after the end of compulsory segregation, precisely because of how protracted the process of that diagnosis was. Like Bacurau, Faustino's childhood was also blighted – not by the actual disease, the fifty-three-year-old says, but by underfunded and incompetent doctors in his home city of Juazeiro do Norte, in the state of Ceará. 'I was diagnosed when I was eighteen, but I actually first got the symptoms when I was nine years old,' he tells me. 'We started looking for treatment but I got misdiagnosed so many times.' He jokes that he probably has super-human immunity against a plethora of diseases he never even had. 'I was given drugs for syphilis; treatment for pano branco, a type of fungal infection. I had syphilis without having syphilis; I had rheumatic fever without having rheumatic fever. I spent two years on antibiotics which were obviously doing nothing for me.' He was then told he might have brain cancer. 'That was very bad, because if it was cancer I'd have to travel to São Paulo for treatment and my dad would have to go with me. Though he had a job – he was in the military – his salary was very low and we'd be on the street and we'd be hungry.' Faustino came to an extraordinary decision for a teenager. 'I decided that if it was cancer, I'd stay and die at home.' At last, after years, his doctor happened to see a public service advert about leprosy on tele-vision. 'He referred me to a medical centre to receive treatment. Having travelled all over the state, almost going to São Paulo, this centre was just ten blocks from my house.'

His joy at receiving a diagnosis was short-lived. 'When I told my parents, they told me not to tell anyone about it.' He refused to keep the secret. 'I was never very good at following orders,' he deadpans. It was a nurse who told Faustino about Morhan originally, but given the organisation's radical reputation, only after they were away from the clinic. 'I was always active in some way, even before I knew the term activism. Standing up for things, even when young,' Faustino says. 'My diagnosis is not what shocked me, what shocked me was seeing how people were being treated in the health centre, so I started complaining and fighting. I wanted things to be better, I wanted to be treated well more than I wanted to get well.'

Morhan takes the motto 'Without the government if possible, with the government if needed and against the government if necessary', and has a long history of militancy. As well as being instrumental in getting the pension for the children and anyone forced into the colonies, other wins include banning the words 'leper' and 'leprosy' in governmental literature and stopping officials from sterilising election booths after patients have cast their vote (which Morhan argued discouraged the suffrage of patients). It has supported research into where medical resources and social programmes are needed most; it has worked with Afro-Brazilian religious groups to ensure traditional priests and healers recognise the symptoms, and run awareness campaigns with the country's biggest football clubs. The compensation awarded to the separated children also makes more urgent a DNA sampling initiative Morhan has in place to find those who were put up for forced adoption, who might not even know the history of their removal (a project based on an Argentinian scheme to trace kids stolen and illegally adopted during its own military dictatorship). The reach of Morhan is international: Faustino and his colleagues travel regularly. He was at Magnus Vollset's conference in Bergen and has travelled from the Vatican to Japan. Yet more important for the Brazilian activist is the work local co-ordinators do beyond these banner initiatives. Morhan has chapters in every state, and in areas where the disease is endemic, most towns will have a representative. They are local campaigners and administrators, helping those affected by the disease with practical issues, but more than that, they build a community among those who have been diagnosed. It is what Hervé Guibert called the 'revolutionary effects' of shared injury (the Frenchman writing in relation to AIDS), the damage of disease invoking 'new complicities, new tenderness, new solidarities'. Likewise, Faustino tells me I should come and see him in Juazeiro do Norte, to see the work he does there. I could fly in to Fortaleza in the north-east – there's a leprosarium there, of course – before getting an overnight coach for eight hours into the Brazilian sertão, the country's scrubby, sun-parched hinterland.

I arrive, legs cramped and eyes dry from the overactive air con, to find a busy town of churches and cheap hotels. They are there to receive over one million religious pilgrims that come four times a year to pay homage to Padre Cícero, a radical nineteenth-century priest considered a heretic in his lifetime, now revered and on his way to sainthood. Faustino is not religious, though, and when the pilgrims come – he had told me when to travel so I'd miss the crowds and price spikes – he stays at home watching Netflix. The suit and tie are reserved for presidents, so when we meet he is in his more habitual shorts and Morhan campaign T-shirts. Over the ensuing days that we hang out, driving around the town, Faustino shows me the sights and makes introductions. He proves a warm and funny host, but it is a humour backed with fiery determination. He's sweet and generous with his time, but I wouldn't want to get on the wrong side of him. (He has met Pope Francis twice and a local health worker wryly tells me that the pontiff is the only person Faustino hasn't picked a fight with.) Faustino relishes his reputation: 'I think I've had battles with every level of government from national to local. I am on the left, I'm a big fan of Lula, but the Workers' Party come with their own agenda and sometimes that might not fit with ours so we are not afraid of standing up to them, too. I am proud to be a nightmare to the politicians.

'We will fight and work with whoever. Even when we had a mayor here in Juazeiro do Norte who was doing a lot of good, sometimes he would get something badly wrong. Well, I don't care, I would march into his office, past his secretary, and I would tell him he was doing wrong, and I would tell him how he was going to correct it.'

One afternoon we're driving down a main thoroughfare of the town, the pavements busy with shoppers and music blaring from electronics stores. Suddenly, at a crossroads, Faustino pulls the car over – he's seen someone I should meet. Cicera, in her seventies, well-built and with a huge roar of a laugh, is both an activist with Morhan and someone whom the group supports. She is a force of nature, giving me a big hug before immediately launching into the news that her left leg, the foot already ending in a stump, will have to be amputated at the ankle. While she no longer has leprosy, the disease severely damaged the nerves and her limbs are prone to infection. I tell her how sorry I am to hear that, a response she shoots down. 'Aff, don't be, I'm not. I'm still going to be dancing.' She later shows me her dancing by twerking round her yard after she's invited us back for coffee and a slice of orange cake. 'These are my people,' Faustino says, laughing at the performance. 'I will do whatever it takes to help them.' Cicera has worked for thirty-five years in a kiosk in Juazeiro do Norte's central market, selling *pastel* and burgers, ice-cold beer and fizzy drinks, to stallholders and shoppers. She was diagnosed after the end of segregation so receives no state money other than her normal pension, which isn't enough to live off.

She tells Faustino that she needs to go to the clinic tomorrow morning, and here the stark economic reality of living with such a condition comes into focus. Cicera has to walk half an hour to the bus stop and travel a further forty-five minutes by bus to the health centre (there's a surgery opposite her house but they don't have the expertise necessary to treat her leg in preparation for the operation). She has put on weight over the years and while she wears a bespoke pair of orthopaedic shoes, walking such distances is painful. Despite this, and despite the ten operations, the amputation of her left foot and the removal of all the bones in her right foot, she says she has no complaints – her daughter is doing well as a manicurist, she has her friends (such as an equally boisterous neighbour, who hears the twerking routine and comes round to offer me what she claims to be better coffee, better cake and a not entirely sincere hand in marriage).

But Faustino says it's not good enough. 'Cicera has been a victim of the system for a very long time. She doesn't get appointments, they make mistakes with her drugs, she gets let down,' he tells me. I would soon see some of his militant spirit in action, as well as how infectious it is among Faustino's peers. 'I've been threatened, sometimes I've felt in danger, I have received death threats. But if I don't fight for these people no one else will.' He offers Cicera a lift to her doctor's appointment the next day; she says she wants us both to accompany her.

The medical unit is a small affair with just a dozen seats in the waiting room, from which patients are called into one of three surgery rooms. Cicera is wearing a nice dress – brightly patterned with red, yellow and blue triangles – because she says I should be taking photographs. As we enter, the receptionist looks disapprovingly at the posse that surrounds the patient, with Faustino the focus of her suspicion. He tells her that I'm a British journalist whom Cicera would like to accompany her. He says I might take photographs. I interrupt to say there's no need, but Faustino holds up his hand and there follows a heated discussion, the speed of which in strongly accented Portuguese eventually loses me. What's clear is that the staff aren't too happy with the idea of the added scrutiny. We agree I won't point my camera, for the photographs I wasn't really planning on taking, anywhere near any of the employees. Faustino says it's a point of principle. 'If Cicera wants to bring someone with her, to her own medical appointment, that's her choice. They don't have anything to hide, so they shouldn't have a problem with your presence.' It is not only an insistence on autonomy for a group of people who have long been denied it, but also a delineation of identity: *these* are my people, don't mess with them.

When we get into the spotless and dazzling white surgery, we wait for an age. Faustino is off chatting to the doctors and other patients; Cicera is lying on the surgical couch, the wipe-clean cover overlaid with disposable paper, impatient because she needs to get to the bank to pay some bills before going to work. The pair of us stave off boredom by sending each other stupid cat memes over WhatsApp. Eventually the doctor arrives, totally anonymised in her surgical mask and hat. She unwraps the bandages around Cicera's foot and first shows us how far up the black patches of infection have spread, a geography that maps out how much of Cicera's leg will have to go, though otherwise everything is fine. The doctor takes a scalpel and starts to remove portions of the blistered, hard skin from the otherwise smooth, rounded end of Cicera's truncated foot. The doctor takes up a device that burns away more of the skin, her patient's leg covered in blue gel that guides the tool, but which also stains the skin for days on end. The doctor checks the right foot, with the boneless toes floppy to the touch, and is satisfied that there is nothing untoward developing. Cicera remains totally desensitised throughout what would otherwise be an extremely painful experience, both physically because of the lack of nerve endings and, it seems, emotionally, worried more about the queue likely forming at the bank.

Faustino introduces me to others in the town. From 2015 to 2022 there were 11,727 new cases reported across the state, 486 of which were in children under fifteen years old. The people I meet are equally sanguine in what I'd have thought must be stressful circumstances. The diagnosis brought a fight, and the fight brought a family, even if not everyone projects the same outward militancy as Faustino. Claudio, handsome in his late thirties, had to give up his job in construction after diagnosis. He seems gloriously unbothered and has opened a small grocery shop from his family's front room to serve the growing favela in which they live. A local spirit brand has painted the front of the concrete-rendered house a jolly yellow alongside their logo; inside are shelves of basic non-perishable supplies for sale: pasta and biscuits, rice and canned veg. The bedroom and bathroom lie behind a pinned-up curtain. Claudio is full of ideas for the store, such as serving rotisserie-roasted chicken or fresh crisps and popcorn, but for now his wife will manage it – he has bought a car on a twelve-payment plan which he hopes to use for Uber driving once they've sorted the ride-hailing app's sign-up bureaucracy. Claudio's two young sons run around as we talk in the shade of the veranda he has built; the oldest, around nine, takes my notebook and pen at one point to carefully tally their keepie-uppie competition, their football slightly deflated (referring back to his notes, I can see his record is an impressive twenty-eight).

I meet hard-working nurses and doctors and administrators, respectful and even appreciative of Faustino's perseverance, doing their best without sufficient funds or decent buildings; in the medical centre, I visit the workshop of a cobbler, the man who produced Cicera's shoes, where he shows me an array of other aids, from straps to help grip cutlery to ingenious exercise devices he has invented to strengthen hand muscles. We meet a community nurse involved in an Internet radio station which broadcasts a mix of funk and samba alongside public health information, and go to a musical instrument library she runs. Everyone seems to know everyone. This is not because of the size of Juazeiro do Norte, a populous and busy place, but because of the network brought together by Faustino and ulti-mately created by the disease. It's a network that taps into state facilities but also sits parallel to it, a system of help based on solid-arity, sometimes anger, but mostly goodwill, as self-reliant as any of the old leprosaria were.

———

Faustino's earliest foray as a spokesperson for patients' rights came when a charity in England published a case study featuring him. It proved successful and helped raise a substantial amount of money. Naturally they were interested in using him again. 'They asked me to come to the UK and I became something like a poster boy. They didn't pay me but they helped with a social project I was starting. Back then I didn't think of it as exploitative or anything like that. I was thankful to them for helping build a better health infrastructure within the state. I thought as long as they are doing good, I'll work with them.' While Faustino does not regret his participation nor reproach the organisation, 'I came to realise that this was not the best approach: it isn't up to a charity in England to fix this stuff, it's the burden of the government. The state should be looking after its citizens, especially citizens who are suffering. So I stopped, and instead we started campaigning.'

It is the conundrum of all social policy in a landscape in which eugenics is a word long banished: how much and in what manner does the state have a duty to intervene in the health of an individual? The strategy of Morhan suggests it is not a question the state should answer itself, but something that should be formulated from the outside – as the body is strengthened by inoculation, so the body politic also needs an outside infection. Faustino and his comrades challenge Brazil's long-held status quo by centring the needs of the vulnerable, pulling out what resources their community requires from the powers that be. It is not a selfish fight, atomising into identity, but rooted in solidarity, improving lives far beyond their own. Disease crystallises the inequity of society, and Faustino's left-wing awakening has illustrious precedent.

Karl Marx suffered 'furuncles', 'boils' and 'carbuncles' that likely helped shape his political outlook; his physical pain – which was excruciating as he wrote *Das Kapital* – was reflected in the pain he saw inflicted on the proletariat. The alienation of disease mirrored the alienation of labour. Marx described to Engels in June 1867, in a series of perversely intimate letters, how the adverse reaction he received from society relating to his skin condition set him apart. 'At all events, I hope the bourgeoisie will remember my carbuncles until their dying day. Here is a fresh sample of what swine they are!'

The 2004 film *The Motorcycle Diaries* romanticises the drama, but certainly the trip then-medical student Che Guevara made across South America with his friend Alberto Granado, six years older and a biochemist specialising in leprosy, was a defining moment on his way to Cuba. The pair scrimped and hustled their way through the continent, making appointments with medical professionals in a bid to gain food and lodging. In Valparaiso, Chile, Guevara, only beginning to give credence to Granado's Marxism, was asked to look in on an older lady, a customer of a shopkeeper who had offered them a room for the night. He found her nearing death, with little he could do. 'It is here in the final moments, for people whose farthest horizon has always been tomorrow, that one comprehends the profound tragedy circumscribing the life of the proletariat the world over,' he wrote in his original journal entry of 7 March 1952. The pair of friends went on to meet exploited mine workers, indigenous labourers, the put-upon and the shut-out, the destitute and the dying. While Guevara's account of the journey is naturally the more famous, Granado's book proves the more insightful. He describes how seminal their encounter with a Peruvian leprologist called Hugo Pesce was to their understanding of society, in which questions of medical ethics catalysed wider questions pertaining to power and economics. When Granado described Pesce as 'the most important person we have met on the journey so far', the reader can assume he meant a political journey as much as a two-wheeled one. 'He has shown us that although environment makes a man, man can change it.' It's a thought that carries through to those whose ostracisation failed to break them but only energised them to fight, to find a familial network through which to enact change.

Granado dismissed most medical professionals as the 'sons of million-aires who get rich exploiting Indians', but Pesce, a member of the Peruvian Communist Party, taught them that the alleviation of stigma was as important as medical science, discussing with his mentees poetry and politics as much as the field research he was conducting.

With this introduction in hand, Guevara and Granado visited several leprosy communities, finding some 'entirely lacking in sanitary or hygienic facilities' – in others, however, under Pesce's radical guidance, a different approach was emerging. Arriving at San Pablo, a leprosarium near Iquitos in the north-east of Peru, in June 1952, Granado writes: 'My first impression of the hospital was that we had arrived at another normal riverside village . . . All the patients live as families.' Several of the shops are run by the sick, he observes:

> These vary from a fishing tackle shop to a bar with a fridge for cold drinks. Others have cleared part of the jungle to grow tomatoes, yuccas, bananas and other crops. Some of them have done so well that they have purchased their own motorboats. This independent way of life – so different from what we knew to be the case in Argentina – instead of propelling patients into flight, ties them closer to the sanatorium and plot of land they own, which has now become their real home.

———

Faustino stops his car at the most grandiose of the shrines overlooking Juazeiro: a mountaintop twenty-seven-metre-high white concrete statue of Padre Cícero, a monument of religious kitsch that surveys a town in which most of the clinics have crumbled façades. We take a disabled spot and Faustino reaches into the seat pocket and pulls out a disability parking permit to display in the windscreen. I realise I haven't really asked him about his own health. Locking the car doors and as we walk to the viewing platform at the feet of the monument, he shakes his head: 'I know I look OK, and I appear fine, but the nerve damage keeps me in constant pain.' He's coming to the end of a new twenty-four-month course of drugs, following a resurgence of the bacteria. 'But I count having Hansen's as something positive. This disease has enabled me to travel to dozens of countries. I've met some incredibly interesting people, I've met celebrities, the Pope, people I would never normally have met coming from my kind of family. Other than having to be hospitalised, and having a lot of episodes that endangered my life, having the disease now, it is a blessing.'

It's a striking attitude, but it makes sense. It is a refusal of 'sameness', a refusal to cover up the 'scars' President Lula acknowledged. Faustino and his comrades were given – forced into – an identity through their condition, one that has long marked them out physically, geographically and psychologically. While modern medicine – if and when efficiently administered – has all but arrested the first, and an unholy alliance of politics and capital is dismantling the second, the third indelibly remains, be it in the trauma of the separated children or the pride and anger driving Faustino's community organisation.

The Bulgarian-French philosopher Julia Kristeva writes in *Powers of Horror* that suffering is where a person's 'subject can be found . . . Where it emerges, where it is differentiated from chaos. An incandescent, unbearable limit between inside and outside, ego and other . . . Being as ill-being.' Ill-being as being became the identity of thousands, *favelados* of the unwell, a subject forged by bad luck and bad politics, by a society that had a vested interest in their marginalisation. Yet people such as Faustino and Cicera have now reclaimed that same identity as a point of pride. In doing so, the erasure of leprosy, they demand, must only be completed on their terms.

KUMAMOTO, JAPAN

O n 31 July 1998, Yasushi Shimura walked into Kumamoto District Court and sued the Japanese government. Flanked by his lawyers, he was wearing dark glasses, a dark shirt and braces holding up well-pressed trousers, his stride determined as he mounted the steps. A small rally of supporters stood outside, and in the coming months this posse would swell. Shimura was joined by twelve other leprosy patients in his lawsuit, three from the National Sanatorium Kikuchi Keifu-en where he still lives, as well as residents of the neighbouring Hoshizuka Keiai-en hospital. Those numbers would also increase as the case progressed, with similar petitions being made to courts around the country.

Their accusation? An 'unprecedented abrogation of human rights' and the 'violation of the Constitution of Japan' carried out systematically, for decades, affecting thousands. Forced labour, unfair incarceration, arbitrary punishment, coerced sterilisations and abortions: the prolonged and purposeful use of stigmatisation as a public health weapon by politicians. Because of strict laws that once mandated sterilisation and abortion for leprosy patients in Japan, Shimura and his fellow claimants are the last few of a generation touched by the state's attempts to control the disease in the twentieth century. Shimura's demands? To be remembered. Once the paperwork had been handed over to the presiding judge, the litigants issued a statement to the waiting media: 'When these have been achieved, we intend to hold memorial services for our forebears who rest in the mausolea in the leprosaria across Japan to bring healing to their sufferings.'

Everything about Shimura's outward appearance that day suggested steely resolve. Anger. Inside, however, he says he was a tumble of nerves and emotions, with little desire for all the publicity. In his pocket he held a small memorial tablet to Misao, the foetus the doctors at Keifu-en had taken away from his wife. 'It is something I rarely discussed even among my friends,' he would later write. 'Even people with the same scars do not want to touch each other.'

———

Keifu-en is a forty-five-minute ride on a two-carriage train from Kumamoto city, on Japan's southern island of Kyushu. It's a journey I would hear about repeatedly. When first diagnosed aged fifteen, Shimura knew something of his fate because his father worked for Japan Railways and told him of the specially sealed carriages that he would sometimes have to couple up. Getting off at the last stop, I wander through a modern medical centre that serves the city's growing suburbs, crossing the road to the drive that leads into the older sanatorium. Keifu-en still feels like a hospital, more than any other leprosaria I've been to. It does share some universal traits with the others: the tranquillity, the nature, the strange uncertainty for a visitor as to whether this is public or private space. Here, however, Japan's Ministry of Health continues to keep the site orderly and clean. Staff wander around in uniforms or ride bikes neatly tagged with the name of the department each vehicle belongs to. The grass is perfectly clipped and signs, which I see a worker soap-sud clean, point to the outpatient dermatology unit or the residents' community hall. On arrival I am proudly shown the room in which I will stay a few nights, located in the new five-unit visitor accommodation block the patients campaigned for. 'We're getting old,' one tells me, 'and so are our visitors.' As I take a pair of slippers from the rack at the front door and swap them for my outdoor shoes, I reply that it's nicer than many hotels I've stayed in.

This sanatorium opened in 1909 to hold the 'national disgrace' of those among the 30,359 people with leprosy at the beginning of the century who had turned to vagrancy or begging. Former police officers were put in charge and invariably brought in their old colleagues to secure what was in effect a poor house. This limited purview changed in the late 1920s when Kensuke Mitsuda, a 'god-like' leprologist with the ear of the Japanese government and the support of the powerful Westernising industrialist Shibusawa Eiichi, began advocating strict segregation for the entire patient population. Mitsuda, like his allies in the colonial offices of the European powers, looked back to a mythic past to justify the 'modernising' action: 'Before the Restoration, as a principle of social order those of leprosy lineages were excluded by the public, and so they naturally came together to form villages and in this way the spread of the disease was forestalled, but after the Restoration . . . all the old ways were destroyed.' The apparent 'old ways' were soon enshrined in law and from then the government zealously pursued what was dubbed the *muraiken undō* policy. Roughly translating as the 'No Leprosy Patients in Our Prefecture Movement', it was a massive government-funded health campaign that 'cleansed' communities of any patients living among them. With the instigation of an annual Leprosy Prevention Day, one observer in Tokyo reported:

> Every street was dotted with tens of thousands of posters advertising leprosy prevention, and on every street corner someone was making an impassioned speech to the passing crowds . . . This shrill noise was accompanied by the sound of a plane overhead making circles while dropping blue leaflets. Standing face-to-face in a crowd, we heard someone say excitedly, 'Ladies and gentlemen! Leprosy is not a disease for which you need feel shame. It is not hereditary. It is within our power to eradicate the leprosy we fear so much. The only way to do this is by strict isolation.'

The 1940 film *Spring on Leper's Island* encapsulated the idea that to submit to the sanatoria was an act of community-mindedness and patriotism. It was distinct from much of the country's cinematic output of the period: less militaristic and nationalistic in tone, the film centred on a female doctor and took inspiration from the memoirs of a sanatorium worker published two years earlier. For all its humanist philosophy and director Shirō Toyoda's lingering shots soaking up the melancholic beauty of Japan's south-east islands, it had no less a propagandistic purpose. Cinemagoers were invited to admire the vocation of Mrs Koyama, the medic, as she gently persuaded patients, otherwise hidden away and dying in shame, to enter a sanatorium where they were well cared-for. The picture was deemed the best of the year by the country's biggest film magazine and unsurprisingly received a recommendation from the Department of Education.

While among the newly institutionalised there were some who entered 'believing wholeheartedly that this was a national project', as one wrote bitterly decades later, for the most part the efforts of *muraiken undō* to segregate patients were bombastic, verging on violent. There's a striking scene in the film in which a group of kids, who are shown searching for fossils in the village stream, observe the health authorities arrive, no less assiduously 'hunting for lepers' among the streets and paths of the island. While the doctors on the silver screen are in suits, their real-life counterparts would arrive at the home of patients masked and dressed in white overalls, pushing trolley-mounted hoses – reminiscent of those used in South Africa, Romania and elsewhere – from which they dispersed disinfectant with such volume and force that property was often left bleached white. While *Spring on Leper's Island* was still playing in local theatres, in contrast to the kindly words of Mrs Koyama, the then-director of Keifu-en wrote to the Ministry of Health to boast of his 'mass sweep' of an area around a shrine that had historically attracted the sick begging for alms:

On July 9th at 5 a.m. a total of 230 people including officials from the two prefectures, under the general command of the Kumamoto prefecture police chief, the Kumamoto north and south police stations, and the Kyushu sanatorium staff, were dispatched. The Honmyoji village was raided all at once and a suspect was arrested for leaking drinking water, taken first to Kyushu sanatorium in a truck and then to the local police detention centre on the premises.

The detention process continued over the next day until all the remaining suspected patients were 'mopped up' – a total of 157 people were taken to the sanatorium that week. Photographs show military-style open-back trucks surrounded by doctors in protective gear and uniformed police in blue tunics. The vehicles are high enough that each patient has to step on a wooden crate as they are manhandled into the back, crammed together like cattle awaiting the abattoir. The resulting explosion in stigma that such spectacle ensured was not limited to the patients themselves. In the kind of testimony that became prosecution evidence decades later, one victim recalled that their name and address was printed in the newspapers the day after she was captured. 'My younger sister and others were working at a company, but when they found out they were fired.' One can gauge the level of hysteria by the fact it inspired a whole new genre of popular mystery fiction, stories serialised in weekly journals which contained all the red herrings, twists and turns familiar of the detective novel, but in which the reader is left guessing not who murdered who, but who infected who with leprosy. Hiding a family history of the disease became the motive for murder in one of the best-loved books by Seichō Matsumoto, the celebrated writer of hard-boiled crime fiction.

Within twenty years the new law necessitated the opening of thirteen national sanatoria which at one time imprisoned around 11,000 patients, representing 91 per cent of all those diagnosed. Now, however, the sanatoria, all still standing, are home to under a thousand residents, most in their eighties or above.

———

At Keifu-en today, aged ninety, Shimura is just as smart and perhaps even a little more chic in his dress than that day in court. Sitting across the table from me in a section of the welfare offices reserved for Zen-Ryo-Kyo – the National Hansen's Disease Sanatoria Residents' Association, for which he is chapter chair – he wears a lounge jacket of fashionable sky blue, smart slacks still neatly pressed at the front and a white T-shirt. If you saw Shimura in the street, there is nothing to suggest he has led and won a revolution, but none of his inner fury has dissipated. He continues to wear sunglasses to protect his damaged eyes. Nerve damage has left his hands permanently clenched; the tips of a few fingers are missing. He now uses an electric wheelchair, travelling the neat roads of the hospital at some speed, requiring the barest of help transferring into a manual to enter the office. He is respectfully received by the staff who are otherwise busy behind desks piled with paperwork. Old photos from the sanatorium's history hang on the walls; a vitrine is filled with shirts and keepsake bats and balls from the baseball team; a whiteboard keeps track of appointments and the association's admin.

'When I first arrived, the doctors here refused to endorse Promin. They said it helped alleviate the symptoms, but that it didn't cure leprosy, despite the rest of the world using it. It drove us to protest,' he says. 'I told the doctors that they were fake, that they didn't know anything and we knew these drugs were effective for us. It drove them mad.' Eventually a limited supply made its way to Keifu-en, but it was nowhere near enough and Shimura was not given any. He was told it would react with the drugs for syphilis – misdiagnosed, like Faustino in Brazil – that he had taken before he'd arrived at the facility. The leprosy was left to progress. He had noticed a spot on his face the year he entered junior high school, but at the hospital, with the most experienced medical staff conscripted into the military and the civilian health system reliant on medical students, he was diagnosed with the sexually transmitted disease. Despite this occurring at the peak of *muraiken undō*, with all the public paranoia, it wasn't until two years later, Shimura's face now swelling and his eyebrows falling out, that the cause of his problems was identified. He was told he had to leave school, though he was not particularly troubled by that. 'I had had enough anyway. It was wartime. Our generation was not one for learning; we had spent our time working the gardens of soldiers who had gone to war.' Militarism permeated every facet of society. Shimura and his year group would have to salute the older kids, who were armed with swords and sent on guard duty.

Arriving at the hospital gates aged fifteen in the spring of 1948, he found the building at bursting point. 'The first person I saw when I arrived with my father was a man in a white coat on crutches, a medic invalided from the war,' he says. Initially he was told the hospital was full and that he would be called back when there was room. He knew he could not go home, though – he would find the house cordoned off, the city sanitation department called in. 'My father had already gathered the whole family around, extended relatives, and told them about my diagnosis. He said that it was likely to cause them problems and that he was deeply sorry about this.' So, rather than risk shame, while they searched for a way of somehow accommodating him, the paperwork was started.

One form would become notorious. Hidden among the stack of papers that the teenager, and thousands of others like him, put his signature to was a consent form for an autopsy to be performed on his body after his death. 'That form is probably still held somewhere here in the hospital,' Shimura says. I glance round to the stacks of filing cabinets that dot the office. More dubiously obtained permission forms would be signed during his stay, including ones allowing the doctors to sterilise him.

Where Brazil built the preventoria, Japan practised eugenics at source well into the late twentieth century. Kensuke Mitsuda explained the policy to the *Asahi Shimbun* newspaper in 1950: 'It will be natural for desperate persons to live only for the pleasure of the moment. But the only pleasures they can obtain in leprosaria are gambling or adultery . . . A moral anarchy has emerged that resulted in more than a dozen babies that should not have been born.' Prior to his vasectomy, Shimura's wife (whom he met at the sanatorium), like thousands of other female patients, was forced to have an abortion. Some women even reported that they went through labour, their baby killed moments after. Though abortion was illegal for the general public, forced sterilisations and the termination of a pregnancy was legalised, in the infamous 1948 Eugenic Protection Law, for 'hereditary' conditions – these included schizophrenia, bipolar disorder, epilepsy, 'remarkable abnormal sexual desire' and 'remarkable criminal inclination'. Consensual operations took place in the case of other diseases. As the Japanese government accepted leprosy as contagious rather than genetic, patients should have been entitled to keep their children, but behind the hospital gates doctors doubled down on the coercion they had already practised for three decades.

———

Those affected by leprosy subscribe to all kinds of politics – indeed many residents' association meetings are fractious occasions because of this – but personally I've met few right-wingers among them. Shimura is no exception to this rule. At first he had little time for politics, kept busy in his work around the hospital. His jobs varied from the mundane – acting as a courier carrying messages between the hospital staff – to being tasked to keep terminal patients company until their last moments. He joined a band (preferring jazz to soul), learned the routine of the sanatorium security and – risking half rations for a week, or worse, imprisonment in the wooden incarceration room that remains preserved on site (near my room, in fact) – he would escape to the cinema (usually to see European rather than American films, though he liked Marlon Brando). He buried his head in books to finish educating himself on his own terms. He started with Guy de Maupassant and the social realism of Tōson Shimazaki. (The story of the school teacher in 'The Broken Commandment', who must hide his *burakumin* background, the lowest caste, resonated.) He soon graduated to Dostoevsky, Camus, Sartre and the proletarian literature of Takiji Kobayashi. 'When the new constitution of Japan was written after the war, I became interested. I started to read about human rights. I didn't want anything special, I didn't start making any particular demands, I just started to see that we deserved the same rights as regular members of society.'

Akira Ota, the deputy to Shimura in the sanatorium's residents' association, wanders into the office. He is a decade younger than the chairman and many others here, slim and full of energy, but he knows the history better than most. He had asked me to send my questions beforehand, which I did, noting that they were probably just a guide to my interest, but nonetheless he carries with him a binder of carefully researched and prepared answers, dates and locations assiduously cross-checked. After the Second World War left Hiroshima and Nagasaki in ash and the Japanese surrendered in the fallout of the USA's atomic bombs, the country was occupied by US forces until 1952. Japan retained administration over most of the country, not least its health policy, and the government renewed the policy of *muraiken undō*. The routine examination of all citizens was implemented and patients were supposed to be hospitalised even if the diagnosis was uncertain. While the residents of the Carville leprosarium and those elsewhere in the US experienced a loosening of the rules from the 1940s onwards, as leprosy became treatable and anything with a whiff of eugenics was found intolerable, there was no such liberation for the Japanese.

Ota personally believes that General Headquarters, as the Americans were known, had a lot to do with that. 'There were going to be bases all over Japan and they were scared that their army would be infected. Wherever the Americans arrived, they sent their sanitation teams first.' The occupiers were interested enough in the sanatoria that they kept a regular tally of resident numbers, but initially that seems as far as it went. Taking a 'pragmatic view', it continued the policy of segregation in the areas of Japan it directly controlled, leaving the Japanese government's policy unchallenged in the rest of the vast archipelago. Having leprosy patients locked away gave the occupiers breathing space to tackle more urgent public health matters including venereal diseases, tuberculosis, dysentery and typhoid. They did, however, aid the importation of Promin, and memoirs of patients kept in the sanatoria in the directly controlled islands of Amami and Okinawa recall convivial baseball games with the American soldiers, who shook their hands and displayed none of the fear and precaution against physical contact that Japanese doctors maintained.

What is certain is that rising militancy within the residents' associations became cause for US concern. The residents' committee at the Hoshizuka sanatorium had started to make contact with other similar patients' groups across the country. It sought to create a national network to bring about change, calling for greater access to Promin, which remained in short supply, demanding better facilities and more freedom. 'The autonomous groups were seen as a dangerous agitation,' Shimura says. By 1950, Mao Zedong had proclaimed the People's Republic of China and the Korean War had broken out. US paranoia in the region was reaching new heights. 'They were stamping down on any organised group, scared of communism. I remember they even tried to stop people gathering at the shrine. They wanted control of all internal affairs, so any sort of organisation was a threat to them.' Suspecting the Communist Party to be behind the militancy, General Headquarters acted decisively and ordered hospital authorities to have the residents' committee in Hoshizuka dissolved. (Likewise, while the Americans had initially encouraged labour rights, they soon reversed their policy as the trade unions strengthened.) Shimura always thought there was a spy planted at Keifu-en. 'There was a particular guy in the welfare office, who we had our suspicions about.' While it is probably unlikely General Headquarters initiated any formal surveillance, they were certainly interested in stamping out burgeoning insurrection and there would have been sympathetic staff members willing to feed them information.

Nor were the Americans entirely irrational in their fear. The Japanese Communist Party, which was a growing political force at the time, *was* interested in the plight of leprosy patients. In 1947 the party kicked up enough of a stink in Gunma prefecture for the Kuryu Rakusen-en Sanatorium to end its policy of forced labour. Afterwards the party publicised the conditions of the on-site prison, in which cells measuring no more than eight square metres kept patients who had attempted to escape the sanatorium or committed other infractions. The prison was unheated, the party's activists pointed out, in winters that fall to way below freezing, and among the ninety-two patients imprisoned, there had been twenty-two deaths. On a national level the party campaigned – unsuccessfully – for leprosy patients' suffrage (something the Americans also supported under the democratisation drive, which had seen women vote for the first time). Were the US forces to look back on past examples of more limited patient self-organisation, they would also find little comfort. In 1932 the director of Sotojima Hoyo-in Sanatorium lost his job after his charges formed the Japanese Proletarian League for the Liberation of Leprosy Sufferers and made ambitious demands for social reform. Believing management had gone too far in placating the patients, a state investigation was ordered, uncovering Esperanto classes and copies of Marx's works in the library, both used as evidence of a dangerously radical left-wing cell.

A few years later the police had to come out to the Nagashima sanatorium, directed by Kensuke Mitsuda, the architect of segregation, to quell a riot. Small concerns over food and wages grew into calls for self-governance, with wooden clogs thrown at staff who turned hoses on their patients. The police found the place in a state of disarray with slogans such as 'Off with the Director's Head!', 'Nagashima Is Hell!' and 'Comrades! Let's Fight Together to the End!' scrawled across the hospital walls. (The US occupation's chief of health and welfare would later assess Mitsuda as 'a first-rate person'.) Was Shimura's residents' group explicitly Marxist? 'No,' he says, before adding with a hint of glee, 'but we were all studying the *Communist Manifesto* and theory of capitalism.' They risked being punished if they were caught with such literature. 'We did it secretly, away from the doctors. The Americans came here several times to investigate.' American personnel began to visit Keifu-en and the other sanatoria regularly – a payday for the rank and file, presumably, as CIA handbooks from 1949 classes contact with leprosy patients abroad as a 'hazardous duty' incurring 'incentive pay'.

———

As the US prepared to withdraw from Japan, the patients took advantage, and the previously thwarted plans for a unified front across the leprosaria came to fruition. Zen-Ryo-Kyo linked residents from all thirteen of the country's hospitals, from the barely populated Miyako Islands way off the southern coast to the Matsuoka Hoyo-en Sanatorium in the north of the country. A network of in-house journals sprang up to share news of campaigns. As well as meeting as a general council, representatives embarked on coalition-making with other organisations, most notably the leftist National Hospital Workers' Union and Japan's Patients' League, the latter originally formed to represent tuberculosis patients. If this emerging solidarity needed a reminder of what they were fighting, one was soon provided. In Yamanashi prefecture, nine members of a single family died by suicide and filicide – cyanide ingestion – after local authorities had performed a very public disinfection of their house, the eldest son having been diagnosed. It was an awful tragedy that enraged the patient body and galvanised their unity.

At the first general meeting of Zen-Ryo-Kyo in 1951, patient representatives sat around a grid of trestle tables, the names of their sanatoria painted on cloth which hung over the edge. While in other countries discriminatory leprosy laws overwhelmingly affected the poor, Japan's regime was so pervasive and efficiently enacted that it touched every stratum of society. The members of the Keifu-en branch come across as a bohemian bunch: glasses, scruffy hair, their hands pushed into the pockets of long coats that wouldn't have looked out of place in the hipper neighbourhoods of

Tokyo. Some Japanese jazz musicians of the era have the same vibe. At the first meeting there was no argument in the calls for Promin; the proposal that *Hansenbyō* ('Hansen's disease') should be adopted as the name of the illness over *rai* ('leprosy') received few objections. The general meeting was also in agreement on the need to challenge cruel or unnecessary characterisations of its sufferers in the media (a struggle, with the legacy of *muraiken undō* deeply ingrained); it was agreed that more doctors were needed and that they would call for improvements to hospital facilities. Divisions appeared, however, in the more fundamental question of whether they should demand an end to forced segregation. If such an action were victorious, would the government just close the sanatoria? If that happened, many patients – those whose family and neighbours had cut all ties – would be left homeless and destitute.

That same year, Mitsuda, now with an Order of Culture to his name, was called as a witness alongside the directors of the Tama Zensho-en and Keifu-en sanatoria to a select committee examining a possible repeal of the 1931 segregation law. Even against the backdrop of tragedies such as that of the family from Yamanashi, Mitsuda was in no mood to budge his support for the tall walls and locked gates. 'Mitsuda frightened the politicians. He said that among the soldiers returning from the war at least 5,000 were likely to have leprosy. Literally an army of leprosy patients was on its way back,' Ota says. He believes that from the seven million demobs it couldn't have been more than 1,000 affected, probably 600 at most. The patients themselves provided evidence from abroad that leprosy wasn't as contagious as previously thought. 'They were the specialists, though, everyone believed them that this disease was so dangerous.'

Despite General Headquarters' remit in the aftermath of the war, residual Japanese nationalism and ideas of racial purity had been allowed to continue, flourish, even, within the country's health policy.

Top political leaders had been tried for war crimes and the military and the powerful Home Ministry were dismantled, but the US was too reliant on much of the old civil structure and personnel to enact any great change. The old guard were also a bulwark against communism, the fight against which increasingly dominated American policy. In 1951 leprosy patients suffered a further blow in the death of the Japanese emperor's mother, who had advocated for them, a loss of a sympathetic voice (though she never spoke out against incarceration). Mitsuda's language became even more uncompromising: 'Leprosy patients must be uprooted, hauled away in shackles, and forcibly quarantined,' he told the politicians. 'Escape must be criminalised and escapees put in prison.'

With attitudes hardening on either side, the authorities feared trouble. On 1 August 1951, a stick of dynamite was thrown into the home of a local Kumamoto official who supported the segregation of leprosy patients. The man survived and a suspect was soon arrested in the village of Suigen: thirty-year-old Matsuo Fujimoto, who police said had recently been diagnosed. By the following year Zen-Ryo-Kyo had agreed internally to call for the dismantling of sanatoria, with the proviso that freedom would go hand in hand with continued material support. They backed their demands up with a threat of mass patient disobedience. 'Our mission and purpose are not only to demand from the government or Diet treatment and improvement in our daily life, but also to be released from suffering and distress in the areas of religion, morals, culture and philosophy,' the group wrote in its new national newsletter. 'Our fundamental aim is rehabilitation into the healthy and cheerful freedom that allows full development as a human being.'

At Keifu-en a general strike was staged, bringing the sanatorium to a halt. The main building and medical offices were occupied throughout May 1952, and the patients unfurled banners that read 'Freedom and humanity even if you have leprosy', 'Patients aren't prisoners'. Anyone entering the offices had to duck under a flag calling for a new social security system. A small stage was built from crates and every day hundreds of the residents would come and sit on the grass, neat in cross-legged rows but boisterous in spirit, to voice their complaints and hear speeches from the strike leaders. The national broadcaster NHK sent a news team and their report initiated a wave of activism. Zen-Ryo-Kyo organised a series of sit-ins outside the Diet, where at one point they were faced with 200 workers from Tokyo's health department dressed in white coats and rubber boots. Nearby, 200 armed police stood ready even more alarmingly attired, head to foot in personal protective wear, including hoods, originally designed in case of a nuclear or chemical attack. In a country in which such catastrophes were so fresh in the memory it was a horrifying spectacle which succeeded in making the patients seem as poisonous as possible. On the last day of July 1953, 350 patients of Tama Zensho-en, a sanatorium thirty kilometres west of Tokyo, broke through its gates and headed to the Diet on foot. When the police stopped them midway along the Tokorozawa Highway, they blockaded the busy road for six hours, the banners intended for the eyes of politicians instead hung from trees by the University of Tokyo's Faculty of Forestry as they stopped the traffic. Residents from Matsuoka Hoyo-en Sanatorium took cars to petition the governor's office of Aomori prefecture; at every hospital the directors were getting nervous.

Shimura was at last able to act on the politics he had imbibed in his reading. He soon joined a few of the patients who took the protest in Keifu-en even further and went on hunger strike. The central leadership council of the Zen-Ryo-Kyo said they couldn't endorse the action, it was too dangerous, and it marked him as an early outlier in patient activism. He lay on a tatami mat alongside several other patients, feeling his pulse slow and the pains in his stomach increase. It was a powerful gesture that spread across the sanatoria, and there were soon eighty-eight men and women around the country getting weaker as they refused food. 'Let's risk death to make soup', one popular slogan ran.

The politicians and doctors remained unmoved. The Diet not only affirmed the old legislation but went even further and enshrined all the discriminatory and coercive tactics already used within the hospitals into the statute books – not least the implementation of thirty-day jail terms for those breaking sanatoria rules, with their directors enjoying something like absolute power. For Shimura, however, the strike ushered in a life of politics: within Zen-Ryo-Kyo and, when he felt constrained by its need for a unified voice, beyond it.

———

Shimura has lived with the Matsuo Fujimoto case since he was eighteen, and he delves deep into the details and his disappointments around the original investigation. He fidgets with frustration as we sit among piles of books and photocopied files, and I get the sense that his days in court back in the 1990s were as much about receiving the recognition of the law that he believes Fujimoto didn't get. On being arrested over the dynamite incident, Fujimoto, an imposing figure with close-cropped hair, was brought to Keifu-en in handcuffs by guards wearing protective masks. The case was already being discussed in parliament in relation to the possible revision of the Leprosy Segregation Law when things took yet another dramatic turn.

A year after his arrest, Fujimoto escaped from his sanatorium cell and went on the run through the flat countryside of the prefecture. Soon after, a child returning home from school along a remote track found a body. The survivor of the dynamite attack, the government functionary, had now been stabbed multiple times. Fujimoto, the obvious suspect, was soon recaptured, injured by a bullet in the process, and faced the death penalty. Representing Zen-Ryo-Kyo, Shimura became a regular visitor. He describes with disgust how Fujimoto's trial was held behind closed doors, the fear of contagion used as an excuse, and how the judge and all the other court officials wore white coats, masks and rubber boots; everyone used tongs to handle paperwork or evidence and Fujimoto was banned from touching anything. Shimura goes into the discrepancies of what type of knife was used; how the court, under the rubric of protecting witnesses from infection, relied on police-gathered statements with no cross-examination; how the witnesses were unreliable; how no blood was found on the suspect's clothes. There is enough counter-evidence to cast doubt on the guilty verdict. Whatever the truth, it is clear the case became swallowed up by both prejudice and the fight for rights, Fujimoto and whatever he might have done inextricably linked with the disease he supposedly had.

For the segregation-supporting elements of the government and the medical establishment the verdict was proof that patients were dangerous, and that whatever draconian measures ushered in via the renewed Leprosy Prevention Law were proportionate and urgently needed. For the patients, it was read as a warning against making trouble. After the Communist Party had had Kuryu Rakusen-en prison shut down, a new national penitentiary for leprosy patients was built opposite Keifu-en and it was here Fuijimoto was kept for a decade on death row. In 1962, still with no visible signs of leprosy, Fujimoto was hanged. 'They never told me,' Shimura says. 'I was cycling over to see him, to talk about where we should go with another appeal, and when I arrived, he was already dead.'

———

During the 1960s an uneasy truce between the Ministry of Health and Zen-Ryo-Kyo emerged. The former listened to the latter more and improvements were made within the sanatoria. Despite the case for mass segregation having been debunked internationally, with life a little more comfortable, calls for revocation of the leprosy laws quietened. Zen-Ryo-Kyo was worried that revisiting the debate would cause splits in the organisation – there were those who viewed the 'free' food and accommodation as a reciprocal arrangement for the confinement, especially as now there was a small chance of some being allowed to leave if treatment could be proved to be effective in the long term. There were even members of the medical staff who flipped the sanatoria image from prison to an abused privilege, characterising those healthy enough to play sport or organise recreational activities as 'people who are idle because of excessive assistance'. In other words, 'if these spongers can't work in the real world, they should be put to hard labour in the sanatoria'.

Ota was one such figure for whom the image of the disfigured 'leper' no longer fitted. He arrived at Keifu-en in 1952, was examined by the director himself and registered as a resident on the day of the diagnosis, moving in immediately. 'I was eight years old, so I didn't really understand what was going on. I wasn't frightened, I think I just took it in my stride,' he says, putting away his notes. He moved into a temporary block for a week before he found a bed in the boys' house, in a dormitory of around thirty-five. There were just as many girls, Ota estimates, receiving rudimentary education that was really just focused on skills they might need for a life within the sanatorium. 'I really loved learning, though, and as long as that was still possible I was happy. The regulations were strict, the kids got punished, but for now it didn't feel like a prison, but a place for education.'

It wasn't until he was fifteen that the limited horizons of the walls began to eat away. Ota was fit, thanks to Promin, and his junior school days had come to an end. He heard that a high school had been established in the island sanatorium of Nagashima Aisei-en, that it was the only chance for kids within the hospital system to continue education. Niirada High School had been founded in 1955 as a small consolation for the failure to overturn the Leprosy Prevention Law. Zen-Ryo-Kyo had originally campaigned for three such educational establishments, but in the end only one materialised, and it could accommodate just a tiny fraction of the teenagers scattered across Japan's leprosaria. Entry was by exam and offered a maximum of thirty kids the chance to become more than just a patient – even if the teachers, with Mitsuda still sanatorium director for the first two years of its life, wore the omnipresent white overalls.

Ota was able to join the fifth intake and soon found that, like him, the boys of Niirada High School were baseball obsessives. The bat and the uniform in the vitrine, here in the office, they're his? 'Of course!' he says, eyes brightening. After classes the boys would gather in their dorms to weigh the batting averages of heroes such as Yasumitsu Toyoda and Futoshi Nakanishi or cheer as Osamu Mihara led the local Nishitetsu Lions to three consecutive Japan Series wins. Nor was it just the statistics of the professional league that they could reel off to each other, but the National High School Championships too. The teenagers had their own team, of course, but despite their talent they knew they would never have a chance to compete, locked away on the island. Their competition was confined to the adults of the sanatorium every Sunday. The kids were at an advantage. Mostly diagnosed after treatment had become more widely available, few of the boys had the kind of disabilities the adults had, and those that did have problems found ways of playing that navigated around whatever damage the disease had left on their bodies. Ota was the shortstop and would be placed third batter.

In the summer of 1960, Ota and his friend Sukeo Hirai, a North Korean, both aged sixteen, were desperate for new challenges on the field. Out of that came a plan which in its own way was as radical as any other protest. They were not allowed to go home for the school holidays, but they were allowed to apply to visit their home sanatoria in certain circumstances. Each of the squad would request to do this, citing different reasons. If they got permission, they would trek to the train station after the boat had dropped them off on the mainland and meet up there. Hidden in their bags would be bats and rubber balls, and the kit they had made with 'Niirada' spelled out in typography borrowed from the Nishitetsu Lions. The boys didn't entirely deviate from the lie they'd told the doctors in Nagashima, sticking to visiting only the sanatoria each of them originally came from and where at least one of the team had friends. The sense of adventure was palpable as the train pulled out of Okayama. Their first stop was Gotemba, where they won their first game against the local patients' team. 'I got a home run, I saw Mount Fuji for the first time,' Ota remembers. 'It is something I never thought I would do in real life. It gave me hope.' They were given food and lodging, the authorities not entirely impressed by their enterprise, but 'we were welcomed, I think we just won them over. We were so young and energetic, full of enthusiasm. They knew we just wanted to play baseball.'

While Shimura takes a break, Ota and I pore over the team photos: they're all so smart and handsome, full of charm in their white tops and shorts, caps and long socks. Strong legs taut as they squat for the camera, they hold their baseball gloves aloft. 'That's Mr Hujisaki. I went to his funeral last week. A great player, my best friend.' Hujisaki stands at the front leaning on two bats he clenches. 'That's Mr Sukeo Hirai. He returned to North Korea and trained as a doctor. Of course, I've not heard of him since.' Hirai is tall with a square jaw, possibly the strongest physically – he would have been one of the tens of thousands of Zainichi Koreans lured back by Pyongyang's 'paradise on earth' repatriation campaign.

The boys would play against the staff teams of the sanatoria, too, promising each time that this would be their last game, that they would go home after this. Their teachers in Nagashima put out a return order, but buoyed by success, the renegade Niirada High School Baseball Team added most of eastern Japan to their stats: wins in Tokyo, wins in Gunma, wins in Miyagi prefecture. Just before the September rains hit Japan's far north, they arrived, confident, at Matsuoka Hoyo-en Sanatorium. They begged for beds as usual, before proceeding to beat the residents' team, also as usual. Then they faced the staff team. Annihilated. 'They were a powerhouse,' Ota says mournfully. 'They had a few former high-school league players among them. It was our last game.' They had reached the end of the country. 'Our only loss.' With that, they packed up their kit.

―――――

Lethargy and division are the enemies of any protest movement. By September 1995, when a patient named Shima Hiroshi received a letter, the original radical spirit of Zen-Ryo-Kyo had dimmed into an acceptance of the status quo. It seemed to Shimura and others that the patients had adopted their prison. They would disappear behind the walls, and all their history would go with them, little known. Hiroshi operated a literary journal from the confines of a sanatorium near the city of Kanoya, also in Kyushu; the letter he received was from a man who had haemophilia and who had become HIV-positive after receiving contaminated blood. It was a major scandal in the country during the 1980s and those affected had sued the government. His question was simple: why weren't leprosy patients enacting similar action for compensation? Why weren't they telling their story?

Hiroshi, galvanised, in turn wrote to the Kyushu Legal Association. He berated them for their apparent lack of interest in those locked away in the sanatoria. 'One would think that no one would have a deeper concern for human rights than the legal profession and yet you continue to sit back, offering no analysis or statement about the Leprosy Prevention Law,' he complained.

The patients found support in unexpected quarters. Anime master Hayao Miyazaki had started to visit the Tama Zensho-en Sanatorium some years earlier and had struck up a friendship with the leader of its residents' group. It inspired him to incorporate leprosy patients into his hit Studio Ghibli film *Princess Mononoke*, those with the disease shown sympathetically as skilled weapons-makers – 'we know what rage feels like' says one – devoid of the cinematic horror and sensationalism that had gone before it. It is perhaps natural that a man as interested in storytelling as Miyazaki would find inspiration here. The residents' history proved to be their most cherished possession. The government took everything else: their homes, their livelihoods and futures, their families and their choice to have children, and the possibility that that son or daughter, grandson or granddaughter, might remember them fondly after they were gone. Their story, whatever version of the history they had written for themselves, was the only thing, a warning based on their lives, that they had to leave the world. Not to disappear in death, as they had done in life, was as important as any change in the law.

'To articulate the past historically does not mean to recognize it "the way it really was",' Walter Benjamin wrote. 'It means to seize hold of a memory as it flashes up at a moment of danger.' In this vein, Zen-Ryo-Kyo began to build its soft power, not just at the movies but also through the construction of a series of museums. Today, all Japan's sanatoria have such institutions, all established by the patients themselves, permanent storage facilities for a collectively lived life, a repository of a people whose social attachments were systematically destroyed. The patients of Tama Zensho-en in Tokyo were the first in this endeavour, opening in 1993, then a ragtag affair of memorabilia and information. I visited a few days before I caught the train to Kumamoto. With professional curators and historians replacing the patient volunteers as age and disability rolls in, I found a slick, sizable institution, its architecture contemporary; money had obviously been spent generously. Inside, the curators told me they struggled with the partisan verve in which the exhibits were organised, an anathema to their academic training, but a person kept apart from society can only be partisan. It is etymologically foretold, as much as emotionally understandable.

This publicity drive sparked attention. With new leprosy cases dropping to insignificant numbers and residents of the sanatoria now at half the number of the population at its peak, there was little appetite to uphold the Leprosy Prevention Law among a new generation of politicians. In the spring of 1996 the government repealed the laws requiring mandatory segregation. There would be no reparations.

That this happened with so little fuss, and with so much history left unresolved and unobserved, did not sit right. After the Kyushu lawyers responded positively, Hiroshi realised he needed allies and knew instantly Shimura would be a likely friend. 'I wanted to go back to society,' Shimura says. 'But how could I go back empty-handed after all those years?' It was about money, yes, but also, again, about erasure. The majority of the patients, who, on average, had been in the sanatoria for forty years each by that point, were approaching or just past retirement age. One, who joined the action later, puts it even more bluntly: the government sought to 'quietly bury the atrocity'. Officially Zen-Ryo-Kyo decided it couldn't lead any action, that for too many of its members such a move would, as Shimura puts it, 'wake the sleeping baby', but it wouldn't stand in any patient's way were they to take charge. Shimura became the first plaintiff in the 1998 action.

Joining Shimura in the witness stand for the best part of three years was Isao Tateyama, a great pitbull of a man who took no prisoners in his testimony (he would go on to be Secretary General of the Nationwide Council of Plaintiffs). Mizoguchi Seiji, whom Shimura calls his 'comrade since a young man', was also present, though he was frail through the disease by this point and found walking hard. There was no need for him to attend court. He could just let the lawyers file the paperwork and present his testimony. He refused, though, telling Shimura he would 'walk the case with my own two feet'. The plaintiffs had all suffered so much; suffering was no longer extraordinary or something to be feared. Mizoguchi, who died in 2011, wanted to be seen.

The lawyers knew that with such a small band of litigants, and with so few willing to risk more public ridicule and stigma in telling their stories directly, they would struggle. The government would likely dismiss them as troublemakers; discredit them as radicals. They knew that sovereign immunity was likely to be asserted, as it had been in cases brought by prisoners of war, Koreans and Chinese forced into hard labour, and foreign atomic bomb survivors. Shimura says he and the others tried to solicit support from their neighbours. Many were sympathetic but 'it was hard to get them over the line'.

Instead, building on the experience of previous class actions, the lawyers put together small support groups – the people who cheered Shimura on the steps of the court the first day. The local law group reached out across the country to colleagues who had, pro bono, represented victims of industrial pollution, defective drugs and the atomic bombs – email was just reaching ubiquity so things were able to move faster and reach further than ever before. They mobilised to bring in more plaintiffs. The Kumamoto lawyers dug deep to find journalists who had been sympathetic to the contaminated blood actions and offered them personal testimonies. They pushed for local press attention, hoping to build momentum for the story to break through to the by-now more homogenous national and mainstream media. The hardest part, Shimura says, looking away from me, was giving these interviews, talking about the coerced operations. I always shift a little uneasy in my seat when someone says something like this. 'In the end, though, I wanted the country to return my child, my lost child. I wanted them remembered and recognised before it was too late,' he says. Thanks to his testimony in court, Misao's name remains preserved in legal perpetuity.

A breakthrough came. A group of residents from Tama Zensho-en joined the action. The government made some tactical missteps. When the state came to lodge its tone-deaf defence, the lawyers for the plaintiffs ensured it was well-publicised:

> In that the quarantine policy for leprosy patients which existed in Japan for ninety years was in no way counter to internationally accepted knowledge, nor to domestic knowledge, and since it provided for the humane treatment of patients, it was not unconstitutional . . . Since vasectomies and abortions were performed with patient consent, they were not forced . . . For ninety years, the government carried out its leprosy policy with charity and generosity.

With such hubris, the trickle of claimants became a stream, a river, until all the sanatoria along the Seto Inland Sea had joined in. Usami Osamu, who had not only lived with Mitsuda's influence on government policy but also experienced the firebrand's attitude towards patients first-hand at the Nagashima sanatorium, wrote in a memoir: 'My blood boiled. How could they say such things? What about the blood and the tears that had been shed? These arguments were completely unacceptable. They offered no excuse or apology to all our forebears who suffered and suffered and were now gone from this world. What spurred my heart and mind into action was this.' A local court soon received his complaint, alongside thirteen of his neighbours, in June 1999.

Two years later, a fifth of the sanatoria survivors that were still alive had put aside fears that legal action might make their situation worse and were suing the government. Over a hundred lawyers were turning up at courts up and down the country to represent almost a thousand residents. They showed how Japanese doctors had been at post-war international leprosy conferences in which forced internment had been discredited, and the lawyers provided evidence of the effectiveness of Promin. The government defence team said reliable drug treatment did not become available until 1981, referring to the multidrug therapy, but even by that measure discriminatory laws were kept in place for a further fifteen years. Inspired by the letter that had started all this, the plaintiffs argued that the treatment of leprosy patients shaped wider government policy towards the most vulnerable. The public indifference the government engineered, the lawyers said, set a precedent, not least the enactment of the AIDs Prevention Law in 1989, which sought to curtail the epidemic through fear and stigma and met with little outcry. Now, however, the national media were reporting on it. The whole country was watching.

———

On the eve of the court's decision, boxes containing a petition of 120,000 signatures calling for a fair verdict were paraded outside the court, and hundreds turned up for a rally in Kumamoto. Poems were read, testimonies were given. Lanterns were lit from each of the san-atorium ossuaries to represent the dead. As they entered court the next day, Shimura says that one of his fellow litigants whispered to him he was wearing new underwear: he would jump from the court roof if it went against them. 'It was our one chance,' Shimura says. On 11 May 2001, the judge sided with the patients and found all previous leprosy prevention laws to be unconstitutional. The government should apologise and pay compensation.

Shimura says elation came slowly. Hearing the judge's words, he felt nothing at first. There were no tears. He has a memory of seeing one of the legal team slip out of the court door. The man was heading to the crowd waiting outside to inform them of the decision. It was only when Shimura heard their delighted roar, muffled by the stone walls of the old building, that it sank in. On the same courtroom steps he'd walked up three years earlier, he gave some interviews before heading back to the sanatorium. Such was the efficiency of the plaintiffs' operation, its newsletter delivered the verdict to each cottage around Keifu-en before the evening paper carried the same news.

The jubilation quickly gave way to greater anxiety. If the government were to appeal, as it had done for every other class action concerning human rights, it would likely draw the already long process out to a decade. If that happened, many of the litigants would be dead before they knew whether justice had been done. Once the judge landed his verdict, a two-week clock started ticking for the government to make its next move in the mandated time limit. All attention turned to the Japanese Diet. The publicity and rallies the campaign had sought were designed with two aims: the first had been to attract more claimants, and the second now came to the fore, the lawyers hoping it would force the government into submission and embarrass them into abiding by the court ruling. The legal team were pessimistic, though, advising that it was likely the government would first appeal and then try to negotiate a settlement behind closed doors.

It was time, once again, like in 1953, to sit on the pavements outside parliament. This time the image was very different. The patients were older, often frail, and elicited more sympathy. Residents of the sanatoria, no longer young men and women downing tools behind impenetrable walls, returned to tatami mats for hunger strikes. The Minister of Justice agreed to meet the plaintiffs. *Sankei Shimbun*, the conservative newspaper, came on side. News cameras turned up to film sacks of postcards and letters being delivered to the government, each missive simply stating: 'NO APPEAL'. As the deadline inched closer, the patients and their supporters maintained their nervous vigil outside parliament. The executive body of Zen-Ryo-Kyo joined them: this was no longer the cause of a few outlier radicals but the fight of all the former patients, whether they were named in court or not. They wore red bibs: 'NO APPEAL, LET'S GET A RESOLUTION'. The red flag of Zen-Ryo-Kyo hung behind them as speeches were made to the media and public. Parliament security said that if they continued this occupation, they would be forcibly moved. In response, a group of female Diet members from across the political spectrum came out and encircled their encampment, urging the parliament police to back off. It was a gesture that allowed some optimism to creep in.

On 23 May, a day before the court's deadline, Prime Minister Koizumi Junichirō agreed to meet Shimura and a small band of the other patients. The newspapers reported that one woman made the premier weep as she told him her story. Twenty-four hours later, in an unprecedented move, the government capitulated. No appeal.

EPILOGUE
THE EDGE OF SETO INLAND SEA

Nagashima Aisei-en and Oku Komyo-en are island sanatoria, divided from the mainland by a hundred-metre strait. For the residents that water was the symbol of their estrangement, and after years of campaigning a bridge was built in 1988. Its blue arches jump into view from around a sharp bend, coming towards the end of my winding bus journey from the city of Okayama, the stops on the road numerous as we make our way through the oyster-shucking villages that feed off the Seto Inland Sea, the waterway connecting the Sea of Japan and the Pacific Ocean. The bridge is an unremarkable construction but is dubbed 'a bridge to restore dignity' – a few months earlier a celebration had been held to mark thirty-five years since its completion. It was always going to be more than a useful piece of transport infrastructure. 'I was happier when the bridge was built than when the leprosy prevention law was abolished in 1996,' a former patient told local media on its anniversary. 'The bridge is visible, isn't it? I thought it would help people in society to understand that it was not a disease to be afraid of.'

The bus has now emptied of the seafood industry's migrant workers and I ring the bell at a stop at which there seems to be little going on. Down a path from the road is Oku Komyo-en. There were never supposed to be two sanatoria on the island, but in 1934 a typhoon hit Japan. The city of Osaka, some 150 kilometres north of here, and its Sotojima Hoyo-in Sanatorium, nearing completion, received the brunt of the storm, leaving both in ruins. Of the 3,036 people who died in the disaster nationally, 187 were patients at the sanatorium, together with several of the construction workers extending the site's capacity, a sanatorium nurse, a hospital cook and a hospital cleaner. Photos of the aftermath show a flattened landscape, the wooden buildings splintered into untold fragments like driftwood littering a beach. The 400 patients who survived, who had made lives in the hospital despite everything, were dispersed around the country while discussions were held on rebuilding. Instead, a new site was proposed, near Mitsuda's fiefdom of Nagashima. With protests by local residents overcome, defined by everyday nimbyism and fear of the disease in equal measure, the building of Oku Komyo-en was finished in 1938. The displaced patients were moved once again, far from any of their original homes, to be cared for by a wartime skeleton staff.

———

Today the remaining seventy or so patients at Oku Komyo-en are possibly the best-represented politically of the sanatoria. Takeshi Oku is both the leader of the local chapter of Zen-Ryo-Kyo and the national president of the patients' association. Oku arrived by boat to the sanatorium later in life than most, aged thirty-two in 1974. He was put in a quarantine unit for two weeks before being assigned a dormitory. Oku remembers being asked lots of questions and meeting them with attitude. He had been pulled up and identified by a public health officer at random, and after confirmation of the diagnosis was brought here within the week. It was all so sudden. He broke up with his girlfriend, though she offered to come with him, thinking that his stay would just be for a year or so; he left a job in the telecoms industry where he'd worked since taking an apprenticeship. For Oku, the doctors waiting for him were like the opponents he used to square up to as an amateur judo and sumo fighter, enemies to face down and force into submission. He refused to take a false name, like many did; he didn't answer their enquiries as to his religion. This aggression was not just reserved for the staff either, Oku says, as he spreads out on a sofa in a plain office to the side of the sanatorium's museum. He felt he didn't fit in; so many of the other patients had arrived young and were institutionalised. 'The place was dark and falling apart,' he says. 'My room was full of people in their sixties – these were old people for me then.' He bought a car and started working as a taxi driver within the confines of the island. Keeping his own counsel for over a decade, he had no time or inclination to be involved in the local politics. He just wanted to make money and get out.

Aged eighty-one, still a bull of a man with closely cropped hair but now in a blue pinstripe suit and open-collar white shirt, Oku's aggression has been replaced with pragmatism. He is writing what he believes will be the concluding chapter to the patients' struggle – he is likely to be the last president of Zen-Ryo-Kyo. Two of the local associations have already ended their activities, the ageing residents of those sanatoria no longer having the energy to continue. The way Oku speaks is akin to an elderly relative who knows that their time in this world is limited; one who has seen too many friends die and wishes to get their affairs in order before it's their time to go too. 'I have seven years to achieve everything,' referring to his term of office prescribed by Zen-Ryo-Kyo's constitution. 'Seven years to ensure that we are comfortable in our old age and to work out how this story of ours ends. How will the government close its century-old Hansen's disease programme? How is our memory preserved? There is a lot to do.' The will needs to be made, the last of the DIY done, the family recipes written down – except the loose ends Oku has to tie up belong to an entire generation.

At Oku Komyo-en, Oku has an ally in Dr Yoshinori Aoki, the supervisor. The days of the patient body and medical faculty having the relationship of prisoner and guard are over. In Aoki's office, I ask how he got into the field. His answer starts in an unexpected place. From a young age he wanted to work the trains, not an unusual childhood dream, but one that Aoki continued to pursue right up to his twenties. By then, however, Japan's rampant neoliberal transformation had seen the lines privatised, with any unprofitable sections and local stations abandoned. 'I grew up in a rural area and it felt like the authorities were just throwing away whole communities, leaving them cut off and isolated. It affected me a lot, and I decided that's not something I wanted to touch, so I abandoned that dream.' Medicine seemed a better route for him, but unlike many in his coterie of student doctors he was as interested in the social aspect to care as the medical, and a field trip to Nagashima put him on the right track.

Aoki's biography lies at the heart of much that I've wrestled with when hearing the stories of questions of governance. Where is the line between the abject anarchy of Cabo Delgado, the control of Robben Island and the abandonment of Hospital Curupaiti in Rio? Aoki is determined to right the biopolitical wrongs of his predecessors. 'After the trial the government apologised, local governments apologised, the education sector apologised, religious groups apologised.' The Anglican Church in Japan apologised for not campaigning on behalf of leprosy patients when asked to do so and the Ohtani Sect of Jōdo Shinshu Buddhism admitted it had been wrong to promote the policy of *muraiken undō*. 'Nothing came from the medical establishment, though, and I still get the feeling that many don't think they did anything wrong, that they have no regrets.'

Shimura's court case laid most of the sanatoria's skeletons bare but it hardly touched on the issue of autopsies. In this hospital alone an estimated 70 per cent of the dead were dissected, either without consent given by the person in their lifetime or with consent improperly obtained. I think back to those specimens in jars that I saw in Hansen's lab in Bergen. When the plaintiffs of 1998 were compiling their case against the government, lawyers took the court to see mortuary and dissection rooms here, having discovered over 800 specimens carelessly stored in plastic containers with no proper labelling, ranging from internal organs to body parts, as well as forty-nine foetuses. Biopolitics to necropolitics: is it surprising a patient's story was given an epilogue of post-mortem politics? It is likely there were many more dissections too, even older, from the days of Sotojima Hoyo-in, which were washed away alongside any records in the typhoon waters. Dr Aoki wished to further the investigation to establish the exact circumstances in which the macabre collection was obtained. He brought together a panel with Oku and other patient representatives, lawyers, and human rights professionals to make a forensic investigation into what went on, discovering not least that post-mortems were continued even after 1998 by his predecessors, the question of consent still a grey area. The fifty-seven-page publication that resulted is the nearest one might get to resolving this crime scene: forensic photos, maps, testimonies from former technicians (many of whom were operating under either the assumption or reassurance that they were working ethically), specimen numbers compared with population figures. 'It is simply there', Aoki says, sliding the grey-covered report across the table, 'to be a record of the truth.'

Neither Oku nor Aoki have an answer to what might be their most pressing issue. The Japanese government has pledged to keep each hospital open until the last patient dies, but neither man really believes that with just 720 people left the politicians mean to keep their promise. Worse still, even discussing the issue has become a huge taboo among the patients, leaving the past scrupulously excavated but the future uncertain. For some of the sanatoria, ensuring their relevance is easier: Keifu-en is surrounded by urban sprawl and could pivot to become a more general site of elderly residential care.

Oku Komyo-en and Nagashima, with the bridge, have villages that
provide small custom for outpatient services. It is unlikely, though,
that people would be willing to send their ageing relatives to the
more remote places. 'At the moment, we don't have enough resources
to open up to a wider public, so for that to happen, instead of winding
the programme down, we would need more money, not less; more
doctors, not fewer,' Aoki says. Of course, it is the Japanese taxpayer
who is paying for this and the country's economy is barely emerging
from a thirty-year torpor, with public spending remaining tight (and
prejudiced towards defence). 'I'm not sure what will happen. As the
populations get smaller, I can see the government requesting sanatoria be merged, or patients moved. I can't say that will happen, but
that would be my guess,' Aoki says. If we were to consider this issue
by the reckoning of the accountant's ledger alone, each hospital is a
terrible inefficiency, and yet the residents here have spent a lifetime
bending to the will of the majority. Oku says he will fight till the end.
'As long as Zen-Ryo-Kyo is around, I won't let the mergers and
closures happen.' If that's the case, it presents perhaps an even greater
fear for the residents of each sanatorium, barely ever even whispered:
don't let me be the last one to go.

———

Look at a map of shipping routes across the Seto Inland Sea and they
all seem to skirt the island of Oshima. It is the next day, a little
further along Japan's southern coast, and I'm trying to make my
appointment with the National Sanatorium Oshima Seishōen. Mr
Shimura had told me that he thought it was perhaps this hospital
that had swayed the judge's decision in the 1998 court action. The
plaintiffs' legal team had taken him on various site visits, but it was
coming here, seeing patients marooned on this remote island, that

persuaded the court that the sanatoria were more prisons than hospitals. My translator Tomo and I are standing outside the administrative offices of Takamatsu Port, unsure of what to do next, since the sanatorium is not served by any of the commercial ferries. The staff at the ticket booths had quizzically asked if we even have the right permission to land there. After Tomo answered yes, they directed us to this nondescript office round the back of the block. It's closed, but at this point a man in overalls comes over. He asks if I'm the British journalist. Tomo tells him I am and he says that we need to ring the hospital administrator. It transpires there's been a death among the residents; we can still come but it's possible that everyone will be too tied up with the funeral to meet us. He tells us that there is a single vessel that goes there, a government ferry taking staff and contractors over. Once we've had our credentials checked, the port worker directs us to the boat and we have just a few minutes to board.

If others on the harbourside were off on sightseeing tours, then our journey proves no less picturesque, though the boat with its plastic seats has none of the cheery livery of the tourist crafts. Navigating beyond the harbour arm and its stacks of shipping containers we are soon out into the clear water, an expanse of shimmering silver from the strong sun. Islands spread like broken patches of moss across the horizon, lushly green and often uninhabited. Bar an elderly woman using a wheelchair – a resident and former leprosy patient returning with a carer from a hospital visit on the mainland – our few fellow passengers are in workers' uniforms and rest hard hats on their laps. Twenty minutes on we come to rest at a wooden pier, its varnished surface in stark contrast to the jagged rocks on which it is built and the postcard sand dunes that trim the island's edge. The ferry door open, the other passengers disperse through the trees towards the sanatorium village. The road markings are fresh and white, the nearest buildings as spotlessly maintained as every other hospital in this country.

Kazao Mori is able to meet me. He is exemplary of the extraordinary amount of intellectual and artistic output that Japanese leprosaria have produced generally, having written both in the media when he was head of Zen-Ryo-Kyo and in academic papers. In this fashion, perhaps these sanatoria aren't so removed from the medieval religious communities patients lived in of old, throwbacks to before extractivist capitalism colonised every waking hour and became the prevailing belief system. Where in the Middle Ages leprosy could usher in a life dedicated to theology – or horology, in the case of the bishop of St Albans – in Japan, poetry emerged. Tankas of exquisite beauty and ennui were written in such profusion by so many residents across the country that it constituted its own genre of so-called 'leper literature'; sanatoria became fissures in society, separated from the requirement to be economically productive, in which learned pursuits were allowed to grow. The residents, albeit against their will, were afforded time.

Mori describes how the sanatoria might be considered 'extra-territorial spaces'. The term is more often used to denote diplomatic or military sites in which the law of the surrounding country holds no sway: embassies, foreign army bases and the like. For Mori, it explains how things illegal under Japanese law were allowed to take place within this site and others: the abuses; exploitative pay levels for heavy labour; the autonomy of sanatoria directors to punish and imprison without trial and right to appeal. The patients undoubtedly suffered as a consequence, but I also wonder whether the 'extra-territorial' nature of their treatment gave a little space for something special: utopian seeds in places separated from the dominant narratives of society.

In Romania, it was escape from the secret police; in Mozambique, a sense of solidarity against the violence; the radical spirit of the Brazilians forged in adversity; those marooned on this island by the Japanese state avoided the stifling nationalism that led the country in and out of war.

These people, reduced to a small community, were a catalyst for good to happen. In Nagashima, where Mr Oku went to school, those residents not interested in baseball founded a stargazing club. Using a donated Newtonian telescope (technology that would have amazed Richard of Wallingford), they passed on seventy years of sunspot data to the Tokyo Astronomical Observatory. It seems natural that patients, extraterrestrials here on earth, a people living in the orbit of society but not of it, would be drawn to space. In a world of nationalism and tribalism, of this and that, us and them, their treatment was a crime – but leprosy also gave space in which empathy and solidarity grew. If anti-leprosy programmes provided a blueprint for segregation and subjugation, then the fight and spirit of the patients offers us a vision of a world mended through care and reparation. Mori and I are talking in this vein when a whirling alarm sounds across the Tannoy system that stretches the entire length of the island. The last rites of his neighbour are about to begin in the community hall. It cuts the conversation short; my last interviewee excuses himself.

———

In Japanese custom the bones of the deceased are usually kept in a family ossuary, close to those one loved in life. For many here there are no relatives with whom their remains will lie. Even worse is that there are families who are still too afraid to admit that the disease has sat in their bloodline, relatives scared of what their neighbours or in-laws might think, who would rather the remains of their dead are hidden in the sanatorium's domed ossuary.

Not wanting to get in the way as people drift over to the hall, I take a walk, and a tinkling instrumental tune takes the place of the funeral call. It's 'Hometown', a century-old Japanese folk song – it continues, changing incrementally the further I go along the sea road. It's there to orientate those who have lost their sight, but with the paths empty it now just seems like a siren call to beyond the water. Behind the low stone wall to the right the ocean soon drops down a cliff, and the steeper the going, the more desolate the island becomes. I'm walking away from where the last thirty-five residents live in neat terraced bungalows. Abandoned on one side is a rowing boat, its white paint slowly being devoured by time; it used to bring the patients to shore before the new pier was built. Native pines close in around allotments gone to seed. A collection of sheds and greenhouses sit idle. Once they would have helped feed the residents, farmed by the sick themselves, but now they accommodate a cluster of spiders and their vast city of cobwebs. As birdsong and the sound of the surf mix with the Tannoy music, I remember reading that some of the residents here used to keep canaries. Every year they would hold an annual competition as to whose bird sang the prettiest tune. The tarmac gives way to sticks and mud underfoot.

Oshima, this lush island under blue skies, feels very far away from the arctic cold of Yakutsk or the dust buckets of Brazil, the villages of Mozambique, yet close, too, a kindred psychic land beyond the walls, occupied by a people whose connection surmounts oceans and continents and climates. The people who have had leprosy, those that have gone through the colony system the world over, past and present, possess a biopolitical identity – they share an alien humanity grown of bacteria as diverse and multifaceted as any culture, but distinct and apart. When talking about their struggle, of how they were used as receptacles to hold all society's ills, living litmus tests for discrimination, there often seeps an inkling of patriotism born of this injury. Despite continuing cases around the world, with the gates now open and bridges built, it is a tribe near extinction, a people passing. Despite it all, these were never lives wasted. I reach the end of the island's path, the Japanese mainland a green blur in the distance; black-tailed gulls above, the waves lapping up the beach below. The tide is coming in, the land gets smaller.

ACKNOWLEDGEMENTS

This book is a small addendum to the work of numerous academics working in the field of leprosy studies. My thanks especially to Carole Rawcliffe for her insight and time; I'm indebted to her superlative *Leprosy in Medieval England* (2006), which helped change my own perspective on the disease and greatly informed the direction of chapter one. Recommended too is *Leprosy and Identity in the Middle Ages*, edited by Elma Brenner and François-Olivier Touati. Thank you to Magnus Vollset, not only for his generosity as an interviewee, but his writing too, not least his 2013 PhD thesis, 'Globalizing Leprosy. A Transnational History of Production and Circulation of Medical Knowledge, 1850s–1930s'. Rod Edmund's *Leprosy and Empire: A Medical and Cultural History* (2006) is an essential text on the history explored in the first half of the book. My thanks to the journalist Kate Marsden, who runs a research project dedicated to her namesake and is working on her own biography of the nurse. My research into Robben Island was made a whole lot easier by the many publications of Harriet Deacon, former Research Coordinator at Robben Island Museum. I'd recommend her book *The Island* (1996) in particular. I'm grateful to Elisabeth Poorman's research into Brazil's history with the disease. Thank you to Carolina Christoph Grillo of Universidade Federal Fluminense for her time talking me through the rise of Brazil's drug gangs and *milícia* groups. Significant background information concerning leprosy in Japan came from the work of Susan L. Burns. While we draw different conclusions, I'd wholeheartedly recommend *Kingdom of the Sick: A History of Leprosy and Japan* (2019). For more on the literature produced by the residents of Japanese sanatoria, as well as some translations into English, the work of Kathryn M. Tanaka is fantastic.

Thank you to David Thorold of St Albans Museums; Grete Eilertsen and the staff of the Leprosy Museum, Bergen; Kristina Marberger for her translation of archaic Norwegian; Julian Porter at Bexhill Museum; Erika le Roux of the Western Cape Archives and Records Service, Cape Town; Cristina Anca Anghelache and the staff of Spitalul Tichileşti; the legendary Emil 'Americanu' Mitrache for translation and driving in Romania; Charlotte Walker at The Leprosy Mission UK; Pedro Safrão, Ana Artur Mabjaia and Graça Maria Ricardo and staff of The Leprosy Mission Mozambique; Joelma Pereira of WHO Mozambique; Titus Kolongei and Shirley Cintura of the WHO sub-office in Pemba; Manuel Maliquito and the residents of ALEMO, Pemba; Tom Bowker for his Mozambique advice; Artur Custodio and the staff and volunteers at Morhan, Rio de Janeiro; Raphael Fonseca, Carol Silveira, Virgínia Pinho and Hakam Youssef for their introductions and logistical help in Brazil; Faustino Pinto for his introductions and hospitality in Juazeiro do Norte; the staff and residents of Colônia Antonio Justa, Ceará; though Agua de Dios, a leprosaria in Colombia I visited, did not end up in the book, my thanks to Zoranyi Romero, the town's council president, and María Teresa Rincón Sánchez, Head of Document Management and Historical Archives; Sam Thorne for introductions in Japan; Tomoya Iwata, Maki Ichijo, Aki Shudo and Satoko Omiya for their Japanese translation; the staff and residents of National Sanatorium Kikuchi Keifu-en for their hospitality; Nao Hoshino at the National Hansen's Disease Museum, Tokyo; Tomohisa Tamura at the Nagashima Aisei-en Historical Museum; Takahiro Nanri and Aya Tobiki at the Sasakawa Health Foundation, Japan, especially Aya for her extraordinary effort co-ordinating my trip.

Thank you to the librarians at Catford Library, the Wellcome Collection and the British Library, all in London; and their peers at

ACKNOWLEDGEMENTS

Biblioteca Mário de Andrade and Biblioteca Monteiro Lobato, in São Paulo. They should all get pay rises. The Mozambique chapter was written while on a residency at Estudio Rural, São Roque – my thanks to Gabriel Lima, Cassio Filho and Cassio's family. Thank you to Rory Steele at The Great Britain Sasakawa Foundation, which provided a much-needed funding grant for my trip to Japan. I was incredibly grateful to also receive the RSL Giles St Aubyn Award for Non-Fiction. I'm indebted to judges Tom Burgis, Fiona St Aubyn and Leila Aboulela, and to Laura Sibbald at The Royal Society of Literature.

Embryonic versions of chapter 6 appeared in the *Times Literary Supplement* and on BBC Radio 4's *From Our Own Correspondent*. Respective thanks to Camille Ralphs, and Joe Kent and Polly Hope, for their early edits and encouragement.

Rodrigo García-Velasco, Gabriel Lima and Dr John Quin read drafts of the book; my thanks for their expert insight, corrections and guidance. All errors are my own.

Thank you to everyone at Faber & Faber for their hard work, especially to Mo Hafeez for being a brilliant editor and taking on the project with such enthusiasm; Sam Matthews for her meticulous copy-editing; Joanna Harwood for patiently stewarding the book to its final form; Robbie Porter for his beautiful design; Jess Kim for marketing; Lauren Nicholl for publicity and Rebecca Hydon in production.

I'm hugely grateful to Emmie Francis for believing in *Outcast* in the first place. Without her, this book wouldn't exist.

Adding to the gratitude expressed in the prologue, I again thank all those who agreed to speak to me about their lives and the disease they lived through. Far more gave their time than those whose names appear in these pages.

Lastly, thanks to my parents (who proved excellent research assistants when it came to Richard of Wallingford's clock); to Selvi May

Akyildiz, Aaron Angell, Maria Vitória Bermejo, Vincent Bevins, Orit Gat, Ben Horandi, Kyla McDonald, Laura McLean-Ferris, Lucy Mercer and Alexia Smith for their friendship. Without the support of Selvi, Vincent and Lucy in particular, this whole thing would have been a lot harder. Thanks to Mathilda Laska for prising me away from the computer. Most of all, thanks to my partner Dan Coopey, who has put up with me all this time.

NOTES

PROLOGUE

leprosy and TB: After the segment was picked up in print media, Fox's press office sent out a clip which it said highlighted anchor Charles Payne challenging Ward's claims.

tremendous infectious diseases: Rupert Neate and Jo Tuckman, 'Donald Trump: Mexican Migrants Bring "Tremendous Infectious Disease" to US', *Guardian* (6 July 2015).

common ancestor: Luigi Santacroce, Raffaele del Prete, Ioannis Alexandros Charitos and Lucrezia Bottalico, '*Mycobacterium leprae*: A Historical Study on the Origins of Leprosy and Its Social Stigma', *InfezMed*, 29/4 (Dec. 2021), 623–32.

202,485 new cases: World Health Organization (WHO). Leprosy. Number of new leprosy cases: 2019. https://apps.who.int/neglected_diseases/ntddata/leprosy/leprosy.html

182,815: World Health Organization (WHO). Leprosy. Number of new leprosy cases: 2023. https://apps.who.int/neglected_diseases/ntddata/leprosy/leprosy.html

7.8 per cent of people: P. R. Klatser, S. van Beers, B. Madjid et al., 'Detection of *Mycobacterium leprae* Nasal Carriers in Populations for which Leprosy Is Endemic', *Journal of Clinical Microbiology*, 31/11 (Nov. 1993), 2947–51.

suffers their condition twice: H. Leloir, *Traité pratique et théorique de la lèpre* (Delahaye et Lecrosnier, 1886).

disease becomes adjectival: Susan Sontag, *Illness as Metaphor* (Farrar, Straus and Giroux, 1978), 58.

Its symptoms are not hidden: Quoted in Mirko D. Grmek, *Diseases in the Ancient Greek World*, trans. Mireille Muellner and Leonard Muellner (Johns Hopkins University Press, 1989), 168.

disfigured, unrecognisable: Charles A. Mercier, *Leper Houses and Mediaeval Hospitals* (H. K. Lewis, 1914), 5.

a language of relationships: Erving Goffman, *Stigma: Notes on the Management of Spoiled Identity* (Penguin, 1990), 13.

regional leper colony: Andrea Jaramillo, 'Brazil Shunned as a Covid Superspreader by Nervous Neighbors', *Bloomberg* (13 March 2021).

how they die: Albert Camus, *The Plague*, trans. Stuart Gilbert (Hamish Hamilton, 1948), p. 4.

ST ALBANS, UK

without difficulty: Matthew Paris, *Gesta Abbatum*, quoted in Peter Bourton, 'The History of the Monastery of St Mary de Pré', St Albans History blog (29 Dec. 2023), stalbanshistory.org/archaeology/st-albans-abbey/the-history-of-the-monastery-of-st-mary-de-pre.

one festival every year: 'Notification of the King's Grant to the Nuns of St Mary de Pré of an Annual Fair', in *The Cartae Antiquae Rolls 1–10*, ed. L. Landon, n.s. 17, 2/54 (Pipe Rolls Society, 1939), no. 375.

1,902,202 years and 270 days: Roland H. Bainton, *Here I Stand: A Life of Martin Luther* (Abingdon-Cokesbury Press, 1950), 71.

dead except to sin: Charles A. Mercier, *Leper Houses and Mediaeval Hospitals* (H. K. Lewis, 1914), 5.

Matilda set a fashion: Carole Rawcliffe, *Leprosy in Medieval England* (Boydell Press, 2006).

detective work: See Timothy S. Miller and John W. Nesbitt, *Walking Corpses: Leprosy in Byzantium and the Medieval West* (Cornell University Press, 2014), and the preface to the 2023 edition of the same book, for a description of how they were able to use Daniel Caner's work on the inscription to come to this conclusion.

thirteenth-century Brive: Miller and Nesbitt, 132.

leprosarium in Genoa: Miller and Nesbitt, 137.

early-fifteenth-century Crete: Miller and Nesbitt, 135.

for lepers alone: Euan Roger, 'Living with Leprosy in Late Medieval England', National Archives blog (4 Dec. 2019), blog.nationalarchives.gov.uk/living-with-leprosy-in-late-medieval-england.

St Bartholomew's in Dover: Rawcliffe, 304.

'pestilential disease: Rawcliffe, 40.

1d. a day: 'Hospitals: St Julian by St Albans', in *A History of the County of Hertford: 4*, ed. William Page (Victoria County History, 1971), *British History Online*, https://www.british-history.ac.uk/vch/herts/vol4.

a skilled tradesman: 'Currency Converter: 1270–2017', National Archives, nationalarchives.gov.uk/currency-converter.

Leprosy has not ceased: Agnes Lambert, 'Leprosy: Present and Past', *The Nineteenth Century*, 16 (Aug. 1884), 212.

rigidly excluded: Agnes Lambert, 'Leprosy: Present and Past', *The Nineteenth Century*, 16 (Sep. 1884).

through fear, not through greed: Agnes Lambert, 'Leprosy: Present and Past', *The Nineteenth Century*, 16 (Sep. 1884).

Again and again: Agnes Lambert, 'Leprosy: Present and Past', *The Nineteenth Century*, 16 (Sep. 1884).

fair, mill, marketplace: Saul Nathaniel Brody, *The Disease of the Soul: Leprosy in Medieval Literature* (Cornell University Press, 1974), 68.

The fourth of these: Agnes Lambert, 'Leprosy: Present and Past', *The Nineteenth Century*, 16 (Sep. 1884).

Maundy Thursday: Carlo Ginzburg, *Ecstasies: Deciphering the Witches' Sabbath*, trans. Raymond Rosenthal (Pantheon Books, 1991), 39.

lordship of towns: Bernard Gui, *Vita Joannis XXII*, quoted in Malcolm Barber, 'Lepers, Jews and Moslems: The Plot to Overthrow Christendom in 1321', *History*, 66/216 (1981), 1–17.

BERGEN, NORWAY

not an outstanding student: G. Armauer Hansen, *The Memories and Reflections of Dr Gerhard Armauer Hansen* (German Leprosy Relief Association, 1976), 35.

I was invited: Quotes from Hansen, *Memories*, 77, 71, 88.

I felt myself growing ill: Quotes from Hansen, *Memories*, 44, 70.

every 10,000 people: Lorentz M. Irgens, 'The Fight against Leprosy in Norway in the Nineteenth Century', *Michael Quarterly*, 7/3 (2010), 307–20, 311.

half the population: R. Melson, 'Daniel Cornelius Danielssen: A Great Leprologist of Norway', *Hansenologia Internationalis*, 1/2 (1976), 172–9, 179.

tearful eye: Johan Ernst Welhaven, 'Beskrifning öfver de spetälske i St Jörgens hospital i staden Bergen i Norrige', in *Svenska Läkare Sällskapets Handlingar*, vol. 3 (A. Gadelius, 1816), 1.

3,000 people: Melson, 179.

the wisdom of old folk: Hansen, *Memories*, 105.

warmth: 'Shamrock', 'Notes by the Wayside', *Nursing Record*, 9 (6 Oct. 1892), 827–8.

Once leprosy has entered a family: Daniel Danielssen, *Den spedalske Sygdom, dens Aarsager og dens Forebyggelsesmidler* (Et Folkeskrift, 1954), 8.

remarkable work endurance: Hansen, *Memories*, 97.

I found sufficient cells: Quotes from Hansen, *Memories*, 97.

Henri Leloir: Robson Roose, *Leprosy and Its Prevention: Illustrated by Norwegian Experience* (H. K. Lewis, 1890), 14.

emotional outburst: Hansen, *Memories*, 99.

the social body: Michel Foucault, *The History of Sexuality: 1*, trans. Robert Hurley (Allen Lane, 1979), 136–7.

stupid: Letter from G. Armauer Hansen to Albert Ashmead (11 Jan. 1896), cited in S. S. Pandya, 'The First International Leprosy Conference, Berlin, 1897: The

Politics of Segregation', *História, Ciências, Saúde-Manguinhos*, 10 (suppl. 1, 2003), 161–77, 166.

no other alternative: Th. M. Vogelsang, 'Gerhard Henrik Armauer Hansen 1841–1912: The Discoverer of the Leprosy Bacillus: His Life and Work', *International Journal of Leprosy and Other Mycobacterial Diseases*, 46/3 (1978), 258–332, cited in Pandya, 166.

do not want contact: G. Armauer Hansen, 'Optional and Obligatory Isolation of Lepers', *Mittheilungen und Verhandlungen der Internationalen Wissenschaftlichen Lepra-conferenz zu Berlin: 2* (1897), 165, cited in Pandya, 172.

In Norway we have achieved: Hansen, 'Optional and Obligatory Isolation', cited in Pandya, 172.

cheeks had swollen: *Madras Mail* (24 Aug. 1889).

a leper of some years' standing: Rudyard Kipling, 'The Mark of the Beast', in *The Mark of the Beast and Other Horror Tales* (Dover Publications, 2013).

chief seat of the disease: *Times of India* (7 Aug. 1889), cited in Pandya, 163.

Are Europeans liable to leprosy?: H. P. Wright, *Leprosy and Segregation* (Parker & Co., 1885), 100.

to a greater or lesser extent: 'Leprosy in the East Indies', *The Times*, 26 November 1862.

Ere we are aware of it: Wright, 101.

colonisation of India: Josephine Robertson, 'Dr Henry Vandyke Carter', *International Leprosy Association – History of Leprosy* (2016), https://leprosyhistory.org/database/person11.

London School of Tropical Medicine: Lioba A. Hirsch and Rebecca Martin, *LSHTM and Colonialism: A Report on the Colonial History of the London School of Hygiene & Tropical Medicine (1899–c.1960)* (London School of Hygiene & Tropical Medicine, 2022).

dread and promise: Edward W. Said, *Culture and Imperialism* (Random House, 2014), 228.

Conan Doyle's characters: A point made by Yumna Siddiqi in 'The Cesspool of Empire: Sherlock Holmes and the Return of the Repressed', *Victorian Literature and Culture*, 34/01 (2006), 233–47.

120,000 people: Sanjiv Kakar, 'Leprosy in British India, 1860–1940: Colonial Politics and Missionary Medicine', *Medical History*, 40 (1996)

I had to explain to him: R. V. Wardekar, *Round the World of Leprosy* (Gandhi Memorial Leprosy Foundation, 1955), 77.

all civilised states: *London Evening Standard* (12 Oct. 1897).

a stern denial: Quoted in Pandya, 165.

Every leper is a danger: James Gatewood, 'Report on the International Conference on Leprosy', in 'Report of the Surgeon General, US Navy, to the Secretary of the Navy' (Government Printing Office, 1896), 138–58, 157.

influence of Middle Ages: L. Rogers and E. Muir, *Leprosy* (Wright, 1946), quoted in James Cameron Purse Logan, *The Initiation of Measures for the Control Of Leprosy . . .* (PhD thesis) (University of Glasgow, 1950), theses.gla.ac.uk/79795.

contradicts the report: *Leprosy in India: Report of the Leprosy Commission in India, 1890–91* (Superintendent of Government Printing, 1893).

Love and affection: *Sheffield Evening Telegraph* (19 Oct. 1897).

three motions: Donald H. Currie, 'The Second International Conference on Leprosy, Held in Bergen, Norway, August 16 to 19, 1909', *Public Health Reports (1896–1970)*, 24/38 (1909), 1357–61.

smoking concert: *London Evening Standard* (13 Oct. 1897).

property of the institution: Jorunn Nerby Vannes, '"Ho óg vart spilt": Kari Nielsdatter Spidsøen (1847–1884) i et lokalhistorisk perspektivl', *Bergensposten*, 4 (Dec. 2011), 25–34, 33.

this paper: Lorentz M. Irgens, 'Hansen, 150 Years after His Birth, the Context of a Medical Discovery', *International Journal of Leprosy and Other Mycobacterial Diseases*, 60/3 (1992), 466–9, 468.

presuppose that the patient: Knut Blom, 'Armauer Hansen and Human Leprosy Transmission: Medical Ethics and Legal Rights', *International Journal of Leprosy and Other Mycobacterial Diseases*, 41/2 (1973), 199–207, 200.

court costs of 90 kroner: Blom, 202.

naming of newly discovered diseases: 'WHO Issues Best Practices for Naming New Human Infectious Diseases', WHO press release (8 May 2015), who.int/news/item/08-05-2015-who-issues-best-practices-for-naming-new-human-infectious-diseases.

reassessed: See, e.g., letters from Patrícia D. Deps, Alice Cruz and Ajit Barve in 'Correspondence: Why We Should Stop Using the Word Leprosy', *The Lancet Infectious Diseases*, 20 (Nov. 2020), 1236.

MOLOKAI, HAWAII, USA

coarse . . . headstrong and bigoted: Hyde, quoted in Robert Louis Stevenson, *Father Damien: An Open Letter to the Reverend Doctor Hyde of Honolulu from Robert Louis Stevenson* (Chatto and Windus, 1890), 7.

We eat what Providence sends: Quoted in Gavan Daws, *Holy Man: Father Damien of Molokai* (University of Hawaii Press, 1984), 40.

uncleanly personal habits,: Arthur Johnstone, *Recollections of Robert Louis Stevenson in the Pacific* (Chatto and Windus, 1905), 86.

unhappy forever: Quoted in Daws, 22.

across the world: For how the news of the arrival was reported in Hawaii, see *Ka*

Nupepa Kuokoa (26 March 1864), nupepa-hawaii.com/2012/12/27/catholic-clergy-arrive-including-someone-named-damien-1864.

The commander manifested: James Jackson Jarves, *History of the Hawaiian or Sandwich Islands . . ., from the Earliest Traditionary Period to the Present Time* (Tappan and Dennet, 1843), 109.

There seems but one way: James Cantlie, 'Report on the Conditions under which Leprosy Occurs in China, Indo-China, Malaya, the Archipelago, and Oceania', in *Prize Essays on Leprosy* (New Sydenham Society, 1897), 363.

683,000 people: David Swanson, 'A New Estimate of the Hawaiian Population for 1778, the Year of First European Contact', *Hūlili* 11/2 (2019), 203–22.

threatening to become more general: Hawaii Board of Health, *Supplement to the Report of the President: 'Leprosy in Hawaii': Extracts from Reports of Presidents of the Board of Health . . . in Regard to Leprosy in the Hawaiian Kingdom* (Daily Bulletin Steam Printing Office, 1886), 5.

slow [but] certain progress: Hawaii Board of Health, 6–7.

seated on the ground: C. S. Stewart, *Private Journal of a Voyage to the Pacific Ocean, and Residence at the Sandwich Islands, in the Years 1822, 1823, 1824, and 1825* (John P. Haven, 1828), 148–50.

sleep with lepers: M. Hagan, 'Leprosy on the Hawaiian Islands', *Southern California Practitioner*, 1/3 (1886), 85–91, 88.

wholesome horror: George Worth Woods, 'The Demographic Effects of Introduced Diseases, and Especially Leprosy, upon the Hawaiian People', *Section on Medical Climatology and Demography of the Ninth International Medical Congress* (W. F. Fell, 1887).

Hawaiians view with ignorant contempt: A. A. St. M. Mouritz, *'The Path of the Destroyer': A History of Leprosy in the Hawaiian Islands, and Thirty Years Research into the Means by which it Has Been Spread* (Honolulu Star-Bulletin, 1916), 59.

any person: 'An Act to Prevent the Spread of Leprosy, 1865', Kalaupapa National Historical Park website (US National Park Service, 2022), nps.gov/kala/learn/historyculture/1865legislation.htm.

an imperial spectacle: Edward W. Said, *Culture and Imperialism* (Chatto and Windus, 1993), 156.

The last king of Hawaii: *Pacific Commercial Advertiser*, 9 Nov. 1909.

a persistent belief: Forrest Wade Young, 'I Hē Koe? Placing Rapa Nui', *The Contemporary Pacific*, 24/1 (2012), 1–30.

the spirit of greed: H. G. Creel, *Hawaii : An International Crime* (Appeal to Reason, 1915), 67.

modern commercialism: Creel, 66.

We have a foul: Hawaii Board of Health, 16.

bankroll dormitories: Arthur D. Baldwin, *A Memoir of Henry Perrin Baldwin* (private printing, 1915), 67.

construct his own home: Mouritz, 205.

aiding their weaker brethren: Hawaii Board of Health, 44.

Drunkenness, pilferings: Hawaii Board of Health, 47.

much addicted: Johnstone, 314.

forgot all decency: Edward Clifford, *Father Damien: A Journey from Cashmere to His Home in Hawaii* (Macmillan and Co., 1889), 87.

roariously drunk: Daws, 111.

The hilarious feasters: Daws, 112.

disintegrating bodies: Jack London, *Tales of the Pacific* (Penguin, 1989), 145.

little else mattered: S. M. Kamakau, *Ruling Chiefs of Hawaii* (Kamehameha Schools Press, 1992).

The terrible disease: Hawaii Board of Health, 44.

mother was ritually impure: Joseph Zias, 'Lust and Leprosy: Confusion or Correlation?', *Bulletin of the American Schools of Oriental Research*, 275 (1989) 27–31.

foetid lust: Kenneth Baxter Wolf, 'St Francis and the Leper', in *The Poverty of Riches: St Francis of Assisi Reconsidered* (Oxford University Press, 2003).

Give Isolde to us: Saul Nathaniel Brody, *The Disease of the Soul: Leprosy in Medieval Literature* (Cornell University Press, 1974), 180.

One night the writer slips away: For further close reading on this episode, see Rod Edmund, *Leprosy and Empire: A Medical and Cultural History* (Cambridge University Press: 2007)

I want to visit you at your hut: Paul Theroux, *My Other Life* (Penguin, 1997), 84.

either of the two ladies, should the circumstances permit: Roald Dahl, 'The Visitor', *Playboy*, May 1965, v. 12. n.5, 78.

earlier anecdote: Dod Orsborne, Master of the Girl Pat (Doubleday, 1949).

Charles Warren Stoddard's relationship to Hawaii: Here I am indebted to Gregory Tomso, 'The Queer History of Leprosy and Same-Sex Love', *American Literary History*, 14/4 (Winter 2002). 747–75.

for the first time: Letter from Charles Warren Stoddard to Walt Whitman (2 April 1870), in *The Walt Whitman Archive*, ed. Matt Cohen, Ed Folsom and Kenneth M. Price (Center for Digital Research in the Humanities, n.d.), whitmanarchive. org/item/loc.01944.

frigid manners: Horace Traubel, *With Walt Whitman in Camden* (University of Pennsylvania Press, 2016).

'Chumming with a Savage': 'Chumming with a Savage' in Charles Warren Stoddard, *Summer Cruising in the South Seas* (Chatto and Windus, 1881), 41

'possessed of much physical beauty': Charles Warren Stoddard, *The Lepers of Molokai* (Ave Maria Press, 1885), 67.

love their friends: Charles Warren Stoddard, *The Lepers of Molokai* (Ave Maria Press, 1885), 20.

The lepers, once gathered: Charles Warren Stoddard, *The Lepers of Molokai* (Ave Maria Press, 1885), 68.

that poisons the air: Quoted in Daws, 83.

core disgust: Jonathan Haidt, Paul Rozin, Clark Mccauley and Sumio Imada, 'Body, Psyche, and Culture: The Relationship Between Disgust and Morality', *Psychology and Developing Societies*, 9/1 (1997), 107–31, 111.

outdoor things indoors: Mary Douglas, *Purity and Danger: An Analysis of the Concepts of Pollution and Taboo* (Routledge, 1992), 43.

treated like dirt: Charles Darwin, *The Expression of the Emotions in Man and Animals* (University of Chicago Press, 1965).

going native: Edward W. Said, *Culture and Imperialism* (Random House, 2014), 215.

The priest had been out walking: Other accounts tell of Father Damien scalding his foot in a bath, but not feeling the pain. This version, one of the closest to the event, is told by Arthur Johnstone in *Stevenson in the Pacific*.

Those microbes: Stoddard, 78.

Ghost of Immorality: Mouritz, 235.

We searched his mouth: Mouritz, 236.

I never heard from anyone: Johnstone, 84.

We who knew the man: Quoted in Stevenson, 6–7.

It may be news to you: Stevenson, 6.

YAKUTSK, SAKHA REPUBLIC, RUSSIA

usual elementary preparation: Henry Johnson, *Life of Kate Marsden* (Simpkin, Marshall & Company, 1895), 2–3.

a very bad girl: Johnson, 8.

perfect Englishwoman: Kate Marsden, *On Sledge and Horseback to Outcast Siberian Lepers* (Record Press, 1892), 173.

Evangelical nunnery: Reprinted *Londonderry Standard* (12 May 1869).

associated with copes: *London Daily News* (22 May 1876).

raise themselves: *Hackney and Kingsland Gazette* (21 March 1881).

81,847: Andrew J. Ringlee, *The Romanovs' Militant Charity: The Red Cross and Public. Mobilization for War in Tsarist Russia, 1853–1914* (University of North Carolina at Chapel Hill, 2016), 185.

weary months of waiting: 'Russian Mistakes', *Daily News* (1 Sept. 1877).

strongly-built physique: '*The Nursing Record* "At Homes": No. 5: Miss Kate Marsden at Our Offices', *Nursing Record*, 9 (3 Nov. 1892), 894.

NOTES

picture of ruin: Henry M. Hozier (ed.), *The Russo-Turkish War: Including an Account of the Rise and Decline of the Ottoman Power, and the History of the Eastern Question: 2* (William MacKenzie, 1880), 780.

remains of a barn: Marsden, typically, provided varying accounts to the media as to the exact circumstances of her first encounter with leprosy, with some reports suggesting that, more prosaically, she had encountered these patients at the military lazaretto. In the October 1891 issue of *The Churchman* and elsewhere she tells the story of the barn.

avoided, despised, and doomed: Kate Marsden, *On Sledge and Horseback to Outcast Siberian Lepers* (Record Press, 1892), 4.

affluence, with excess: Susan Sontag, *Illness as Metaphor* (Farrar, Straus and Giroux, 1978), 15.

Before this time: Marsden, 4.

self-sacrificing nature: Quoted by Joseph Frank, *Dostoevsky: A Writer in His Time* (Princeton University Press, 2009), 698.

hoped and prayed: Johnson, 15.

many backward steps: Marsden, 3.

a memory: Marsden, 3.

What am I: Radclyffe Hall, *The Well of Loneliness* (Jonathan Cape, 1928), 127.

full on the lips: Hall, 121.

impure relationships: Quoted in Hilary Chapman, 'The New Zealand Campaign against Kate Marsden, Traveller to Siberia', *New Zealand Slavonic Journal* (2000), 123–40.

I am not in the least afraid: Emma Brewer, 'Kate Marsden, and Her Mission to Russia and Siberia', *Girl's Own Paper*, 12/565 (25 Oct. 1890).

immorality of the most shocking kind: *Evening Star* (25 Feb. 1896).

everything and everyone: Henry James, *The Bostonians: A Novel* (Modern Library, 1956), 125.

known amongst the Maoris: *Wellington Evening Post* (10 Nov. 1890).

extending its ravages: Morell Mackenzie, 'The Dreadful Revival of Leprosy', *The Nineteenth Century*, 26 (July–Dec. 1889), 925–41, 933, 927.

roving commission: Johnson, 29.

For hundreds of years: Johnson, 32–3.

the Great Healer Himself: Johnson, 31.

A dreadful sight: Johnson, 33.

too awful to describe: Johnson, 35.

Your limbs ache: Marsden, 69.

Divine summons: Marsden, 84.

all but dead, half crushed: Quotes from Marsden, 162, 99, 72, 4.

mauled about: Quotes from Marsden, 31, 59, 147.

I can never forget: Marsden, 117.

blood-stained snow: Marsden, 56.

80 per cent: Alan Wood, *The History of Siberia* (Taylor & Francis, 1991), 82.

a myth among the Yukaghir: Vladimir Jochelson, *The Yukaghir and the Yukaghirized Tungus* (E. J. Brill, 1910), 27–8.

105 gulags: Yekaterina Karpukhina and Robert Coalson, 'Stalin's Great Terror: Sakha's Mountain of Tin and Bones', Radio Free Europe/Radio Liberty (4 Oct. 2017), rferl.org/a/great-terror-stalin-sakha-far-east-victims-not-forgotten-mines/ 28773826.html.

one of her horses: Marsden, 103–4, 136–7.

cattle refused to drink the water: Marsden, 32.

a mining operation: Susan A. Crate, 'Silent Spring in Siberia: The Plight of the Vilyuy Sakha', Cultural Survival (25 March 2010), culturalsurvival.org/publications/ cultural-survival-quarterly/silent-spring-siberia-plight-vilyuy-sakha.

In 1974 and 1978, two detonations: Susan A. Crate, 'Co-option in Siberia: The Case of Diamonds and the Vilyuy Sakha', *Polar Geography*, 26/4 (2002), 418–35.

plutonium-239: Crate, 'Co-option in Siberia', 426.

exact number of rocket components: Crate, 'Co-option in Siberia'.

this poor woman: Quotes in this paragraph from Marsden, 133, 141, 60.

if human love is denied: Simone de Beauvoir, *The Second Sex* (Jonathan Cape, 1953), 633.

The erotomaniac feels: De Beauvoir, 635.

almost powerless'; '*After wishing*: Marsden, 145, 60.

What do you think of Querry: Graham Greene, *A Burnt-Out Case* (Penguin, 1975), 22.

The beverage flooded us: Quoted in De Beauvoir, 638.

he communicated his pain: Georges Bataille, *Inner Experience*, trans. Leslie Anne Boldt (State University of New York Press, 1988), 120.

a dear English lady: Marsden, 14.

thrilling story: *Bayswater Chronicle* (4 March 1893).

courageous and heroic: *The Queen* (4 Feb. 1893).

a tall fine-looking woman: *Osceola Times* (11 July 1891).

absolutely devoid: '"Philanthropy" on Horseback', *The Nation* (6 April 1893).

ROBBEN ISLAND, SOUTH AFRICA

One group, banished: J. C. Wells, *The Return of Makhanda: Exploring the Legend* (University of KwaZulu-Natal Press, 2012), 231.

'low-lying' island: Cape of Good Hope Legislative Council, 'Report of the Select Committee on Robben Island Leper Asylums' (Cape Times Limited, 1909), vi.

doorstep dormitory: Martin Hall, *Archaeology and the Modern World* (Psychology Press, 2000) 157.

I can speak merely: Cape of Good Hope Legislative Council, 'Report of the Select Committee on the Spread of Leprosy' (25 July 1883), Western Cape Archives and Records Service.

chiefly to the pauper class: S. P. Impey, 'Leprosy in South Africa', in *Prize Essays on Leprosy* (New Sydenham Society, 1895), 195.

a descent upon the house: 'Report of the Select Committee on Robben Island Leper Asylums', 55.

Admitting such a practice: 'Report of the Select Committee on Robben Island Leper Asylums', 7.

a very different population: 'Minutes of Evidence, 1909 Commission', 22, quoted in Harriet Deacon, 'Leprosy and Racism at Robben Island', *Studies in the History of Cape Town*, 7 (1994), 45–83, 52.

Hottentots and Bushmen: Impey, 197.

the reign of the East India Company: Impey, 192.

dreaded bubonic plague: Howard Phillips, *Epidemics: The Story of South Africa's Five Most Lethal Human Diseases* (Ohio University Press, 2012), 43.

the cup of woe of the Indians: *Times of India* (weekly edition), 22 April 1899.

Gandhi: Rajni Kant and Balram Bhargava, 'Medical Legacy of Gandhi: Demystifying Human Diseases', *Indian Journal of Medical Research*, 149 (Suppl. 1, 2019), S25–S37.

A Lesson from the Plague: Francis Dube, 'Public Health and Racial Segregation in South Africa: Mahatma (M. K.) Gandhi Debates Colonial Authorities on Public Health Measures, 1896–1904', *Journal of the Historical Society of Nigeria*, 21 (2012), 21–40.

For many, the exposure: 'Report of the Select Committee on Robben Island Leper Asylums'.

their testimonies: 'Report of the Select Committee on Robben Island Leper Asylums', 158, 164, 152.

There are places established: Erving Goffman, *Asylums: Essays on the Social Situation of Mental Patients and Other Inmates* (Penguin, 1961), 4.

In no sense of the word: John Iliffe, *The African Poor: A History* (Cambridge University Press, 1987), 114–42.

in 1887 two blind residents: Letter from Ross to Under-Colonial Secretary (6 Jan. 1888), TNA: PRO, CO 14 14.

They have no baths: 'Report of the Select Committee on the Spread of Leprosy'.

Goffman's observation: Goffman, 7.

the Europeans have a stand to themselves: 'Report of the Select Committee on Robben Island Leper Asylums', 39–40.

The whites have really a lot of liberty: 'Report of the Select Committee on Robben Island Leper Asylums', 115.

whites mix up freely: Harriet Deacon (ed.), *The Island: A History of Robben Island, 1488–1990* (New Africa Books 1996), 72.

request of Female Coloured Leper Patients of corsets: Memorandum from the Under-Colonial Secretary to Commissioner, 17 March 1905. MOH 353 C121A. Leper Administration, Leper Cases, General Correspondence. Western Cape Archives and Records Service.

I never thought of corsets: Memorandum from the Commissioner to Under-Colonial Secretary, 24 March 1905. MOH 353 C121A. Leper Administration, Leper Cases, General Correspondence. Western Cape Archives and Records Service.

Cecil Rhodes himself: Deacon, 'Leprosy and Racism'.

The whites got tinned sardines: Deacon, *The Island*, 72.

sulky idle people: Quoted in Deacon, 'Leprosy and Racism', 62.

went on strike: Deacon, *The Island*, 70.

£4,000 a year in wages: 'Report of the Select Committee on Robben Island Leper Asylums', 94.

111,600 eggs: 'Report of the Select Committee on Robben Island Leper Asylums', 95.

They will never do a single thing: 'Report of the Select Committee on Robben Island Leper Asylums', 95.

two carpenters on the island: 'Report of the Select Committee on Robben Island Leper Asylums', 60.

treated as . . . free British Subject[s]: Deacon, 'Leprosy and Racism', 63.

Our request and entreaty: Letter from F. J. A. Jacobs, Robben Island, to Queen Victoria (10 Aug. 1892), the (UK) National Archives: Public Record Office (TNA: PRO), CO 48/521, 642–51.

war and riot: From 'Memorandum by the Under-Colonial Secretary on the subject of the Leper Settlement on RI' (29 Aug. 1893), TNA: PRO, CO 48/522.

delicacies of all kinds: Deacon, 'Leprosy and Racism'.

The campaign to improve: Nelson Mandela, *Long Walk To Freedom* (1994).

in whom all sympathy: 'Report of the Select Committee on Robben Island Leper Asylums', 141.

of considerable education: Under-Colonial Secretary (6 Feb. 1909), Cape Town Archives.

a religious lunatic: Letter from Henry B. Loch to Lord Marquis as a report on conditions on Robben Island (Sept. 1893), Letter 94, TNA: PRO, CO 48/522, quoted in Ato Quayson, *Aesthetic Nervousness: Disability and the Crisis of Representation* (2007).

threatened to strike: Loch.

where the social boundaries: Quayson, 388.

'first prize in a state lottery': Barbara Hutton, *Robben Island: Symbol of Resistance* (Mayibuye Books and Sached Books, 1994), 33.

TICHILEŞTI, ROMANIA

The building looks like an old mansion: F. Brunea-Fox, 'Five Days among Lepers', *Dimineaţa* (Aug. 1928), quoted in *Historia*, no. 213 (Oct. 2019), historia.ro/sectiune/general/cinci-zile-printre-leprosi-o-pagina-uitata-de-568574.html.

terrorise: *Seward Daily Gateway* (1 Aug. 1933).

Leprosy Patients to be Sent to the Leper Colony: 'Bolnavi de Lepră Ce Urmează a Fi Trimişi La Leprozerie', Holocaust Survivors and Victims Database (United States Holocaust Memorial Museum, n.d.), ID: 47598, ushmm.org/online/hsv/source_view.php?SourceId=47598.

all the problems of healthcare: Michel Foucault, *The Birth of Biopolitics: Lectures at the Collège de France, 1978–1979* (Palgrave Macmillan, 2008), 230.

Every sick man: 'Report of the Surgeon General, US Navy, to the Secretary of the Navy' (Government Printing Office, 1896).

The Germans found a leper: Quoted in Michael A. Grodin and Myron Winick, *Jewish Medical Resistance in the Holocaust* (Berghahn Books, 2014), 46.

Brauns accused: Joshua Rubenstein and Ilya Altman, *The Unknown Black Book: The Holocaust in the German-Occupied Soviet Territories* (Indiana University Press/United States Holocaust Memorial Museum, 2008).

We are not allowed: Avraham Tory, diary entry, 25 Feb. 1943, quoted in Dennis B. Klein (ed.), *Hidden History of the Kovno Ghetto* (Little Brown/United States Holocaust Memorial Museum, 1997), 180.

[The State] must see to it: Adolf Hitler, *Mein Kampf*, trans. Ralph Manheim (Houghton Mifflin, 1943), 403–4.

Nazism and Stalinism: Achille Mbembe, 'Necropolitics', trans. Libby Meintjes, *Public Culture*, 15/1 (Winter 2003), 11–40.

an injury to the head: John of Salisbury, Policraticus, VI, 25, in *The Statesman's Book of John of Salisbury*, trans. John Dickinson (Alfred A. Knopf, 1927), 259.

Finally the city of Chişinău: 'In Sfârşit, Chişinăul a Scăpat de Lepra Iudaică', *Basarabia* (4 Nov. 1941), kehilalinks.jewishgen.org/chisinau/LIF_Shoah_Ghetto.asp.

170,000 abandoned youngsters: James C. Rosapepe, 'Half Way Home: Romania's Abandoned Children Ten Years after the Revolution', Report to Americans from the US Embassy, Bucharest, Romania (2001), 2.

territory of confinement: Michel Foucault, *History of Madness* (Routledge, 2006), 355.

great spiritual depths: Andrey Tarkovsky, *Time Within Time: The Diaries 1970–1986*, trans. Kitty Hunter-Blair (Faber & Faber, 1994), 174.

smiling leper: E. M. Cioran, *A Short History of Decay*, trans. Richard Howard (Penguin, 2010), 40.

nostalgia: Radu Dumitrescu, 'Half of Romanians Now Believe Life Under Communist Regime Was Better', *Romania Insider* (13 December 2023).

CABO DELGADO, MOZAMBIQUE

mercenaries: Tim Lister and Sebastian Shukla, 'Russian Mercenaries Fight Shadowy Battle in Gas-Rich Mozambique', CNN.com (29 Nov. 2019).

Just before dawn: Peter Fabricius, 'Mozambique's First Islamist Attacks Shock the Region', *ISS Today* (27 Oct. 2017).

They told residents: Saide Habibe, Salvador Forquilha and João Pereira, *Islamic Radicalization in Northern Mozambique: The Case of Mocímboa da Praia* (Cadernos IESE 17, IESE Scientific Council, 2019).

began to carry machetes: Habibe et al.

new leprosy cases: WHO, 'Number of New Leprosy Cases', Global Health Observatory Data Repository (12 Sept. 2023), who.int/data/gho/data/indicators/indicator-details/GHO/number-of-new-leprosy-cases.

$20 billion project: 'Total Announces the Signing of Mozambique LNG Project Financing' (press release), total.com (17 July 2020), totalenergies.com/media/news/news/total-announces-signing-mozambique-lng-project-financing.

Plans to build shipyards: Cristina Krippahl, *Mozambique: 'Hidden Debt' Trial Exposes Corruption*, dw.com (1 Sept. 2021).

$200 million: Susan Comrie for amaBhungane, 'The Banker Bros Who Bankrupted Mozambique', *Daily Maverick* (8 Jan. 2019).

Chinese companies have spirited away: Susan Njanji and Adrien Barbier, 'Mozambique Battles Illegal Logging to Save Tropical Forests', Phys.org (26 April 2017), phys.org/news/2017-04-mozambique-illegal-tropical-forests.html.

Gemfields: Gemfields press statement (29 Jan. 2019), www.gemfieldsgroup.com/gemfields-press-statement.

human rights lawyers have claimed: Leigh Day, 'Gemfields' (press release) (n.d.), https://www.leighday.co.uk/news/cases-and-testimonials/cases/gemfields.

550 families: Ilham Rawoot, 'Gas-rich Mozambique May Be Headed for a Disaster', *Al Jazeera* (24 Feb. 2000).

NOTES

745 new cases: Alberto Massango, 'Heath Authorities Record 3,115 Cases of Leprosy from 2021 to 2023', *AIM News* (1 Feb. 2024).

Several villages around here: CCCM Cluster Mozambique, 'Ancuabe Displacement Flash Report', ReliefWeb (12 June 2022), reliefweb.int/report/mozambique/cccm-cluster-mozambique-ancuabe-displacement-flash-report-12-june-2022.

went on to target: Cabo Delgado (Twitter post and video) (10.11 a.m., 20 Oct. 2022), twitter.com/DelgadoCabo/status/1583023118691356672.

the star pupil for Western capitalism: Joseph Hanlon, 'Postal Service Closures Show Mozambique Is a Star Pupil of Western Capitalism', LSE blogs (4 Aug. 2021), blogs.lse.ac.uk/africaatlse/2021/08/04/postal-service-closures-mozambique-frelimo-star-pupil-western-capitalism-neoliberalism-lobbying.

A sixteen-year-old boy: Amnesty International, 'Mozambique: Authorities Must Investigate Police Violence against Peaceful Protesters' (press release), amnesty.org (21 Oct. 2023), amnesty.org/en/latest/news/2023/10/mozambique-authorities-must-investigate-police-violence-against-peaceful-protesters.

nearly one million people: UNHCR, 'Nearly 1 Million People Have Fled Five Years of Northern Mozambique Violence' (briefing note) (4 Oct. 2022), unhcr.org/uk/news/briefing-notes/nearly-1-million-people-have-fled-five-years-northern-mozambique-violence.

the vast majority of survivors: Ruth Castel-Branco, 'The Fragility of the Mozambican State', *Africa Is a Country* (25 March 2019).

Before the conflict: International Organization for Migration (IOM), 'DTM Northern Mozambique Crisis: Baseline Assessment District Profiles Round 12 (April 2021)' (7 June 2021), dtm.iom.int/reports/northern-mozambique-crisis-%E2%80%94-baseline-assessment-district-profiles-round-12-april-2021.

11,000 people : IOM, 'Metuge District Sites Situation Report' (2 Nov. 2023).

mobs targeted health facilities and health workers: Peter Mwai and Paul Brown, 'Mozambique Cholera: Why Outbreaks Have Sparked Unrest', BBC News (28 May 2023).

In Namogelia: Tom Gould, 'At Least Four Killed in Cholera Riot in Cabo Delgado', Zitamar.com (18 Dec. 2023).

Such violence is nothing new: Joseph Hanlon made a similar observation as far back as 1999 in his preface to Carlos Serra, *Cólera E Catarse: Infra-estruturas Sociais De Um Mito Nas Zonas Costeiras De Nampula (1998/2002)* (Imprensa Universitária, Universidade Eduardo Mondlane, 2003).

300,000 people: 'Cabo Delgado: An Estimated 300,000 People Returned to their Places of Origin', *Club of Mozambique* (24 May 2023), clubofmozambique.com/news/cabo-delgado-an-estimated-300000-people-returned-to-their-places-of-origin-watch-237955.

a growing problem: 'When (New) Drugs Don't Work: Mozambique Faces Alarming

Multidrug-resistant Tuberculosis Epidemic' (press release), Research Centre Borstel Leibniz Lung Centre (10 Nov. 2023), dzif.de/en/when-new-drugs-dont-work-mozambique-faces-alarming-multidrug-resistant-tuberculosis-epidemic.

1,800 people with active leprosy: 'ALEMO preocupada com desaparecimento de doentes durante os ataques terroristas em Cabo Delgado', *Carta de Moçambique* (2 Feb. 2023), cartamz.com/index.php/sociedade/item/12893-alemo-preocupada-com-desaparecimento-de-doentes-durante-os-ataques-terroristas-em-cabo-delgado.

Twenty-six out of a total of thirty-nine: Agência Lusa, 'Moçambique: 26 Unidades de Saúde Destruídas por Rebeldes Continuam Encerradas' (21 Sept. 2023), observador.pt/2023/09/21/mocambique-26-unidades-de-saude-destruidas-por-rebeldes-continuam-encerradas.

RIO DE JANEIRO, BRAZIL

The Shame of Rio de Janeiro: Matt Roper, 'The Shame of Rio de Janeiro: Squalid Hospital Just Five Miles from Olympic Park', *Daily Mirror* (22 May 2016).

22,773 new diagnoses: World Health Organization (WHO). Leprosy. Number of new leprosy cases: 2023. https://apps.who.int/neglected_diseases/ntddata/leprosy/leprosy.html

that leprosy is mixed up: Letter from William MacArthur to Leonard Rogers (1 Oct. 1923), Papers of Sir Leonard Rogers, Wellcome Collection.

A Brazilian study on tuberculosis: Ricardo Arraes de Alencar Ximenes, Maria de Fátima Pessoa Militão de Albuquerque, Wayner V. Souza et al., 'Is It Better to be Rich in a Poor Area or Poor in a Rich Area? A Multilevel Analysis of a Case-control Study of Social Determinants of Tuberculosis', *International Journal of Epidemiology*, 38/5 (Oct. 2009), 1285–96, 1285.

study focusing on young people: Louisa Chenciner, Kristi Sidney Annerstedt, Julia M. Pescarini and Tom Wingfield, 'Social and Health Factors Associated with Unfavourable Treatment Outcome in Adolescents and Young Adults with Tuberculosis in Brazil: A National Retrospective Cohort Study', *The Lancet Global Health*, 9 (Oct. 2021), e1380–e1390.

22 per cent: Julia M. Pescarini, Elizabeth Williamson, Joilda S. Nery et al., 'Effect of a Conditional Cash Transfer Programme on Leprosy Treatment Adherence and Cure in Patients from the Nationwide 100 Million Brazilian Cohort: A Quasi-experimental Study', *The Lancet Infectious Diseases*, 20 (May 2020), 618–27.

leprosy has a colour: Interview with Artur Custodio (19 Jan. 2023).

these patients need isolation: Quoted in Elisabeth Poorman, 'The Legacy of Brazil's Leper Colonies', *Cadernos Saúde Coletiva*, 16/2 (2008), 307–26, 318.

NOTES

Leprosy, Mr. President: Quoted in Letícia Pumar Alves de Souza, 'Sentidos de um "País Tropical": A Lepra e a Chaulmoogra Brasileira' (Fundação Oswaldo Cruz, Casa de Oswaldo Cruz, 2009).

healthy and able to work: Coleção de Leis do Brasil, vol. 1, fasc.VI (Imprensa Nacional do Brasill, 1890), 1424.

Under Vargas: Tanya Katerí Hernández, 'Colorism and the Law in Latin America: Global Perspectives on Colorism Conference Remarks', *Washington University Global Studies Law Review*, 14/4 (2015), 683–93, 690.

Theodore Roosevelt wrote: Theodore Roosevelt, 'Brazil and the Negro', *Outlook*, 106 (21 Feb. 1914), 409–11, 409.

Leprosy, a bad advert: A point made in Poorman, 320.

It is a tremendous calamity: Quoted in Poorman, 320.

That our government imitate: Quoted in Poorman, 313.

alarming sanitary experts: *Washington Times* (9 Dec 1931).

thirty-three new hospitals: Josephine Robertson, 'Brazil', *International Leprosy Association – History of Leprosy* (2016), https://leprosyhistory.org/geographical_region/country/brazil.

The evidence: Janice E. Perlman, *The Myth of Marginality: Urban Poverty and Politics in Rio de Janeiro* (University of California Press, 1976), 195.

In 2023 police in Rio killed: Constance Malleret, 'Police Bullets in Rio Aren't just Deadly, They're a Public Health Hazard', *Brazilian Report* (23 Aug. 2023).

The last count: Editorial staff, 'Favelas se Distribuem no Antigo Leprosário', *Diário do Nordeste* (19 July 2008).

those who have brute strength: Ricarlos Pereira de Melo, 'Parque Aquático da Colônia Antônio Justa: Quais Foram os Estudos Feitos para a sua Implantação, e de Onde vem á Água para o seu Funcionamento?', Blog do Melo (29 Jan. 2018), blogdomelo32.blogspot.com/2018/01/parque-aquatico-da-colonia-antonio.html.

As with the other new developments: De Melo.

The state government admitted: Elmar Bones and Cleber Dioni Tentardini, 'Três Pacientes Travam o Fechamento do Último Hospital Colônia do Brasil: "Nós Não Caminhamos Sós"', *Jornal Já* (30 Sept. 2023).

intangible heritage: 'Projeto Aprovado na AL Torna Hospital Colônia Itapuã Patrimônio Histórico e Cultural do RS', *Sul21* (22 Nov. 2023), sul21.com.br/noticias/geral/2023/11/projeto-aprovado-na-al-torna-hospital-colonia-itapua-patrimonio-historico-e-cultural-do-rs.

Map of Armed Groups: 'Mapa dos Grupos Armados do Rio de Janeiro', Fogo Cruzado, NEV-USP, Grupo de Estudos dos Novos Ilegalismos UFF, Disque-Denúncia and Pista News (2020), geni.uff.br/2021/03/26/mapa-dos-grupos-armados.

JUAZEIRO DO NORTE, BRAZIL

At present we have in operation: Eunice Weaver, 'Importance of the Preventorium in the Rehabilitation of the Child of the Leper', *International Journal of Leprosy and Other Mycobacterial Diseases*, 8/4 (Oct. 1940), 495–500, 496.

not merely to rehabilitate the child: Weaver, 499.

The child, because of its susceptibility: Weaver, 495.

twenty or thirty children: Weaver, 497.

removed from its original environment: Weaver, 498–9.

Her vision is reflected: 'A Campanha Sanitária do Governo – Rio: O Educandário Santa Maria e o combate ao mal de Hansen', *Cine Jornal Brasileiro* 3/029 (DIP, Cinemateca Brasileira, 6 Nov. 1943).

Bacurau: 'Linha de Tempo', Casa de Bacurau (n.d.), web.archive.org/web/20180903204440/http://www.casadebacurau.org.br/linha_do_tempo.

revolutionary effects: Hervé Guibert, *To the Friend Who Did Not Save My Life*, trans. Linda Coverdale (Serpent's Tail, 2021), 35.

11,727 new cases: Evelyn Barreto, 'Hanseníase: Saúde Do Ceará Cria Guia de Bolso Para Profissionais Da Atenção Primária' (press release), Secretaria da Saúde do Ceará (24 Jan. 2023), www.saude.ce.gov.br/2023/01/10/hanseniase-saude-do-ceara-cria-guia-de-bolso-para-profissionais-da-atencao-primaria.

I hope the bourgeoisie: *Marx and Engels Collected Works*, volume 42 (Lawrence & Wishart, 1987). 383.

It is here in the final moments: Ernesto Guevara, *The Motorcycle Diaries: Notes on a Latin American Journey*, trans. Che Guevara Studies Center of Havana (Ocean Press, 2004), 70.

the most important person we have met: Alberto Granado, *Traveling with Che Guevara: The Making of a Revolutionary*, trans. Lucía Álvarez de Toledo (Pimlico, 2003), 70.

sons of millionaires: Granado, 65.

My first impression of the hospital: Granado, 80–1.

subject can be found: Julia Kristeva, *Powers of Horror: An Essay on Abjection*, trans. Leon S. Roudiez (Columbia University Press, 1982), 40.

KUMAMOTO, JAPAN

When these have been achieved: Gregory Vanderbilt, 'Hansen's Disease and Human Rights Activism in Postwar Japan: The Life of Usami Osamu (1926–2018)', *Asia-Pacific Journal: Japan Focus* (15 June 2018).

rarely discussed: Yasushi Shimura, *Ningen kaifuku: Hansen-byō o ikiru* (Kadensha, 2021), 121.

NOTES

national disgrace: National Hansen's Disease Museum, 'Issues Related to Hansen's Disease' (26 April 2021), www.nhdm.jp/en/about/issue.

30,359 people with leprosy: Michio Miyasaka, 'Punishing Paternalism: An Ethical Analysis of Japan's Leprosy Control Policy', *Eubios Journal of Asian and International Bioethics*, 19/4 (July 2009), 103–6, 104.

god-like: According to former patient Usami Osamu.

Before the Restoration: Mitsuda Kensuke, 'Raibyō kakurijo setsuritsu no hitsuyō ni tsuite', in *Mitsuda Kensuke to Nihon no rai yobō jigyō: Rai yobōhō gojūnen kinen*, ed. Tōfū Kyōkai (Tōfū Kyōkai, 1958), 3–7, quoted in Susan L. Burns, *Kingdom of the Sick: A History of Leprosy and Japan* (University of Hawaii Press, 2019), 122.

No Leprosy Patients in Our Prefecture Movement: With much controversy, other translations have it more simply as the 'Leprosy-Free Prefecture Movement'.

Every street: Rai Yobō Kyōkai (ed.), *Raisha sakuhin eiga sosaishū* (Rai Yobō Kyōkai, 1933), 119, quoted in Burns, 167.

believing wholeheartedly: Matsuoka Hiroyuki, 'Kakuri no shima ni ikiru: Okayama Hansenbyō mondai kiroku', quoted in Burns, 206.

On July 9th at 5 a.m.: National Hansen's Disease Patients' Council, 'Zenkyo Kyōkai Movement History' (2002), 18.

My younger sister: Exhibit at the National Hansen's Disease Museum, Higashimurayama, Tokyo.

best-loved books: Seichō Matsumoto, *Inspector Imanishi Investigates*, trans. Beth Cary (Penguin, 2024).

thirteen national sanatoria: Tōfū Kyōkai, *Mitsuda Kensuke and Leprosy Prevention in Japan* (Tōfū Kyōkai, 1958), figure quoted in Miyasaka, 104.

It will be natural for desperate persons: K. Mitsuda, 'Kaishun byoshitsu', *Asahi Shimbun* (1950), 204–5, quoted in Miyasaka, 104–5.

Some women: Miyasaka, 105.

1948 Eugenic Protection Law: Takashi Tsuchiya, 'Eugenic Sterilizations in Japan and Recent Demands for an Apology: A Report', *Ethics and Intellectual Disability*, 3/1 (Fall 1997), 1–4.

pragmatic view: Verification Committee Concerning Hansen's Disease Problem, 'Final Report' (Japan Law Society, 2005).

ninety-two patients imprisoned: Miyasaka, 105.

Believing management had gone too far: Burns, 207.

Small concerns over food: Nagashima Aiseien Nyūensha Jichikai, *Kakuzetsu no ritei*, quoted in Burns, 207.

a first-rate person: Verification Committee Concerning Hansen's Disease Problem, 'Final Report'.

hazardous duty: 'Pay and Allowances of the Uniformed Services', Title 37, §235, 236, 237 USCA (12 Oct. 1949).

Leprosy patients must be uprooted: Quoted in Vanderbilt.

Our mission and purpose: Zen-Rai-Kan-Kyo Newsletter, 13 (1 Jan. 1952). Quoted in Miwako Hosoda, 'Hansen's Disease Recoverers as Agents of Change: A Case Study in Japan', *Leprosy Review* (2010) 81, 5–16.

people who are idle: Mori Mikio, 'Atarashiki jidai no atarashiki ryōyōjo', *Kaede* (Sept. 1956), quoted in Burns.

One would think: Quoted in Vanderbilt.

To articulate the past historically: Walter Benjamin, 'Theses on the Philosophy of History', in *Illuminations*, trans. Harry Zohn (Harcourt, Brace & World, 1968), 255.

quietly bury the atrocity: Quoted in Vanderbilt.

In that the quarantine policy: Quoted in Vanderbilt.

My blood boiled: Quoted in Vanderbilt.

EPILOGUE: THE EDGE OF SETO INLAND SEA

I was happier: Chugoku Shimbun, 'Bridge Marks 35 Years Connecting Island Isolated under Past Leprosy Policy', *Japan Times* (5 June 2023).

70 per cent of the dead: Hanami Matsumuro 'Autopsy Records for 3,000 Leprosy Patients found at 2 West Japan Sanatoriums', *The Mainichi* (25 April 2021), mainichi.jp/english/articles/20210423/p2a/00m/0na/047000c.

720 people left: 'Survey in Japan Reveals Discrimination Against Hansen's Disease Patients Persists', nippon.com (16 June 2024), nippon.com/en/japan-data/h02001.

INDEX